Women's Voices in Hawaii

To the Holy Spirit

Mother, my ancient tree,
Your hands inside heaven
O, my old one,
Beside you I dare to be
Young
Tell me your stories, my auntie,
Legends you learned at a queen's knee,
Chant me your lullabye of
Wakening, O my warrior,
Teach me your love of this land
And this life
Wearing the bone tongue of heaven
Under your heart,
Wearing your praise of creation
Mother, my everlasting tree
Your branches raised in knowledge,
Here at your prayers
Here, with the spirit

Women's Voices in Hawaii

Joyce Chapman Lebra

UNIVERSITY PRESS OF COLORADO

10   9 8 7 6 5 4 3 2

Front cover: The pride of being Hawaiian. No. BM50129. Courtesy of the Bishop
Museum.

The University Press of Colorado is a cooperative publishing enterprise supported, in
part, by Adams State College, Colorado State University, Fort Lewis College, Mesa State
College, Metropolitan State College of Denver, University of Colorado, University of
Northern Colorado, University of Southern Colorado, and Western State College.

Library of Congress Cataloging-in-Publication Data

Women's voices in Hawaii / [edited by] Joyce Chapman Lebra.
        p.   cm.
    Includes bibliographical references and index.
    ISBN 0-87081-299-8 (alk. paper)
    1. Women — Hawaii — History. 2. Hawaii — Ethnic relations. 3. Oral his-
tory. I. Lebra, Joyce Chapman, 1925–
HQ1438.H3W66 1991
996.9'03'082 — dc20   91-29092
                                                                    CIP

The paper used in this publication meets the minimum requirements of the American
National Standard for Information Sciences—Permanence of Paper for Printed Library
Materials. ANSI Z39.48–1984
∞

To the women whose voices we hear

Contents

Preface

An invitation to teach in the Women's Studies Program at the University of Hawaii Manoa Campus in the fall of 1985 gave me an unexpected opportunity to develop an oral history project there. I decided to carry out oral history interviews with women in their eighties to learn what life was like in Hawaii for members of various ethnic groups at the turn of the century. I still have with me as an adult the strong imprinting of my barefoot Hawaiian childhood and share with my respondents many memories — of Chinese peddlers carrying buckets on long poles over their shoulders; of the smell of burning sugarcane when the fields are cut; of women with bent, bound feet, barely able to hobble; of bantam cockfights surrounded by shouting bettors; of the red earth of pineapple fields; of the sound of waves against rocks; of friends of every ethnic group, and more.

I initially intended to focus on generations of mothers and daughters to learn how cultural messages are transmitted across generations and how they serve in some areas to maintain cultural continuity while transformations occur in others. After a few interviews, however, I decided instead to concentrate on the older generation. The octogenarians I interviewed retained much in their memories about the lives of their parents and grandparents, and with the passing of this generation a rich oral repository dating from the turn of the century will be lost. These octogenarians were better able than their daughters to inform us about the goals, perceptions, work, life-styles, survival strategies, and aspirations of the settlers of Hawaii, women and men who contributed so vitally ethnically, culturally, and economically to the peopling of Hawaii and to its rich and diverse heritage. The goal of this volume, then, is to illuminate this heritage through the voices of the women who helped to create it.

I carried out interviews with approximately fifty women in their eighties and upper seventies on Oahu, Maui, Kauai, and the Big Island (a few respondents were in their sixties, a few in their nineties). Because the focus of my concern was sociocultural history, I did not include groups that immigrated to Hawaii principally after World War II, such as Samoans and Southeast Asians. The ethnic groups from which my respondents were selected are: Hawaiian–part Hawaiian, Chinese, Scottish-English, Portuguese, Japanese, Okinawan, Puerto Rican, Korean, and Filipino. They are presented in this order in this volume, an ordering that approximates their chronological appearance in Hawaii. Although I selected the respondents by ethnic group and not from particular socio-economic or occupational strata, many had been teachers. Others had completed little schooling and were only slightly literate. All, or nearly all, had worked beyond raising their families, performing multiple economic roles.

Interviews ranged in length from an hour and a half to three hours or more and in some cases involved more than one sitting. All interviews were taped and transcribed in their entirety. I found that my Hawaiian background enhanced interviewer/interviewee rapport in all cases. With Japanese and Okinawan respondents, interviews were aided by the fact that I speak Japanese, and with other respondents, my familiarity with pidgin proved useful. Several respondents and I have formed continuing friendships.

The questions I asked and the principles I adopted for editing the interviews were based on providing information on immigration, childhood, education, food, clothing, language, religious beliefs, work experience, courtship, marriage, children, and relations with other ethnic groups, as well as on furnishing more personal data reflecting values, philosophy, and life experience. Some interviews are far more comprehensive than others due to individual differences. Some interview segments were included because they provide distinctive data. That the chapter on the Japanese is longer than the others reflects the larger proportion of Japanese in Hawaii's total population.

Oral history offers some advantages over reliance on written sources, but it is also attended by some shortcomings. The memory of respondents is not always total or entirely reliable, for example, with regard to dates, places, or public political events. Yet individual voices lend data an authenticity, an immediacy, and a poignancy not apparent when we rely on documentary sources alone. We gain a sense almost of having been there, sharing the joys and sorrows of the respondents. Memories of happenings in the daily lives of women tell us about the social and cultural history of an era and make history live.

In every interview segment, I have sought to protect the anonymity of the respondent (although in some cases she may be recognized by her achievements), and for this reason I have not included names or photographs of interviewees, however tempted I may have been. Illustrations have been selected rather from collections in the Bishop Museum, Honolulu, Hawaii, the Alexander & Baldwin Sugar Museum at Puunene, Maui, and the Pioneer Museum at Lahaina, Maui. I used interview techniques that I developed during similar oral history projects in three parts of Asia — Japan, Southeast Asia, and India. I have also made use of guidelines developed by Warren Nishimoto and Michi Kodama-Nishimoto in the Oral History Project at the University of Hawaii.

In the chapters that follow, women of Hawaii speak in their own words, which convey far better than mine how they feel about their lives. Where I felt it would aid mainland readers, I have transcribed pidgin into more standard English. Otherwise I have not altered the respondent's words beyond editing for inclusion or exclusion of data.

That other researchers preceded me in conducting oral history research in recent years in Hawaii presented both advantages and disadvantages. On the one hand, I found that many researchers and resource persons were generously willing to share knowledge and advice; but on the other hand, I found that many well-known octogenarians had already been interviewed or had developed a resistance to being interviewed. This situation made it difficult at times to identify appropriate respondents, particularly in Honolulu. On the Outer Islands, introductions were in most cases provided by the efficient and helpful county offices on aging. Criteria of selection were age, ethnic group, and clarity of recall.

My purpose in organizing interviews and chapters by ethnic group is not to overemphasize ethnicity but rather to reflect the identity of Hawaii's people, who thought of themselves — and often still do — more as haole (white), Hawaiian, Chinese, Japanese, Korean, Filipino, or Puerto Rican than as doctors, lawyers, teachers, shopkeepers, or plantation hands. Prior to World War II, every ethnic group in Hawaii was a minority, though some groups were, of course, larger than others.

Acknowledgments

I was assisted in identifying prospective interviewees by many individuals and agencies in Hawaii. I would like to express my gratitude to them for the aid, suggestions, and encouragement that made this research possible in the limited time I had available. It goes without saying that my sincere gratitude goes first of all to the women who generously shared memories and stories of their own lives, stories that I feel certain will impress and move readers as they did me.

Although it is not possible to mention all those who in various ways helped in the process of this research, I would like to express my special thanks to the following individuals, many of whom work in the county offices on aging in Hawaii's highly developed network of services for senior citizens.

In Honolulu: Warren Nishimoto and Michi Kodama-Nishimoto, Robert Watada, Renji Goto, Karen Motosue, Blase Souza, Amy Agbayani, Helen Nagtalon Miller, Franklin Odo, Barbara Kawakami, Abraham Piianaia, Genevieve Correa, Beatrice Krauss, Esther Arinaga, Ruth Lieban, Madeleine Goodman, Bernhard Hormann, the Makua Alii staff, and the Lanakila Senior Center staff.

On Maui: Takashi Yamashita, the Reverend Charles Haruo Yamamoto, Roy Fusato and his staff, the Reverend Heather Mueller, Natalie Powell, Martha Martin, Inez Ashdown, Charlotte Nakamura, the Hale Mahaolu staff, and the Wailuku and Kahului library staffs.

On Kauai: Eleanor Lloyd, Richard Chun, Martha Hoverson, Georgia Mossman, and the Koloa Senior Center staff.

On the Big Island: Julie Tulang, George Yoshida, William Takaba, and their staffs.

In Colorado: Ernest Andrade, Jr., Kyung Namkoong Menkick, Elnora Mercado, and Teresinha Pereira.

In Carbondale, Illinois: Hua-ling Hu.

I also would like to thank my two graduate students at the University of Hawaii at Manoa — Deborah Zabarenko, who interviewed two Okinawan respondents, and Lily Liu, who interviewed two Chinese respondents in Chinese. I am also grateful to Barbara Mori for transcribing several tapes. They and the others already mentioned contributed stimulus and encouragement and in other ways added to the project. Responsibility for any errors or misrepresentation of course rests with me.

J.C.L.

Women's Voices in Hawaii

I   Introduction

Immigrants came to the Hawaiian Islands, as to America generally, looking for a better life than they left behind, for a place where they would find work, education for their children, enough food for their families, and a secure and peaceful old age. They came from Polynesia more than a thousand years ago, and more recently from the countries bordering the Pacific, in larger numbers than to the continental United States. They also made their way to Hawaii from parts of Western Europe — from England, Scotland, Portugal, Spain, Norway, and even from Russia.

The voyagers left their homes by ship: the specially built canoes in which Polynesians navigated hundreds of miles by the stars and tides, the early nineteenth-century whaling ships in which European sailors from Norway, England, and Portugal traveled around the continent of South America and across the Pacific, and the sailing ships from New England bound for China in the clipper trade. All of these travelers encountered in the Hawaiian Islands an environment such as they had never seen before, islands whose balmy climate and lush foliage so enchanted them that many chose to stay. Often European sailors jumped ship when they saw the dark-skinned Hawaiian women who greeted them, and they stayed to marry them.

By the beginning of the nineteenth century, by far the most numerous of the arrivals were men recruited by agents of the sugar planters as labor contracted for three or five years. They came primarily from the countries of Asia. These men were recruited from one country after another as a result of shifts in the policy of the Hawaiian Sugar Planters' Association. They came because they lacked work or food in their homelands and because of the enticements offered by the labor recruiters. The work of these plantation recruits was the motive force of Hawaii's plantation economy, an economy that rested on sugar and to a lesser degree on pineapples until World War II brought change. Most of the early arrivals were single men or were men who left their wives behind in the expectation that they would make fortunes and return home. Once in the new land, most settled and did not return. In the early decades of the twentieth century, the gender ratio remained disproportionately male; in some ethnic groups, there were as many as ten men to one woman. This gender asymmetry had many social and economic consequences for the lives of the new islanders.

Early Female Immigrants

The women who made these adventurous voyages brought with them rich cultural backgrounds and disparate personal aspirations. They came as the wives of the Polynesian immigrants and missionaries; they were sent for from their homelands by sailors and labor recruits. Single women who made the journey found themselves in great demand as wives, workers, and also as prostitutes. Although there was no shortage of potential husbands, the burden of work was heavy for women in Hawaii, and the demands on their labor were often far more arduous than had they not left home. Yet most of them remained, raised families, and made new lives in the Islands. Not that they never regretted leaving home or never wished to return, but for most of them, going back was not feasible financially. And for most, life in Hawaii, difficult though it was, was satisfying. Even if they did not always realize their hopes, they knew that their children would have a better opportunity than they for getting an education and moving up out of the plantation and into occupations where they could make their own decisions, where there was a chance that achievements might match aspirations and effort expended.

Churches, where they existed, were an important focus for the lives of the early settlers, especially the women. In some cases in which a church failed to offer needed support to new arrivals, women shifted their religious affiliation. This was true, for example, for some Filipinas on Oahu who left the Catholic faith and became Protestants. The proportionately large number of churches in Hawaii today attests to the early significance of the church as the center of social and religious life for ethnic communities as well as to the efforts of missionaries from New England.

Beyond the churches, women devised a variety of formal and

informal groups that would provide mutual support and aid in the new environment. On the plantation, women cooperated in the use of scarce conveniences, such as the ovens that were essential to Portuguese cuisine and the baths that the Japanese cherished. For other needs, they organized more formal groups that functioned as mutual aid societies or savings and loan clubs. Midwives served plantation women when doctors and nurses were lacking and often did not charge for their services or accepted food in return. In most ethnic groups, women displayed a strong sense of service and cooperation, sharing work loads and helping those less fortunate or more recently arrived than they.

Family unity and filial duty were also strong themes in the lives of these women. Often every family member worked for the welfare of the family as a whole rather than for individual personal advancement. Devotion to filial duty was particularly apparent in the lives of women from East Asia, in whom the Confucian tradition was entrenched.

Like pioneers wherever they are found, these women discovered that they were tough, resilient, adaptive, and ingenious. They developed strategies and innovations that enabled them to survive in a strange, new environment without the support of the friends and relatives they left behind, without the comfort of familiar surroundings and belongings. In most cases, they devised networks within their own ethnic groups for mutual aid and support. Midwives typically attended women from their own ethnic groups. Immigrants lived in ethnic enclaves on the plantations and helped each other prepare food and sew clothing for their families. Many did much more. Beyond caring for their own large families, they cooked and did laundry, ironing, and mending for the bachelors on the plantations. These women learned to do whatever their situation required, and they performed these tasks with a minimum of complaint or illness. Their stories make strong statements about these everyday heroines who peopled Hawaii and gave it its distinctive character.

Arrival in Hawaii

First to traverse the Pacific more than a thousand years ago, navigating by the stars and tides and arriving in their ingeniously constructed capsize-proof double canoes, were the Polynesians from the

South Pacific. For more than a thousand years, they lived on the Islands, undisturbed by other visitors, and evolved a society and culture based on their Polynesian heritage.

At the time of Captain James Cook's "voyage of discovery" in 1778, some 300,000 Hawaiians populated the Islands and employed Stone Age technology. Less than a century later, in 1853, contact with Western diseases had reduced the population to 71,019.[1] One percent of the population in 1853 were part-Hawaiian mixtures, or hapa haole. There is no suggestion of gender asymmetry in the Hawaiian population at the time of Captain Cook's voyage. The Hawaiian culture and society were noted for hospitality, sensitivity to and dependence on nature, and fondness for poetry, song, and dance.[2]

In the nineteenth century, Hawaii was visited by an assortment of whaling and clipper ships from New England and from countries in Europe: Norway, Germany, Portugal, Spain, Britain and Russia. Some sailors were so enchanted by the beauty of the Islands and attracted to Hawaiian women that they jumped ship and married the Island women; others left after briefer liaisons and escapades. In 1853 the Caucasian population numbered only 1,687.[3]

The early decades of the nineteenth century also brought Christian missionaries. Sent primarily by the Congregational Church based in Boston, the first shipload came aboard the *Thaddeus* under the direction of the Reverend Hiram Bingham and his new bride, Sybil. The long, arduous voyage around the coast of Latin America often called on all the health, energy, and messianic certitude these men and women could summon before they finally reached their tropical destination. Although their numbers were not large, the significance of their work reached beyond preaching the Gospel and spread into the school system and economy of the Islands. Their language soon dominated, and they lent Hawaii the character of a New England settlement. Within a generation or two, their descendants became the directors of the pineapple and sugar enterprises, the banks, and the railroads. They formed a haole elite that controlled the "Big Five" corporations.[4] Successors of these firms still operate today.

The first workers hired on the plantations were Hawaiians, but because their value system and work habits did not suit the haole planters and because of the high death rate among Hawaiians, they were soon replaced by workers imported from parts of Asia and Europe. The first recruits to be brought in as plantation labor were Chinese, and they dominated the plantation work force in the last half of the nineteenth century. By 1900 the number of Chinese in Hawaii reached 25,767, which approached the size of the decimated Hawaiian population (29,799) and the Caucasian population (26,819).[5]

The early Chinese immigrants were predominantly male. Like the Chinese who emigrated to Southeast Asia and elsewhere, many of these men intended to work out their contracts and return to the wives they left behind in their villages. Women made up only 2 to 3 percent of the Chinese population.[6] About half of the Chinese immigrants did return to their homeland in the nineteenth century. Many of the men who remained in Hawaii married Hawaiian women, although they may have left wives in China as well. Today the most common Hawaiian ethnic mixture is Chinese-Hawaiian.

By 1900 the sugar planters for several reasons altered their view of the desirability of Chinese labor. For one thing, when the Chinese laborers worked out their contracts, most moved to the cities, where they competed for jobs with Hawaiians and Caucasians. Of more importance, the Chinese Exclusion Act, as applied to Hawaii in 1900, effectively cut off Chinese immigration. Thereafter, only professional men, merchants, and government officials could bring wives in from China.[7] In addition, by 1884 more than 22 percent of the population of the Islands and 50 percent of the foreigners were "Celestials." In the view of the sugar planters, it was time to look to another labor group. Not only was the Hawaiian population on the wane, but some planters had come to view the Chinese as too numerous.

The next group to be imported in large numbers as laborers were the Portuguese, who were recruited between 1878 and 1888. So long as they worked and lived on the plantations, they were treated as separate from the other Caucasians, the haoles, as will be discussed in Chapter V. They were also treated differently from the other plantation labor. They were favored by government and sugar planters alike because they brought their wives with them, settled permanently, and were good workers. Moreover, the Bureau of Immigration welcomed them as a peasant people whose "education and ideas of comfort and social requirements [were] just low enough to make them contented with the lot of an isolated settler and its attendant privations."[8] By 1910 people of Portuguese descent were more numerous than people of Chinese descent in the Islands. Coming mainly from the Azores and the Madeira Islands, they were reminded of home by the flora and geography of the Hawaiian

Islands. Many became overseers, or *lunas*, on the plantations. By the last decade of the nineteenth century, however, many of the Portuguese laborers had moved from the plantations to the cities and had intermarried, with the result being that the Portuguese lost their identity as a separate ethnic group.

Next to arrive were the Japanese. An emissary of King Kalakaua of Hawaii was sent to Japan in 1883 to recruit immigrants in the expectation that they would "revive the dying native population, His Majesty believes." He relayed Kalakaua's message "that the Japanese and Hawaiians spring from one cognate race and . . . he hopes our peoples will more and more be brought together in a common brotherhood."[9]

An agreement signed between the Japanese and Hawaiian governments allowed more than 60,000 Japanese immigrants to enter Hawaii by 1900. The planters were as pleased as was the monarch at the Japanese immigration. "No laborers have ever been introduced here on such easy terms. And what is still better, the Japanese readily learn the English language and habits, and make good house, farm, and plantation servants . . . and they are provident and thrifty," stated an article in the *Plantation Monthly* in April 1889.[10] Moreover, the Japanese were more likely than the Chinese to bring their wives with them and did not move to the cities as rapidly. Nor were they banned by the Chinese Exclusion Act. By 1900, 40 percent of the Hawaiian population was Japanese; the group was twice as numerous as any other single group, including Hawaiians. Although the 1907 Gentlemen's Agreement for voluntary restriction on Japanese immigration to the United States did not apply to Hawaii, the Japanese government prohibited the emigration of Japanese laborers to Hawaii in 1907.[11] The 1924 Immigration Act finally cut off all Japanese immigration to the United States, including Hawaii. During the years between 1907 and 1924, Japanese women came in by the shipload as the famous picture brides. Men never exceeded women in the Japanese population by more than two to one.

The planters began to look elsewhere for labor even before 1907, and other groups arrived in smaller numbers. Six thousand Puerto Ricans arrived in 1900–1901 following a major tidal wave in San Juan, and 8,000 Koreans came in 1904–1905 as Japan began to assume control of Korea in the aftermath of the Russo-Japanese War. As a smaller group, the Koreans had to assimilate rapidly with regard to language, and most became Christians if they were not already converts.

Although 8,000 Spaniards arrived between 1907 and 1913, most of them left for the U.S. mainland within a decade.[12]

The last major ethnic group to be imported by the planters as contract labor were the Filipinos, 120,000 of whom arrived between 1907 and 1913. As with the Chinese, there was a large excess of males over females, with the ratio being between four to one and seven to one. Most Filipinos were Christians and came from Ilocos Norte, Ilocos Sur, and Visayan provinces; a small number of Filipino immigrants were Tagalog speakers from the Manila area.

Each ethnic group, because of historical and cultural conditioning, developed a distinctive life-style in Hawaii. As Lawrence Fuchs puts it: "For the kamaaina [old-timer] haoles, the goal was to control; for the Hawaiians, to recapture the past; for the Portuguese, to be considered haole; for the Chinese, to win economic independence; for the Japanese, to be accepted; for the Filipinos, to return to their home in the Philippines."[13]

Haole Control in Hawaii

For over a thousand years, the Hawaiians lived and worked on the land, dependent on its abundance. They fished, cultivated taro, and ate a variety of tropical fruit. Their arts and culture flourished, their chiefs fought battles to unify the Islands, and they did not know tuberculosis, leprosy, smallpox, or venereal disease.

The arrival of Caucasian sailors and missionaries and then Asians began the transformation of the population and, shortly thereafter, the transformation of the economy and politics of the Hawaiian Kingdom. So long as Hawaiian land could not be purchased by the Caucasians and other arrivals, economic change was minimal. However, the alienation of land to foreigners initiated the economic revolution that generated the development of the plantation economy.

By ancient theory, all land belonged to the king. In 1848 King Kamehameha III instituted the Great Mahele, through which a portion of royal lands was allotted to the *alii* (nobility) and a portion to commoners. Titles were settled by the payment of fees. Once in private ownership, the lands could be resold, and by 1850 aliens could purchase the Mahele land directly. Some of the new owners, in fact, sold land to haoles in exchange for services. The government in 1846 offered land for sale in Manoa and Makawao at $1 per acre. Aliens were able to buy land fee simple, and the production of sugar accelerated the haole demand for land. Missionary children were able to purchase land cheaply. When, in addition, the 1850 Masters' and Servants' Act established a Bureau of Immigration to import labor to work on the plantations, the plantation economy controlled by the haoles began to boom. Haoles also engineered the downfall of the Hawaiian monarchy and the annexation of Hawaii to the United States in 1898.[14] The haoles, although fewer than 5 percent of the population, within a few decades of settling in Hawaii controlled the land, enterprise, labor, and finally the politics in Hawaii.

During the reign of Kalakaua, Robert Wilcox, a half-Hawaiian, planned a coup against the 1887 Constitution, and in 1889 he carried out the coup but was caught, tried, and acquitted by a Hawaiian jury. Perhaps he acted out of sympathy for Kalakaua, who had been forced to accept the constitution; perhaps he acted in his own interest.

Queen Liliuokalani came to the throne as the last Hawaiian monarch in 1891, when her brother King Kalakaua died. Because foreigners had been jockeying for power during her brother's reign, Liliuokalani was determined to rule in her own right, to appoint Hawaiians to key positions in the administration, and to promulgate a new constitution restoring crown control over the House of Nobles and limiting suffrage to actual subjects. She felt the need for a constitutional revision to achieve these goals because the constitution of 1887 had been forced on King Kalakaua.[15]

Several haoles worked to stop the queen. Lorrin Thurston, the son of missionaries, agitated for a revolution against the monarchy and for the annexation of Hawaii to the United States. Henry Baldwin suggested dethroning the queen by constitutional means. When U.S. minister Stevens landed troops in Hawaii, the queen was urged not to resist the revolution. She surrendered, but she expected that she would be reinstated when the U.S. government learned the facts. She was disappointed. The first president of the Revolutionary Republic was Sanford Dole, another missionary son, who, however, spoke Hawaiian and defended Hawaiian interests as a lawyer. In the Republic's newspaper, *Punch Bowl*, he attacked the contract labor system.[16]

Immediately after the revolution, Lorrin Thurston, William Wilder, and William Castle went to Washington to secure territorial status for the Islands. Queen Liliuokalani was put under house arrest, and the American flag was hoisted over Iolani Palace.

The Sugar Plantation Economy

The first sugar plantation was established in 1835 by William Hooper of Boston, who was sent to Koloa, Kauai, by Ladd and Company, a mercantile trading house in Honolulu. The company leased 980 acres of land from Kamehameha III and hired his Hawaiian workers, for which a tax was paid to the king.[17] The workers were paid not in cash but in scrip, with which they could purchase goods at the company store. Hooper hired Caucasian overseers and complained about the native labor. He wrote to the company office in Honolulu suggesting that "a colony of Chinese would probably put the plantation in order."[18] Accordingly, he hired a few Chinese bachelors for the Koloa plantation and housed them in barracks.

Sugar production flourished in Hawaii for a variety of reasons. Rich soil, a warm climate, and abundant water were the geographic preconditions. The Great Mahele enabled haoles to purchase or lease land in large plots. The Gold Rush stimulated emigration from the mainland, and the Civil War gave added impetus to the sugar industry. The most important political boost to Hawaii's sugar industry was the Reciprocity Treaty of 1876, which gave Hawaiian sugar a preferred place in American markets.[19] For a number of years Hawaiian sugar enjoyed this privileged position, but the situation was reversed by the McKinley Tariff of 1891, which allowed all sugar to enter the United States duty-free. In addition, under the tariff, subsidies were paid to domestic sugar producers.[20]

The Masters' and Servants' Act solved the problem of how to keep a cheap labor supply. Contracts were generally signed for three years, though in some cases they were signed for two or five years. Each plantation had its own rules governing working conditions, including hours (not only working but sleeping hours), pay scale, and housing. Fines and a docking system were used to reduce absenteeism and tardiness. The planters developed a system of occupational stratification based on race even before that became the policy of the Hawaiian Sugar Planters' Association (HSPA). Eighty-eight percent of the *lunas*, engineers, foremen, and clerks, were white. Wages for the same tasks also varied by race and sex. In William Hooper's day at Koloa, women were paid 6¢ a day, men 12¢. In 1910 Filipino cane cutters were paid 69¢ a day; Japanese cane cutters received 99¢. White carpenters were paid $4.26 per day, Japanese $1.28; white overseers were paid $3.01, Japanese $1.25.[21] To encourage Caucasians to have children and thus settle more permanently, the Lihue Plantation following annexation gave a $5 bonus to mothers of German and Portuguese infants.[22] At Grove Farm on Kauai, "children [went] to work at the same hour as adults, 6 A.M. and [stopped] at the same hour as adults, 4:30 P.M.," during their vacations.[23]

The HSPA fixed wages for all workers and used a passbook system, which made it impossible for a worker who left one plantation to find work on another. Some got around this by altering their surnames. As low as the plantation wages were, however, they compared well with wages elsewhere at the time.[24] Workers were provided housing — barracks in the earlier years and later the more typical square frame houses that were raised above ground level to protect against rains, insects, and small animals. Workers were also furnished with plots of land for gardens, with seeds, and with kerosene for lamps; primary school education and medical care of sorts were sometimes provided, depending on the time and place.

Under the Homestead Act, passed in 1895, no more than one thousand acres of land could be sold in a single parcel. It was possible under the same act for homesteaders to acquire parcels of land for thirteen years. But the sugar companies subverted this law by using "straw buyers" as homesteaders and thereby diverted land for plantation use.[25] The philosophy behind the Homestead Act, to return Hawaiians to the land and to encourage independent farming, was thus circumvented. It should be noted, nevertheless, that the Homestead Act was passed by the government of the Republic, the same government reviled as the creature of the planters and haoles.

When the contract labor system was abolished by the Organic Act of 1900 and workers were released from their legal obligations, planters had to entice laborers to remain on the plantations. Many planters decided it was the better part of virtue to employ men with families as workers. Japanese and Filipino workers were encouraged to obtain brides from home. The decade of the picture bride ensued, 1910–1920.

Long hours, poor food, and penalties for illness and absenteeism sometimes became too onerous, and planters could no longer count on passive acceptance by workers. In 1905 the first strike broke out at Lahaina after a *luna* beat a worker so badly that he lost the sight in one eye. Planters called in the National Guard. In 1909 Japanese workers organized the Great Strike at Aiea to demand higher wages. Similar strikes followed at Kahuku, Waianae, and Waimanalo.[26]

The outburst of strikes by Japanese laborers (following the 1907 restriction on emigration by the Japanese government) led planters to change their tactics: They decided to focus on importing Filipinos, who, they felt, would not strike. This tactic was not entirely successful. The largest of all strikes, organized on all four islands in 1920, was the result of activity not only by Japanese workers but also by a Filipino activist named Pablo Manlapit.[27] These strikes were serious challenges for the planters, challenges that signaled the beginning of a gradual shift in the political and economic balance among the classes and ethnic groups and eventually ushered in a new distribution of land and power in Hawaii. In the resulting new dispensation, the haole monopoly on political and economic power was broken, and power came to be shared more equitably among Hawaii's many ethnic groups.

Women's Roles

It is the multiple roles of the women within ethnic groups that is the focus of our concern. These women were not feminists — feminism had yet to appear except in pockets on the mainland and is still a different phenomenon in Hawaii from what exists in other states. For the women who settled Hawaii, the chief concern was survival. Yet in their struggle to feed and clothe their large families, their lives made eloquent statements about their courage and fortitude. When they sacrificed their own interests for the welfare of their families, they did so without complaint. "There was just no question," as one Okinawan respondent put it.

In historical retrospect, we see these women living in a colonial society as being doubly colonized, even triply colonized in the case of Okinawan women. Female, and a minority within a Japanese minority, they sometimes commented on being discriminated against by other Japanese for being Okinawan. Yet seldom if ever did the women of any ethnic group complain of being discriminated against for being female — though their brothers were more often than not given preference in education. Even a Korean respondent whose father advised her to give away her siblings after her mother died because "they're only girls" reacted not so much with anger against her father as with a dedicated determination to keep the family together.

It is to the voices of these women that we turn our attention as they recall the events and emotions of their lives and relate what it meant to be growing up female in a particular ethnic community in Hawaii at the turn of the century.

II   Hawaiians–
Part-Hawaiians

The Tradition

The cultural tradition the Polynesians brought to the Hawaiian Islands more than a thousand years ago was an oral one; the islanders learned no means of written recording until the arrival of the missionaries in the nineteenth century. This early tradition — the collective memory of an island people — was the expression of a poetic vision carried and transmitted by chanters, who recited the genealogies of chiefs and *alii*, the nobility. Most chanters were men, though in the more recent past some women as well learned the art. Today, few traditional chanters survive. The chant did not tell of a succession of generations but rather told of events arranged under symbolic titles and memorialized by families in the name of deities believed to have assisted in their achievements.[1]

Polynesians living in their new Hawaiian home maintained their strong sense of identity with the sea and land. The fruits of the earth and ocean nourished them, and knowledge of the ways of animals and fish and of the shifting of the tides, seas, and sands imparted to them a sense of well-being. Hawaiian poetry reflects this strong emotional orientation to the natural environment.

Because of the absence of a literate tradition, there is no written ancient history of the Hawaiians. When Captain Cook visited the Islands in 1778, an estimated 300,000 Hawaiians lived there; less than a century later, in 1850, their number had dwindled to some 84,000 because of contact with Western diseases to which they had no immunity. Of the population in 1850, fewer than 1 percent were part-Hawaiian, indicating that intermarriage had just begun.

At present, the "pure Hawaiian" population, if in fact it can be called that, is extremely small. Within the ethnic Hawaiian–part-Hawaiian populace, a resurgence of Hawaiian national pride and a movement to revive and preserve Hawaiian culture have appeared. Individuals whose ancestry is one-eighth Hawaiian are proud to consider themselves Hawaiian. This movement is a response to the active suppression of Hawaiian culture that occurred early in this century. Many octogenarians remember the time when the Hawaiian language was not taught even at the Kamehameha Schools and Hawaiian children were exhorted by their parents to "speak English" if they expected to get ahead.

Recovery of the Hawaiian heritage has prompted such events as a recent voyage by some Hawaiians to retrace the migration route taken by the original Polynesians. They navigated the Hokulea, a double canoe built after the model of the original outriggers, through the South Pacific without benefit of modern technology, relying on the stars and tides as did the Polynesian voyagers over a thousand years ago.

Women's Lives

As in most societies, the nurturing of children and preparation of food were primarily the province of women. Care of children was, however, not always provided by the mother; in the loosely structured *ohana* (Hawaiian family), it was frequently the *kupunas*, grandparents, who raised the children. The oldest woman in the *ohana*, the matriarch, was a focal figure. A distinctive feature of the family was the custom of *hanai*, giving one or more children to members of an older generation to raise. The custom evolved because couples without children in the home, even if they were grandparents, were viewed as incomplete and as being lonely. It was thus common for grandparents to raise children other than their own, at times children of more than one couple. When the *ohana* could not provide for children, they were cared for in orphanages and schools established by women of the *alii*.

Grandmothers were social engineers of the *ohana*, preservers of aspects of tradition and harmony within the family. When discord threatened the domestic peace, it was the grandmother (sometimes the grandfather) who presided over *hooponopono*, a structured mechanism for conflict resolution through discussion, prayer, and forgiveness. "We were taught in the family never to go to bed angry with our brothers and sisters," said one respondent.

Many of the traditional crafts were also performed predominantly by women. Common but cherished arts were the making of flower and feather leis and preparation and weaving of *lauhala,* leaves of the pandanus tree. Most Hawaiian respondents described the lengthy process of preparing and weaving hats and floor-covering mats, skills that were passed from mother to daughter. Women also made *tapa* cloth from bark and colored it with natural dyes. The missionaries taught women to quilt, an art that was adopted widely and evolved with distinctive Hawaiian permutations. "Quilting was a must for girls," in the words of one respondent.

Men did most of the fishing — whether by net, using a torch at night, or gathering shellfish on the reefs — and pounding of poi, the staple food made from taro root. Taro was used also as a thickening agent for stews. Women prepared and cooked the fish and other foods, including a favorite sweet potato pudding made with honey and coconut milk. Children helped with drying certain varieties of fish.

Religion and Mythology

Some aspects of Hawaiian myth, religion, and cosmology apotheosized female power, others male power. The most important body of Hawaiian myth is the Pele cycle. The myth is "closely associated with *aumakua* worship of the deities of the volcano, with the development of the hula dance," and with stories of odd rock and cone edifices that formed as a result of contests between Pele — the volcano, or fire, goddess — and her human and divine rivals.[2] The myth describes the migration or expulsion of Pele from a distant homeland (referring probably to the migration of Polynesians to Hawaii) and Pele's digging of a cool pit deep enough to house her whole family. Other phases of the myth "demonstrate [Pele and her family's] spirit forms of flame and cloud and other volcanic phenomena."[3] Anyone who dares to offend Pele will suffer swift retribution, for her power is to be feared. Pele falls in love with a handsome young chief on Kauai and, determined to have him as her husband, she sends her sister off to fetch him but then becomes suspicious of her sister. One respondent in Hilo showed me some of "Pele's hair" and reported that Pele was extremely beautiful but also dangerous and that anyone who spoke ill of her would "get it."

Fig. 2.1. Woman wearing *niho palaoa*, holding hand *kahili*. CP97199. *Courtesy of the Bishop Museum, Honolulu, Hawaii.*

Hina, the cosmic female force, is brought into the Pele cycle as one of the forms taken on earth by the fire goddess.

Hawaiian myth and legend reflect also the importance of the sea, not only for the original migration but also for the life-style of the Hawaiians. Each family had a totemic protector deity, an *aumakua*. The most common *aumakua* was the shark. The shark was viewed as an important ally and protector of fishermen, and some families had their own particular shark *aumakua* that watched over them when they were on or in the sea. Some legends tell of half-shark, half-men or -women born of human mothers. When returned to the sea, these hybrid sharks become family *aumakuas* that help fishermen when they are in distress or increase their catches. Another common *aumakua* was the *mo-o*, lizard, which, like the shark, offered protection to certain families. Many respondents in this study mentioned either the shark or the *mo-o* as their family's *aumakua*. Stories also abound of men or gods assuming shark form.

The *aumakua* also guided the soul to its final resting place after a family member's death. The worst fate that could befall one was to be abandoned by one's *aumakua*, left to wander eternally. Such restless spirits are believed to be dangerous and to delight in leading travelers astray.[4]

The importance of animals in Hawaiian lore is also reflected in the Kupua stories, which are tales of heroes who are part human and part animal. Some consider them part divine as well because they believe that the spirit of an animal ancestor entered them at birth. Although they are born as animals, they are raised as humans by their human, maternal grandparents. In the tales, some of the semidivine heroes were allowed to marry the daughters of chiefs as a reward for going to fight the enemy.[5] Such legends, moreover, reflect the importance of the maternal grandparents in the Hawaiian kin grouping. In present-day society this traditional importance of maternal grandparents is perpetuated in the *hanai*. Several respondents in this study were raised by grandparents; others felt especially close to maternal grandparents.

Rocks also figured prominently in the stories of the respondents. Some of them recalled legends of children with twin bodies, one a rock and the other human. Rocks also figure importantly in the construction of *heiaus*, or traditional temples, and in family grave sites. In addition, stones are considered folk representations of Ku and Hina, the male and female cosmic forces. One part-Hawaiian respondent reported that her

Fig. 2.2. Hawaiian girl, ca. 1909. *Photo by C. H. Gurrey. No. CP101,977. Courtesy of the Bishop Museum, Honolulu, Hawaii.*

mother told her that whenever she returned to their ancestral home she should first go to the river and touch two rocks, which apparently were associated with the family *aumakua.*

Stones also had great utility for the Hawaiian life-style. They were used for pounding poi, polishing canoes, forming wooden dishes, and fashioning axes.[6]

Another body of Hawaiian legend deals with the Menehune people. Regarded by Hawaiians as their ancestral spirits, these "little people" acted as benevolent godparents to their descendants.[7] Some anthropologists have identified them as aboriginal pygmies who lived on the Islands in prehistoric times. The Menehunes are reputed to have built walls and *heiaus* and prepared feasts for their descendants, generally working at night when ordinary humans are not about. According to legend, they lived in caves on Kauai and Oahu, planted taro and sweet potatoes, enjoyed sports and games, and could even control the weather.[8] One of the Kauai respondents in this study told me that she and her father had seen a photograph of a Menehune, but according to the story she had been told, the Menehune did not appear to the photographer's naked eye — the figure appeared only in the photograph.

The trickster god of Polynesia, Maui, also plays a part in Hawaiian legend. He has numerous quarrels and adventures in the Islands, including snaring the sun. He is the son of Hina and has the power to draw the Islands together if he wishes.

Another body of belief in the supernatural centers around the ghostly night marchers. Spirits who march to the beat of drums on the nights at the end of the lunar cycle, they are believed to be ancestral spirits or family gods. If one hears the marchers coming, one must lie face down or hide behind a rock; death will come to those who are in the path of the marchers or are seen by them. There is only one other way to be saved: If some of the phantom marchers happen to be one's own ancestral spirits, they may prevail on the other spirit marchers to spare the unlucky human who happens to be in the path of the march.

Taboos and *Kahunas*

Male power was represented in the early part of the century by beliefs in taboos and *kahunas,* as well as by the organization of society under male rulers. Each island was owned by a king, under whom were numerous chiefs and *alii*. The lives of the *alii* were surrounded by many taboos, known collectively as *kapu*, and people who transgressed these taboos were killed. The highest line of chiefs were *kapu* chiefs, and to preserve the purity of their lineage, these chiefs were often married to their sisters. Their offspring were then entitled to inherit the throne. The chiefs were sacred, or taboo. To cross the shadow of a king or *kapu* chief meant death for a commoner. A commoner could appeal for his life to the king; if the king raised his head and looked at him, he was saved, but if the king refused to look up, the person was put to death.[9] Each chief had a priest empowered by the gods he worshipped. The priest supervised the religious rites of the chief's household and accompanied the chief in battle.

Despite the cosmic female power as exemplified by Pele and Hina, taboos for women were extensive and enforced. This dichotomy — female cosmic power but social disempowerment — has analogies in other ancient societies. In Japan, for example, the sun deity, Amaterasu, was female, and women sat on the throne as rulers in the eighth century. By contrast, in more recent times, women in Japan have been rendered powerless in many spheres by androcentric controls. Similarly, in India the traditional cosmic power, Shakti, was female, yet numerous disabilities have faced women in recent and historical eras.

Hawaiian women traditionally could not eat with men, including their husbands. Bananas, coconuts, and certain fish were forbidden to them on penalty of death. Nor could women worship with men in temples.[10] Queen Kaahumanu, queen regent and companion of Kamehameha I (Kamehameha the Great), was a convert to Christianity and a friend of missionaries. She wished to abolish these taboos for women and is reputed to have daringly eaten a banana as an experiment. Nothing happened to her, and the taboo was thereby broken. King Liholiho, Kamehameha's son, broke another taboo by sitting at a women's table. The king then ordered that *heiaus* be destroyed and images burned.[11] Although some challenged this royal order, hid images, and continued to observe the *kapu*, its power was officially broken.

Kahunas were priests believed to possess special powers, including the most notorious — the ability to pray a person to death or to health. There were several schools of *kahunas*, and the power was passed from father to son. To succeed in his lethal prayers, the *kahuna* needed to obtain something connected with the intended victim — a lock of hair or nail parings, for example. Such omens left at the doorstep inspired such fear that the targeted victims often, in fact, died. In 1850, during the reign of Kamehameha II, a law was passed against the practice, but it continued surreptitiously until long after. I recall one instance that occurred during my childhood in the 1930s.

Some *kahunas* dealt with healing rather than death, and these healing *kahunas* were often women. *Kahunas* were also consulted before new ventures were undertaken.

Another religious practice was human sacrifice. Instances of people eating the eyes of sacrificed humans and pigs are reported by David Malo, an early Hawaiian who traveled to the U.S. mainland.[12]

The Hula

The hula originated in association with ancient temple worship. The dance was accompanied by chanting in honor of gods, chiefs, and war heroes. These chants relayed the oral history of the people. Unlike the modern hula, the ancient form of the dance was inseparable from worship and the sacrosanct. After the taboo was broken and before the missionaries arrived, the hula came out of the *heiau*. There is some debate regarding the nature of the early hula because Cook refers to dances that were not religious. The dance the missionaries describe was also a late, nonreligious form or was perceived as such.[13] It is conceivable that the arrival of Western sailors, followed by missionaries, altered the dance and gave it a more sensual connotation.

The wearing of flower leis, today associated with the hula and known as a symbol of friendship, is another tradition that probably derived from Polynesia. Oldest of all leis is the maile lei made of fragrant leaves; the yellow ilima lei was worn in old Hawaii by people of highest rank. One repondent stated that a lei should never be given to a pregnant woman, for fear that the baby will be strangled by the umbilical cord and born dead.

Several respondents reported that their parents and grandparents taught them never to ask questions about Hawaiian customs and beliefs. One Hawaiian anthropologist reports that some Hawaiians believe the gods will punish those who reveal family secrets or stories about the gods.[14] Today, however, many Hawaiians are anxious to preserve if not revive their traditions, and the women we met did speak of some of these traditions.

The Land

Hawaiians have a strong feeling for the land, as reflected in much of their poetry and song. The issue of separation of the Hawaiian people from the land is one of crucial importance today. This issue is discussed more fully in Chapters I and IV. It should be reiterated here that although under the feudal system it was only the *alii* who owned land and the commoners were tenants, there is no gainsaying that some Hawaiians lost land in the decade following the Great Mahele. They were driven off by alien concepts of sale and purchase, by requirements that they present claims to land on which they had always lived. It was not only the loss of land but also an alien social system that made them in many respects strangers in their own land. Instances of loss of land through deceit were legion.

The clash of cultures was especially apparent with regard to the land. Whereas the Caucasian philosophy of life was closely bound to the concept of private property and its acquisition — and the absence of a similar philosophy among Hawaiians was a source of puzzlement and irritation — for Hawaiians, land was for the support and use of the whole community, though the original theory was that it belonged to the king and nobility.

Hawaiians began to form societies to protect their interests and way of life, beginning with the establishment of a secret organization in 1902, the Order of Kamehameha. Among the respondents in this study were several who mentioned the clash of cultures over land or were themselves involved in seeking to protect their claims to land. The Order of Kamehameha and other later groups formed "a focus for Hawaiian introspection, for the never-ending Hawaiian quest to recapture the past."[15]

We turn now to the voices of Hawaiian respondents recalling facets of their heritage and what it meant to be Hawaiian and female growing up in Hawaii several decades ago.

AMANDA

Amanda was born in Hilo. She taught high school for several years and is also a journalist. She has worked through the Kupuna program in primary schools to preserve the Hawaiian language and culture. She is married and has three sons and a daughter. Two of her granddaughters are scholarship students.

I'm three-eighths Hawaiian and five-eighths Chinese. My father was pure Chinese. His idol was Sun Yat-sen, who came to the Islands, went to Iolani School, and had gone among the Chinese soliciting funds. My mother was Chinese-Hawaiian. Her mother was also Chinese-Hawaiian, but her father was pure Hawaiian, though many of his relatives spoke of the fact that he was very fair and that he was probably not pure Hawaiian. He was a schoolteacher and lighthouse keeper in the rural areas. My grandmother brought up her two daughters — my mother was the oldest. There were many other children that came later, totaling a family, I think, of ten. My grandmother was determined to pass on what she knew to her children, especially to her daughters. Because my mother was the oldest and had just gone to elementary school and remained at home, much of the Hawaiian tradition was taught to her. . . . In *hanai*, if the oldest child was a boy he went to the father's parents. If it was a girl she went to the mother's parents.

The saddest time was when I saw my father leave. It was during the Depression, and there was very little money here. And so he felt that if he went back to China he'd give himself a start. Maybe my mother would go and some members of the family. And so he went. I saw him leave on the steamer. It was 1929. He never came back. I can still see him waving to me, because I was seventeen then. That saddened me. I never saw him again. . . .

My grandmother was very watchful of any kind of disturbances in the family. If among her siblings and all her own relatives she noted some little trouble, little *pilikia*, she would search it out and search it out, and if it bothered her she thought nothing of gathering all the members of the family and putting everybody through what was called *hooponopono*. And at that time — [in what] was very similar to what we would do in problem solving — everybody was assembled, quiet, quiet, quiet, before midday and a prayer said by her [and] at the time of the prayer she would designate why we were assembled and what she hoped would eventually end. A Hawaiian prayer, it was always a Hawaiian prayer, for guidance. And then she would take the oldest individual, and it would go all the way down to the youngest — what was bothering them. If the older individual who was having the problem would speak up, that other person who was present and was being accused as part of the problem said nothing — and she was very emphatic about that — said nothing until that person's time came. Because the idea was to settle what was causing the upheaval. And most of us younger children just sat there. It was my grandmother that did it. And when it was all finished you were asked to *kalamihi*, to forgive, and say in the tone of voice that you were sorry and that you would not repeat this kind of disharmony, and, you know, the room would be lighter and brighter. People would be kissing each other and talking to each other. Then there was always a big meal afterwards. Never was anything allowed to be taken out that was not eaten. It was all wrapped in ti leaves. . . .

Hooponopono was an accepted method of problem solving that was in all Hawaiian families of my grandmother's generation. That was approximately in the year 1880. It is still practiced today. It's been kind of altered, but basically it is almost the same.

I remember once when my grandfather was present. It involved, I think, a son or two in the family. He was very emphatic about this not repeating itself. The blame was here and the blame was there and the blame was shared elsewhere, but he tried to reconcile the differences. . . .

We had this home in the country that was just above the cliffs. We had our uncles and aunts that made the trails down to the ocean floor. And so they would go down. There were three trails that they would use. But the particular one that they liked was called *kanahaa*. *Kanahaa* was almost directly back of the lighthouse. But it went along the edge of the cliff, and then it would cut back, and then they went down to where the rocks were. Because there was no beach, just rocks. This was a ritual that we all understood and accepted. And when we were called to it, we went. We didn't hide. We just went.

And my mother would want to see my grandmother in her country place. She would come over to our house. And I remember once when my grandmother came all the way here to Honolulu and came to my home with my mother because of a land deal she felt was being unfairly apportioned out between herself and her half-sister, older half-sister. But it was eventually solved.

My mother always served a very heavy lunch of Hawaiian food

among her women friends and relatives almost daily, because my father could afford it. And she would cook the things that her mother taught her, the native foods of meat — salt meat — with taro leaves. A luau. Always the great pots of stew with taro instead of potato, and the thickening agent was the poi. Then she would have, quite often, dessert that only my grandmother knew how to do, because we would go out to my grandmother during the summer, and she would have taro that she would steam and fry in butter. And my grandmother was always fond of my father because always when we went out to my grandmother during the summer vacation, my father took a bag of rice. I think it was fifty pounds. And many pounds of butter called *waiu buta*. And they were big one-pound slabs, butter cut in quarters, the big slabs. And always a case of corn beef, sardines, pork and beans. To this day I am not fond of any of those things. Always, too, my father would include cheese, jellies, because there was just guava jelly.

My grandfather used to love the strawberry jelly that would come in the huge round crocks. That was eaten with coffee in the morning. It was not unusual for us in the morning to have papaya or banana if it was available. And some of the same hardtack with the jelly. And then, of course, my grandmother would make other kinds of dessert with the coconut, and we would have what is called *bhaupia*. And then sometimes she would scrape the green banana and pour either honey on it [or] coconut. Then she'd wrap it in ti leaves and steam it for many hours. And it was a quite a delicacy to us. Then, of course, there was a lot of sweet potato growing around, and she would go out there and add coconut milk to it, and more honey, and this was called *koele palau*, and it was a pudding of sweet potatoes. After three or four days, especially around the fifth day, it was so well liked by the men because it had fermented. . . .

I do remember this — my grandfather was a very good fisherman, because that was how he supplied food to his family. He would go to one of the places he used to go near the lighthouse. He would go where there seemed to be tide pools and a lot of fish, a lot of rockfish. I don't remember what was said, but I know if it was the first time he went down my grandmother would say something about did he leave some? Yes, the biggest one, you know, because that was the Hawaiian custom.

I remember when at New Year's it was always the custom of my father to leave a $10 gold piece because members of my mother's family would come and serenade. They'd come at New Year's and this old fellow played the violin, and it was here that it ended. All Hawaiian. They came at midnight, more or less. We were the last people they'd come to. They knew that they were going to have this gold piece, they knew that my father was going to have a big meal ready for them, they knew that there was enough to drink. Because this was how the New Year was greeted. . . .

My mother told me this story — we tell it to our children. In the river was a stone that was U-shaped. You didn't know this U-shaped rock was in the river, except maybe at very low tide these points would stick up. My grandmother, after Grandfather died, lived with one of her daughters who was married to some rather educated person who built this two-story home down there. Now here my grandmother lived there with this family. But prior to this two-story home being built, there was an old family home with two of her — I think — first cousins, because they were close, she and these two first cousins. We would come as children, and this was a great big picnic idea — go down and swim here and then in the afternoon hightail it up this high hill and walk up the railroad track and go home. Well, our grandmother would tell us [this story], especially if the points were above the water. And it was cold water because it was a spring, and it wasn't exactly clear water. It was a little murky, green and brown. And always, always, on the side of the house was watercress growing. It was a spring, and we would dip our head in and drink the water. Lots of mountain apples back here and pigs running around. And this was the story — that there was a birth, twins, twin sons, of a great-great-aunt of this grandmother I'm talking about. And that with the birth of these two, one child seemed to take on the aspects of a shark, young shark, and so that child was allowed into the stream, and that child would come back up, the little fish, to be nursed by this mother. And the fish grew up. And so the story was about our *aumakua*, our family *aumakua*, so if we were ever in the water and sharks were there, that they would help us, they'd take care of us. *Aumakua* is known as a family god. And there are many kinds, but in our family that was it. So my mother would say to us — and especially she'd point the finger at me — when you leave the island, when you come back, you just dive into that stream and you go there and you touch that rock. I used to do that. I'm home. My sons have not gone there. It's still there. The land has been sold — it's been a kind of sad thing. It's been sold and it's gone into the hands of three people, but the third person that bought it has told us that we're welcome to come down.

And I feel that our children should have the chance to do that. They must, because it's part of this family's background.

ALONA

Alona was born on the Big Island and is of Hawaiian-Chinese-Italian-haole descent. She attended normal school in Honolulu and also studied at Columbia University and the University of Southern California. She taught for forty-two years. She is widowed and has a son and two grandchildren.

I was born right here. Many years ago, my father was managing the family meat market. My mother was a housewife. I'm one of these mixed-up potpourris because my mother was Italian-Hawaiian. Her father had come out here on a sailing ship and somehow or other had jumped ship and remained, then took an American name and married a pure Hawaiian woman. My father came from an old missionary family. His mother was Chinese-Hawaiian. His father was one of the sons of the original missionaries who came out here. I have a very faint recollection of Grandfather as being a very stalwart man. He told me, "You don't say how do you do if a man is smoking and doesn't remove his pipe and hat." That's all I remember about him. . . . I remember just once my father sitting at the organ playing a hymn. I was sewing a dress to finish so I could wear it to school. He said, "You're not to sew on Sunday — it's the Sabbath."

But I do remember my mother's family. Grandfather, that's my mother's father, was a small man for a man, but, oh, such a dear, gentle person he was. He was fair and had blue eyes. And Grandmother was a heavyset woman. I remember her so definitely sitting on the floor quilting. And whenever we went over to Grandfather's place to spend a vacation, and Grandmother would be sitting there on the floor with her friends at a quilting frame quilting, she would say, "You small kids stay outside. Don't come in here with your dirty feet." And if we dared to go in, she had a guava switch, and she would say, "You see this? I going to use this on your legs." Grandmother spoke very little, oh, she spoke broken English. And Grandfather had insisted on his family — that was a large family — speaking in Hawaiian to Grandmother. So as a result they all spoke Hawaiian. I speak no Hawaiian. Whenever my father and mother wanted to say anything to each other that they didn't want us to know, they talked in Hawaiian. And if we dared to ask, "What are you saying?" they'd say, "It's not for your ears. If we want you to know, we'd speak to you." So that was it. . . .

The men did the fishing, and the women did the rest. I don't know why, but whenever we went down to the beach it was always the men who took the nets out. They would lay the nets out there. We had a great big mullet pond, and especially during the dry weather we had to rely on catchment water down there. Well, the men would take the nets out, and in the pond they would close the mouth of the pond after the tide had gone in and before it turned. . . . And fish would try to get out, and that's when the nets had been placed. Then we had to go in. That was fun. The children would get into the water and splash and all that to get the fish to go there. Then at night many of the men, the younger men especially, would go out and do torch fishing around the beach. Oh, that was so pretty. I remember that. And then they would come back, maybe early in the morning, with a bucket full of crabs. And, of course, all the children, all of us, would be still sleeping on the floor. And these men would empty these buckets of crabs. I can remember that so well. Crabs crawling all over, and you'd hear them on these mats. Then they would bring in the *opihis* [limpets] and the *wana* [urchins], but certain men attended to that because they knew how to handle the *wana*. They left them in a great big bag, and they would simply roll the bag along the rocks and break all those spines. But when it came to the *opihis*, I loved to shell them.

They would have some to cook, some they would fix to have raw. The rest of it would have to be dried. We dried all our fish on the rooftop. We had a little shed, and that was fine. The children took the fish up there to dry. No covering. We took the fish and lay them out on the roof. That was okay until the fish began to get dried, and every evening we had to bring the fish back down. And after the fish began to get dry, we'd go up there supposedly to be turning the fish over, and we'd sit there eating it. Then my father would say, "You know, I don't know what's happening to these fish."

Grandmother belonged to the Kamehameha line, and she had always said that the white shark was our *aumakua*. I didn't know too much about it. But my sister drowned, and it took almost all day before they were able to locate her body, and it had drifted. There were people along the shoreline spotting, and they said they saw these two white sharks on either side of her body going along. And they felt that as long as those sharks were keeping her body that they'd be able to retrieve it, but they would have to retrieve it in some way that wouldn't disturb the sharks. The Coast Guard cutter came along, and they lowered one of their boats and were able to get her body untouched. . . .

My dad was sent out to look after the family ranch. They had a small cattle ranch out there. And so besides looking after the ranch, he eventually went into planting sugarcane. They needed someone to be there, and so they hired my father and he became the . . . I don't know what they called them. But he was in charge of the area down there. . . .

My mother was asked if she would go down there to teach. So without any training she went down. And I can remember her teaching these youngsters. They weren't small. Many of them were grown youngsters who had come in with their parents. Most of them were Japanese. And they would all come to school without any knowledge of English, and my mother would say to them, "Dress — this is a dress. Slip — this is a slip." And "shoes," and all the rest of it. And then with food it was the same way. She taught them that way. She kept going to teachers' training groups on weekends, and in that way it was picked up. She taught there until she passed away, even after we moved. . . .

My brother and I commuted to school by train, leaving at 6:30 in the morning, and we'd get to town and hurry up to the school. We usually got there at 8:30, quarter of nine, although school had begun at 8:30. In the afternoon we had to hurry to get back down to the station to catch the train. We would leave at 2:30 in the afternoon and get home anytime after 4:30, depending on how many cattle there were on the tracks and whether they wanted to get out of the way or not. We lived in a plantation house. It's no longer there. It has been taken down. . . .

As I grew older I knew that I wanted to be a dress designer. I wanted so badly to be that. I wanted to go to the mainland. I used to tell my mother I was going to learn to be a dressmaker, and she'd say, "Oh, no, you're not." Oh, yes, I was. I think Mother wanted me right from the beginning to be a schoolteacher. I wanted to go away so badly to be a dress designer. And, oh, she and my father had all the reasons why I shouldn't go . . . So, okay, alright, I'll go to Honolulu then. I'll go to normal school. So I did . . . I went to normal school two years. I taught down there. The students were giants alongside me, great big Hawaiian boys and girls, and they all called me Sista.

ESTHER

Esther was born of Hawaiian-Chinese-English parentage on Kauai. She was raised by Mormon grandparents, Tutus. She attended normal school and the University of Hawaii and taught for several years. She has four sons and raised an adopted daughter. She has recently worked in a museum library.

My father was pure Chinese from Canton. He came here because the Chinese people here asked that a teacher be sent here. They noticed their children were getting to speak English or even the Hawaiian language, so they were losing the privilege of learning about their own homeland. So my father came as an instructor. However, when he got here he found that he had to go to work rather than teach school in order to support a family. So he began to raise rice. That was the crop, so he thought he'd go there and plant rice. But when he got out there, because of his status they felt that he did not belong in a rice field. So they made him a sort of bookkeeper for the rice planters, a Chinese group. He did that for many years, and he also wrote their letters for them. And would send home money for them. . . .

The Chinese people here had married Hawaiian women. And a lot of them, Hawaiian women and children, refused to learn Chinese. I was one of them. Mother didn't learn Chinese, and my father didn't learn Hawaiian. It was broken English. My mother got to the point where she could understand him, yes. But to really speak it, no. And we just spoke very few Chinese words. . . .

My grandmother . . . Actually, she wasn't my grandmother, she was my grandmother's sister. My grandmother died, and she was my grandmother's stepsister. They had no children. They kept everybody else's children, *hanai*. So when I was born, she took me and raised me. My mother had thirteen children. I was number four. . . .

I got to love my Tutus, grandparents. To me they were my only parents. I don't think I can do justice in what I say about my adopted parents. She gave me all the love, everything I learned. I think with her it was always that slogan, "Charity never faileth." She was always giving. They were religiously inclined, all Christians. They were converted. My grandmother was educated by the missionary families. My grandparents were not poor, but they were not rich. When I became eight years old my grandparents felt that it was time for me to make a decision as to whether I wanted to go and live with my parents. I often went to visit them, and my grandfather would say, "Wouldn't you like to go and stay with your other brothers and sisters?" Now my oldest sister was raised by my mother's stepmother, also my own grandmother's sister, another sister. So we both had very little to do with our parents, and my grandparents, I think, legally adopted me. I could not live without my grandparents. I absolutely refused to go back. And so when my grandparents went out of town and left me with my parents, I would go through a crying siege all night and never could stop until daylight.

My Tutus taught me values, like spiritual values, things that were important in life. Loving and sharing, and that material things would only add to your comfort but they weren't the greatest. They shouldn't be foremost. You know the little things that would enrich my life? She would stop at the store and buy a little package of crackseed and have it ready for me after school. . . .

We spoke Hawaiian with Tutu. Not in the beginning. We spoke English. But my grandmother, when we were young, would put on a deaf ear. No Hawaiian, no answer to our questions or requests. If we asked in English, she didn't answer. That meant we didn't get what we wanted. My grandfather would be told to do the same. But my grandfather was always at work, and it was she who really taught us. My grandmother had a very lasting influence on my life. . . .

My grandmother taught all the Hawaiian crafts. Making *lauhala*. I never go that far but I learned to weave mats. The preparation of the *lauhala* is the thing. That was a task in itself. Oh! You go and you pick. You don't pick *lauhala* from any tree. It had to be certain areas. They'd go and test the area, and they'd get it only from that place. And you'd pick up the dry leaves, you'd bundle them all up. Off the tree and off the ground. You must have an eye to know which one is good and which was not. Then you'd bundle them up, you'd take them home, and then comes the task of scraping all those leaves. Scrape them with a metal — an iron piece — scraping off the part on the top that was no good. Then you had to clean the thorns on both sides. You had to get that off. We'd peel that off. My grandmother showed me a stone that they used before. But when I was young they used a metal, like a comb or brush, very thin bristle. We had to soak it in water, dry it in the sun. Then you scrape it again. Then, when you thought it was good, you roll it all up. Sometimes you don't need to soak. It depends on the texture of the *lauhala*. Then we didn't need to soak it. Then we would roll it up in bundles. Then, when you were ready to make the *lauhala* mats, we would have metal pieces that would have two metal pins that would cut the width of the strip you need to make the mat. Then again you go and scrape, and then you cut this. Then you put them all in bundles. Then you begin your mat. It took a long time to get ready. In the meantime, you're going to get more so that you always have ready *lauhala* on hand.

Then we learned to quilt. It was a must for girls. Grandmother always had a quilt. She did not quilt herself, but she made us learn. My mother did a lot of quilting. My grandmother learned when she went away to school, from the missionaries. My mother quilted, so therefore there would always be a quilt in our home. I was the one that would stay with my grandmother and we would have to quilt. If the stitches were too big I had to take them all off. But, you know, I never regretted that I learned to do these things. We were also taught to do feather leis. We had to. I'd rather go out swimming or play baseball or some other kind of game with the children of the community, but my grandmother always said there was a time for work, time for play, time for learning. There was always time for learning, so that by the time I had gone to school, you know, I had learned the Ten Commandments. . . .

My grandfather would go and catch fish, throw a net. They never took more than what was needed. If one throw of the net would bring in more than what was needed, he'd put the rest back. If they were small they'd go back, but if they were big it would be my job to go and give it to the neighbor. Across this time — the next time we'd give it to someone else. We made poi, and we steamed the taro, and then we cleaned it. And then he pounded it. I was never taught to pound the poi because he thought it was a man's job. He wouldn't let my grandmother do it. But he did get her a poi pounder, a small one, a woman's poi pounder. And he would say that with her poi pounder it was a waste of time. He would do it better. But as we grew up, I must say another thing, that [they began] accepting what they felt was God-given, like the use of machinery. He saw other people grinding rice. Why couldn't we have a machine to grind poi? And the idea developed. I think he was the first in our area to have a machine to grind poi and that meant he would have more poi to give to neighbors. And he sold poi, but was always giving. He'd say, "When you give, you get something in return." What he got in return was not what he got from these neighbors. The health and strength to do what he could do. His taro fields grew and got bigger and bigger. And materially, he could sell more poi. And that's how he sent me to school, to high school. My grandmother raised chickens, so that we gathered our own eggs. And whenever we wanted chickens . . . My grandfather raised two cows. . . .

No, Grandmother didn't teach about the *aumakua*. These were things she didn't want me to know. She said we've become Christianized, and all those things were to be left behind. My grandmother would not give me a Hawaiian name. She said, "If you had this name, you become that person. It was dangerous." Therefore she would not give me any Hawaiian name. My grandfather told me about Hawaiian lore. My grandmother was from royalty, *alii*. They don't speak. I guess it was something that was handed down. They don't talk about their royal lineage. No chanter. My grandmother said when she became a Christian she left all these things behind. She didn't want us to be implicated with any of the taboos that went along with her early life. Nothing. But my grandfather was always with this one thought — you know, if you hide a people's heritage it would be lost. So he was a great storyteller, and he was willing to speak to anyone who would listen to him. Many have been written down.

You see, my grandfather came from a long line of retainers. They lived with the *alii* because they were of the royal blood too. They originated on this island, and they came over this side to live with the kings and queens. And he would tell us [he] was the last of the retainers. My husband told me after my grandfather died — he said, "I think I can tell you now because Grandfather has passed on. But before he died he took me to this cave and he said it was a ritual with him to go into this cave and clean the canoes, the capes, the wooden implements, everything that went with the king, and that he wanted a witness to show that these things were actually the truth. That what he told about the kings of this area and what they did." But I told my husband, "Why didn't you say something before?" I said I knew my grandfather would go many times by himself. I knew that my grandfather, whenever he came home, would be in a very . . . as though he was very tired, as though he had worked hard. I often said I wondered what he did on those days. Dry caves. "There were times," my husband told me, "your grandfather had to swim under the river to get into the cave. And he said we wouldn't do it this time. We went from the top down. Partly underwater." The caves were also used for burial. My husband said my grandfather told him that he would come one day to blast the entrance. That no one must go there, and he must never reveal. So to this day I don't know where it is. . . .

I want to tell you something true. This really actually happened. My grandfather told us a lot of legends about the Menehunes. My grandfather had a friend who was a photographer and would tell him about the Menehunes. And about the *heiau* that was built, the one above the Waialua Falls. He and his friend went up there. Now in those days you couldn't get one panoramic view of the whole valley unless you took the pictures in parts. And that's what he did.

And so one day he rushed to see me and said, "I want to show you something." And he said, "Now, promise — this is not a trick of the trade. It was not prepared by my man who developed it. And I didn't plant it there. So promise that you won't make fun. But I want you to know . . . Before I show you this picture, I want to tell you that I'll never, never make fun of your grandfather again. Nor will I belittle any of the Hawaiian legends and stories."

And I said, "Okay, I'm getting anxious. Please, what is all this about?" So he takes from his book this picture, and he said, "You look at it closely, and you tell me what you see." And there in the picture you see the background is the valley and the mountain, and across Waialua, and there was this little man. I could see him coming up, part of his body, and he held on to a cane. He had on an old straw hat, like one of those *lauhala* hats on his head, but he was a very short man. I looked at it and I looked at it, and I said, "No, this can't be."

And he said, "I always considered the Menehunes were mythical, and whenever your grandfather told me these legends I took it for granted that was what he was brought up on, just a story." But he said, "Now I cannot deny it." And he said, "I believe that if the veil were removed from our eyes, we could see a lot more things." And I said, "You sound like my grandfather." And he said, "Well, it's something I've learned from him. When I took the picture, there was nothing there."

My youngest grandchild is three years old, and I teach her very simple Hawaiian, like parts of the body, her eyes, nose, and she catches on real fast and makes me real happy. Now she's going to nursery school, and I don't know if it's too much for her because now she lives with her parents, and no more Hawaiian until she comes to me. I find myself talking in Hawaiian to her and she says, "Grandma, I didn't understand." I don't tell them the stories I remember from my grandfather, no.

Well, it seems as if none of them, perhaps, have shown an interest. They're too busy in their own — going here, going there. You know, my sister and I feel very strongly that we should put all our knowledge down on paper so that our children — if they have not had all that we have to offer — can someday have it. So that it won't be lost. . . .

HANNAH

Hannah was born in Honolulu of a Hawaiian mother, but she knows nothing about her father because she spent much of her childhood in an orphanage and never met him or heard about him. She practices and teaches Hawaiian massage and is also versed in Hawaiian herbs. Married to a Portuguese-Hawaiian husband, she has five children. Two daughters are nurses, the third teaches handicapped children. Hannah recently adopted a daughter.

My mother was pure Hawaiian. I was less than two and a half years old when I was put in a missionary home, and it was her request. It was a home for children, unwanted children and girls. It was a girls' home, and there were a lot of grown girls. I went to school right there. After graduating from high school, I came home to my aunt and uncle here. But at the age of ten, I came to know I had relatives through my grandfather. In my family, he was a chanter and just like a seer because all the people look up to him. My grandfather came to see me once with his youngest daughter when I was in the missionary home, and he gave me the family blessing, the family heritage blessing, you know. It was a family heritage blessing that was passed on to only one child. Because there were many grandchildren, but I was the only one chosen from all the grandchildren. He chanted on me in Hawaiian. I only spoke the English language. I was brought up the American way. All I know is that it was a family heritage chant that he blessed me with. He never said a thing because he spoke only Hawaiian. He just placed his two hands on my head and embraced me, and he breathed on me. Hawaiians breathe — they don't kiss. They all breathe. On my head. Well, now that people are talking about Hawaiian culture, I feel honored. Because my grandfather gave me the family blessing instead of all the others, and they all spoke Hawaiian. . . .

I missed a family when I was a child. When I was a little girl — I must have been about five or six years old — I'd get up at night and go to the bathroom, and I'd wash and I'd sprinkle water all over my nightie, and I'd knock at the matron's door, and I'd say, "Mrs. K., Hannah's all wet. She wet her nightie. Wake up!" And she'd wake up, and she'd say, "You poor little dear," and she'd change my nightie, and she'd open the foot of her bed, and she'd tuck me in. Oh, I liked that! And maybe the next week I'd do the same thing. So she knew this little girl wanted to be loved. And I loved her. She was a beautiful woman, so pretty. And after my grandfather came to see me, I was so happy because someone else loved me too. He came to the missionary home. Only once. . . .

My grandfather taught *hooponopono* — make things right with your family before the sun sets. Go and kiss your sister. Tell her you're sorry. Then go to the piano and sing. If something went wrong and we maybe scratch one another and hurt one another and bite one another, we got a spanking and a cold shower. And we had to sing this song: " 'Tis love that makes us happy, 'tis love that smoothes the way, it helps us smile, it makes us fine to others every day."

I play the piano — I play the piano and the organ. We sing together a lot of songs. My husband and I sing a few Hawaiian songs together, and I sing a few Hawaiian songs for other people. They have parts, you know, and you have to have someone to sing with, the male part. You have to have somebody that knows the song, and they can sing the male part and I sing the soprano part. My oldest girl sings, but the youngest one plays the guitar and the ukulele and sings. She sings Spanish songs, American songs, and Hawaiian songs. . . .

I teach Hawaiian herbs and lomi lomi massage. It's a gift. And two of my daughters are nurses. The first word and first sentence in Hawaiian massage is a praying word. And my aunt prayed before she went out and picked the herbs for the family.

My husband is Hawaiian–Portuguese–Spanish–American Indian. When we first got married and came here, we opened a general merchandise store. . . .

What happens when anyone comes to my door? I take them in, even if they have no money. If they want help, I take them in. Sometimes my husband doesn't like it, but I say, "Well, the Lord brought them, and I'm going to take care of them." . . . I use vegetarian diet, and fertile eggs. . . . My daughters are all in healing work. We educated the children, sewing seed leis and selling them to the tourists.

SARAH

Sarah was born on Maui of Hawaiian-Chinese parents. She spent part of her childhood in an orphanage. She is a musician, and she also drove a tour truck for over twenty-three years. She is divorced, as her parents were also. She is active in a Hawaiian Congregational church.

I'm three-quarters Hawaiian, one-quarter Chinese. My mother is part-Hawaiian, part-Chinese. My dad was pure Hawaiian. I knew my grandmother but not my grandfather, because when I was born he was already gone. But I had a stepgrandfather, pure Chinese. My grandparents were Congregational and my parents were involved in the church. My grandfather had eleven boys, one girl. These eleven boys — from my dad telling me — most of them were educated at Mid-Pacific Institute. My father just finished grammar school. He went away to China, just to go on a tour with someone, and also later I heard that my Chinese grandfather sent them to China with the idea in mind that he would pick up a Chinese bride, you know. In the meantime, he had gone to Chinese school, so he knew five Chinese dialects. Then he wanted me to go to Chinese school, and today when I think of it I regret that I didn't continue. I did go for a short while, but it was hard because I go to English school, and in English school you learn to be quiet and to read silently, whereas in Chinese school the louder you read the better student you are. Besides trying to learn Japanese at the same time. My dad thought it would be nice to learn another language, and of course there were quite a bit of Japanese. Now, my mother can speak, just from learning, in fact a little of almost everything. She can speak Spanish, and Japanese, Chinese, Filipino, enough so that she can carry on a conversation. Well, she lived among these people, and every now and then they'd get together and have card games. I guess she just gradually picked it up.

I started school late, public school, English. I never went to a Hawaiian school. The only way I learned my Hawaiian was through her, my grandmother. She did not accept our speaking English to her. We had to converse in Hawaiian. And I had the hardest time because my sister and my cousin were brought up with her all the way and they were good, but when I got there it was really hard. I hadn't gone to school yet, then, at six or seven. So my sisters and them were good in Hawaiian, being with her when they were quite young. So I worked hard until I really can speak, and I can always answer her back the way she wants us to.

At church I started to go to Sunday school, and of course we had a Japanese section and a haole, and the Japanese would meet at six and have their worship service at six to 7:30, and then the regular English service begins at 8:30, and then the Hawaiian department comes in at ten. We have it both in English and Hawaiian because there were some younger ones. From that we learned all our lessons when we had church rallies all in Hawaiian. They'd give us a little slip, and we'd go over and study our prayers, and they'd help us. So that's one way the language was kept. But as we grew up and got married . . .

One day I waited for the bus. I could understand Hawaiian but I couldn't converse, except maybe to put one or two Hawaiian words and English. That's what we call pidgin. And so this lady asked me if the bus we were waiting for was going to a certain area. And I said yes — but in English, but she was speaking to me in Hawaiian. And then she said how much was it, so I told her it was 25¢, but I always answered her in English. Finally she said, "You know, it's a shame that our children cannot speak Hawaiian." And I felt kind of shameful.

So when I got home, I went to see an uncle of mine who lived right next door, and I said, "Uncle, you better teach me Hawaiian." I said I can understand but I can answer back only in English. So he told me, "Look, Baby, you go get your Hawaiian Bible." And I had one — Hawaiian and English. "So you go get your Hawaiian Bible. You read the Hawaiian part and you read the English. You read the English part and you read the Hawaiian." Later on there was a Hawaiian school, and so I went. It was held, I think, three times a week in the afternoon. So I would go just to learn the language. We had no dictionary. So what he'd give us, we'd write it down in our book in Hawaiian and then have the English on the side, so that we'd understand. Then, after learning Hawaiian from the teacher, he asked me to help him teach the beginners, so I started that. The older ones, grandparents, would speak Hawaiian, but not so that it would confuse us, but just enough that we would understand a few words.

We had a Hawaiian group, and I used to sing quite often with orchestras. I played the ukulele, also danced. He [her future husband] came to help out with the music, and we got acquainted. Three years later, we were married. Ever since my granddaughter was three, we've been taking her with us.

More fortunate, I have a great-grandchild. Look, I'm very happy, and I'm thankful to the Lord I lived to see my third generation. If counting with me, yes, fourth generation. . . .

I would say at least three times a week I come to church. Sometimes there's something going on here, so I just come and sit around and have someone to talk to instead of [staying] at home. . . . We meet every Wednesday, and we have a lot of fun. Then we do handwork, bringing some handwork and a brown bag, you know, and we'd sit in the lanai and sew or crochet, whatever. And these articles are for the bazaar. . . . That's one of the projects for the church, besides the luau on Kamehameha Day. In between, of course, we have our lunches on Sunday.

BERNICE

Bernice was born on Oahu of Hawaiian-Chinese-English parentage. She attended college and taught and also worked as a marriage license recorder, as did her grandfather and aunt before her. Widowed, she has three daughters. Her husband was Japanese.

My grandfather's family lived in Laie. They were pure Hawaiian. They pulled up stakes and moved with the rest of the converts [to Mormonism] to the island of Lanai. They were happy, but the Civil War was brewing, so the missionaries were recalled. . . . I don't know my Chinese grandparents because by the time I was four years old, my parents were divorced. . . .

I was born here right on this street. I remember when I was about four, my parents were divorced. My mother was so busy working that her parents raised me, my grandparents. We all lived together. . . . I accompanied my grandfather in all the things that he did because I truly loved my grandfather. He was tax assessor for the territory. He was also the marriage license agent as well as a notary and one who drew up deeds and wills. Now I do these things. On this two-seater drawn by a horse, I would sit on the front with Grandfather and hold the reins. I loved to drive with him. . . . I would accompany my grandfather down to Kaneohe to turn over his report and money to his supervisor, a Caucasian named Cob Adams. . . .

My grandmother was a blond who had yellowish-greenish eyes. With the other women under the trees weaving, making mats, cleaning pandanus [the botanical name for *lauhala*], they would tease her. Her friends would say to her, "Marion, you're a Caucasian." And she would pucker up and say to them, "I'm pure Hawaiian!" And some of my schoolmates said to me as I was growing up, "Hey, Bernice! You have haole blood!" But I said, "No, I'm a Chinese-Hawaiian."

I remember as I was growing up that we had breakfast, lunch, and dinner, fish and poi. Now, we had other varieties of ocean food, like we had crabs, either sand crabs or *aama*. *Aama* is a big black crab, but when it's boiled it turns red. They're delicious. We had dried fish. Grandfather was more of a torcher. He would wait for dark nights. Then he would get his torch ready. Then I would ask him . . . I was scolded for asking. You're not supposed to ask because "You can look at me and see I'm getting ready, but don't ask if I'm going fishing." That was their custom. Not that they didn't want us to know. But his chance of getting a good harvest would be interrupted, would be spoiled. . . .

My aunt lived here. This is where we peeled our taro and cooked our taro. And where we had our banana fields, right in the back here. Grandfather was very industrious. He had bananas, sugarcane, we had ti leaves. Ti leaves are very important to cook with and to decorate, make leis. Oh yes, we had papayas. Grandfather had another property at the foothills, where we had coconuts and bananas, also mangoes, our mango grove. We had, I think, two taro patches where the TV housing is now. Those were our taro patches. . . .

Besides *aama*, we had *pipipi*, a small snail that clings on the rocks. Then we had *ina*, urchin . . . in the deep water. [For] *wana*, you have to go on the reef that's in the water, it's underwater, and when the tide is kinda high. Grandfather didn't do that. It's a big urchin with porcupines, really dangerous. They were younger men who would dive under the reef there, and with this strong, curved wire reach in and pull it out. What Grandfather did was to reach down from the reef, because the water would be only about to his knees. They had to wear shoes. I remember him taking a gunnysack, and he would come up on the reef above water. There were openings in the reef, so he would reach down and hold the top and making sure his hands were not anywhere near the top [of the bag] just push the *wana* back and forth, back and forth, so the porcupines got off, and [he'd] put it in the bag. . . .

When we got married, we lived in Haleiwa because my husband was disowned by his family because it was a disgrace for a Japanese to marry a Hawaiian. My grandfather didn't approve either. He didn't want me to marry a man with three children, but I talked to him and he finally agreed. . . .

My own heritage is that during the days of the monarchy, Laie was the land of refuge for the oppressed. My aunt, who was a beautiful storyteller, to impress us children would tell us [a story about] how Laie was a favorite land for commoners . . . There was a lovely girl in Kaneohe who had her own lover, and they were deeply in love. But one day the chief of that district spotted her talking with her friends. He went to her parents and told them that he had chosen their daughter as one of his concubines. And when she reached home, her parents told her that the chief had stopped over to request her. They felt they had to because that was the way they lived. They obeyed the chief.

This maiden said, "No, I love my own friend, so I won't be one of his concubines." So the mother said, "Then you have to leave as soon as possible and get over to Laie, where you'll be free." So the mother prepared a little knapsack [with food] for her to eat along the way, and under the protection of darkness of night she left. There was a little bird that was a favorite of the family that joined her. Flew ahead and along with her. In daylight he would fly ahead and then come back and talk to her that she shouldn't take the path she was taking but should get closer to the ocean so she wouldn't get lost in the woods. And so they traveled together in haste. Then the bird said, "I'd better go back and see if all is normal, then I'll come back." So then he flew and flew, and right outside Kaneohe he saw the chief's soldiers, a couple of them. They were talking about the daughter who had not wanted to be one of the chief's concubines and had left for the land of refuge. So they were ordered to pursue. So the bird got all this knowledge and flew back. She was near, just past Kaaawa, near this area here. The bird told her the trouble that had arisen. So she said, "Then I can't take my time and I must start running." So she started running and ran and ran. Then the bird said, "You have to rest also." So she'd rest a little while under the protection of the shrubs. And so the bird flew back, and [it] came back to her and said, "They're advancing pretty fast. You can't rest any longer. You'll have to run."

So at that time she was at Laie Malo'o. Now, that is the boundary of the land of refuge, the south boundary. Now, from the mountains to the sea is the Laie land of refuge. All the districts are divided to the mountains and the sea. She could hear the men panting not too far behind her. But she had nearly reached that boundary. There was no bridge, just a sort of ditch. You have to scramble over the rocks. She barely got over the rocks, but she stumbled. When she stumbled, she stumbled over the boundary. And the men were behind her, but they couldn't touch her. She was in the land of refuge. During the days of the monarchy, the land of refuge was recognized by everyone. . . .

After we were married and our children came, we stressed English. I only wish I had taught them Hawaiian! Even Kamehameha Schools when I was there, they didn't allow the hula. And my husband [I wish] had taught them Japanese. But we didn't do so. With my own mother was English most of the time. But it was with my grandparents that I spoke Hawaiian. So you can see I was fortunate to have my grandparents — otherwise I wouldn't be able to speak Hawaiian. And my children can't speak Hawaiian because I didn't speak Hawaiian to them. One culture I didn't teach my children, I think I got it from my grandmother. We're not the kissing Hawaiians. So my daughters found themselves like that too. . . . They're not the one to go forward.

RACHEL

Rachel is Hawaiian-Chinese, was born on Kauai, and has five sons and three daughters.

Both my parents were part-Hawaiian, part-Chinese. My father was . . . I think he had a little German in him. Eight years I went to school, that's the farthest I went.

I remember my grandmother. She was a nice grandmother, tall and slim, and she was a hardworking grandma. She was pure Hawaiian. My grandmother used to teach us, those days, how the Hawaiians used to live, what they were interested in — fishing and planting taro — and they always tell us as long as you have a taro patch you'll never go hungry, because that's the main food. And the ocean is right there, and they go to the ocean and get their fish, and in those days there were plenty of fish. So they just go and get what they needed. There was a river close by. If the ocean would get too rough, then they would depend on the river. They had nets — they'd lay their nets and catch fish. There was plenty of mullet. Grandmother would take me down to the beach, and she would teach me how to hook fish. Bait is either shrimp or squid. We'd go early in the morning. About six o'clock we would leave the house because they go when the tide goes down. And in the early morning it's so nice and cool. It was fun. The ladies would go and catch shrimp with shrimp net. I love it. We used to do that when I was about thirteen years old. With my girlfriends, we used to go after we get through eating breakfast. Our house was close to the river, so we'd go down [to] the river with our little nets and pan, tie a string to our waist and [to] a pan floating by, and get shrimp. And, those days, they had plenty of fish. They didn't have to worry. Not like nowadays. Today, sometimes you go with a bamboo and you stay all day and you catch maybe one fish, or nothing.

Grandmother taught me how to make patch quilts [and] this other kind [of] quilt besides patch quilts, the Hawaiian quilts. Patch, you just make these strips of material. But the Hawaiian quilt is the one you cut the pattern and baste them on the foundation that you want. Then she used to teach me and my sisters how to sew our own clothes. She said, "You girls should learn how to sew your own dresses." So she used to teach us.

Grandmother does the hula. She loves to dance. Well, I guess those days most of the Hawaiian did know how to dance, because when they had parties, birthday parties for their babies, they would have a grand time. The menfolks would play the guitar and ukulele, and the ladies would dance.

And our grandfather used to tell us, "Watch them, how they pound the poi and cook the taro, clean the taro and then pound the poi." Oh, ya, we did just for the fun. They had these long boards, cook the taro, and pound it. But we did it just for the fun — we cannot do really a good job.

Part of our *aumakua* in the river and in the ocean, it's the shark. They didn't tell too much of that. It's like a secret to them. They say every now and then they would go and feed the shark. They would go at night. They would go in the water as far as up to their breast, and they get the food for the shark. They would prepare at home. At night when it's quiet, they would go down to the beach and go in the water and throw it. I guess they would call the shark by name. They said they can tell when the shark is coming because the water splashes, and then when it gets close, the water gets warm. And then they throw this food. Then they would go home. In the river it's a *mo-o*. A *mo-o* is something like a lizard.

Yes, they still have night marchers, certain nights. They have certain nights for those marchers to march. My grandmother passed away, and she never did tell us those things. But when my grandfather bought a place up there and we were living there, the road was something like this — our house and the road. And these things would march on the road. No, you don't see anything. All you hear is the drum and the footsteps, and they must be singing or something, but just a mumbling sound. And they are marching, but you can hear the footsteps and you can hear the drum. And they say that road is their road, and when it comes to the night for them to march, they would march on that road. Not full moon — it's on a very dark, dark night. And when everything is quiet, then you can hear them. I think it's only one or two nights a month. They say if you're in their way and if you don't have any relatives that passed away that's in the group that's marching, they can kill you. Because if you're in their way, they're not gonna go off their way for you. They'll march right through, and if you're in their way you can die. But if you have a family that passed away that is in that group marching, then the family would tell them, would tell these boys, that I'm not to hurt you because I am related to you, so they'll let you go. Nobody sees them, they only heard them. Until today up there they still have that. And the people that live close by, they say, oh, certain nights, they hear these marchers marching.

III   Chinese

The Chinese Diaspora

Beginning at the end of the eighteenth century and continuing at an accelerated pace during the nineteenth century, the migration of Chinese people from their homeland was one of the largest migrations in the history of the world. Prompted by poverty, floods, war, and economic insecurity, the emigrants left southern China for Southeast Asia and Africa, Hawaii and California, where they sought a chance for a better life, for jobs and the prospect of making money to take back home to their villages. Once abroad, however, many became permanent exiles in strange lands, unable or ultimately unwilling to return to their places of birth. A few did in old age fulfill their dreams and return to their villages and families with more money than they had when they left. These fortunate rich returned in larger numbers in the eighteenth and nineteenth centuries than later.

Abroad, the first and often second generations were slow to assimilate. The first-generation immigrants wished to remain Chinese. Wherever possible, they lived in discrete community ethnic enclaves, where they retained their own language, food, and culture. Transplanted, their outstanding characteristics were their enterprising spirit, their willingness to follow wherever opportunity beckoned, and their concern for the future. Chinatowns sprang up wherever the immigrants settled, from San Francisco to Jakarta.

The first Chinese to settle in the "Sandalwood Mountains," one of the early names for the Hawaiian Islands, arrived almost immediately after Captain Cook's "voyage of discovery" in 1778. By 1828 between 20 and 30 were living in Honolulu, where they bargained with Hawaiian chiefs for sandalwood to ship to Asia. In 1865 the first 500 laborers were recruited from Hong Kong, and others came in the same decade of their own volition. In 1878 another 2,484 Chinese males arrived, and a steady stream followed. By 1882, 95 percent of all the Chinese in

Hawaii were male.[1] The Chinese Exclusion Act of 1882, aimed at interdicting all Chinese immigration to the United States, did not affect Hawaii until 1900, following annexation. Other legislation, however, did affect Hawaii's Chinese. With annexation in 1898 further Chinese immigration to Hawaii was forbidden, and Chinese residents were required to register and obtain certificates of residence within one year. Chinese in the Islands were also forbidden to travel to the mainland United States. And in 1904, legislation extended and continued all Chinese exclusion laws for an indefinite period of time.[2]

Female Immigration

Many, if not most, of these emigrants married before they departed from China and left their wives at home to await their return. Many waited in vain. Some of the wives later joined their husbands, but most remained in their villages waiting. Some husbands found second wives abroad yet continued to work with the expectation of later returning to their first wives in honor and wealth. The "Singapore wife" was the prototype for these local, second wives. She helped her husband manage the family business, whether small or large, and raised a family besides. Many of the emigrants lived as bachelors until they died. In some cases, marriage was arranged by mail, and the bride arrived from China after the exchange of photographs, a picture bride.

Some fathers sent their sons, even those who were part-Hawaiian, to China for schooling, in the expectation that they would also acquire Chinese brides. Few daughters were given the opportunity to go to China to school; usually they were sent out to work or worked with their mothers in family stores. When they worked outside the home, they contributed their earnings to help support the family. Some female immigrants had bound feet, which meant they were not able to work outside the home. Older women with bound feet were a common sight in Honolulu in the 1930s. These disabled women spent their time sewing clothing from rice sacks and flour bags, a practice adopted by other immigrant women as well because all were faced with the scarcity of fabrics with which to make clothing. Most women contributed to the family economically by becoming dressmakers or by helping in family stores, or both. Despite the shortage of women within the ethnic Chinese communities, some wealthy merchants managed to acquire Chinese concubines, a custom transplanted from their homeland.

In addition to performing these roles, Chinese wives raised large numbers of children. Families with as many as ten or eleven children were not uncommon. Women also preserved and transmitted cultural traditions as seen, for example, in their preparation of traditional foods for the important New Year's and Dragon Boat festivals. Chinese women did not typically work on the plantations in the early stages of the sugar plantation economy, and even male workers on plantations left for other employment as soon as they could.

Chinese immigrants in Hawaii, unlike those in California and other states, were able to intermarry. When the men married Hawaiian women, moreover, they acquired more than wives. They became landowners, although the land was held in their wives' names. Before the Great Mahele, non-Hawaiians could not acquire land, and even after that reform, the acquisition of land was difficult for aliens. Chinese immigrants were quick to see the advantages of having Hawaiian wives, and more Chinese married Hawaiians than they did any other ethnic group — except, of course, their own. The consequence is that the largest Hawaiian ethnic admixture even today is Hawaiian-Chinese.

Today, many Chinese women in Hawaii are employed in banks and savings and loan institutions. The same is true of Chinese women in Southeast Asia. Apparently financial institutions are quicker than other businesses to recognize the abilities of these women.[3]

Economic Activity

Chinese workers entered sectors of the Hawaiian economy serially. The earliest immigrants arrived before the time of the large plantations and contract labor recruitment and worked on small sugar and rice plantations. Some early arrivals came as independent merchants and craftsmen, others came as language teachers. Still others earned a living as gamblers, moving from camp to camp in search of winnings. Many immigrants who came without connections became itinerant peddlers or urban hawkers, selling their own garden produce and fish from baskets, which they hung from both ends of a bamboo pole carried on their shoulders. From such modest beginnings, many went on to become large entrepreneurs.

Fig. 3.1. Second family, the first wife having been left in China. *Courtesy of Mrs. Helen Wong.*

Enterprising Chinese workers were some of the earliest to move off the plantations and into towns in search of better wages. Under the 1870 labor contracts, the Chinese plantation workers earned $6 a month for twenty-six days of work; by 1888, they were no longer indentured but worked as "free" day labor.[4] Many took advantage of their new freedom to move to the cities in search of better pay. The 1884 census listed thirteen Chinese druggists; the 1896 census reported fifteen Chinese physicians. By the 1930s, there were two Chinese banks — the Liberty Bank, opened in 1922, and the American Security Bank, founded in 1935.[5] Several Chinese immigrants owned investment and trust companies and building and loan organizations. Real estate and construction also had large ethnic Chinese representation.[6] As with overseas Chinese communities elsewhere, Cantonese and Hakka were the major languages, reflecting the southern origin of the immigrants. The two languages were not mutually intelligible. Another sharp division separated the Hakkas and the Puntis, whose languages were also mutually unintelligible. Most of the Chinese came from four districts in Kwangtung Province.

The Hakka population numbered over 20 percent of the Chinese immigrants, but they came from several districts and did not concentrate in Honolulu as did the Puntis. They assimilated more quickly in

Hawaii than did other groups and became successful more rapidly. Many of them had become Christian converts. Some sources suggest that the Hakkas were a land-poor seafaring people who were less concerned than others with maintaining Chinese customs. Unlike some other groups, the Hakkas did not practice footbinding, and Hakka women were thus more able to work.[7]

Societies, Secret and Otherwise

When enough immigrants from China gathered in one place, they organized societies for mutual support and aid, for social interaction, and for assistance in dealing with the government in a strange land. Membership in these societies was for life, and there were no dues. These organizations assumed some of the functions of the clan organization in China, such as burial rites. In Hawaii, clan members exhumed graves, cleaned the bones, and prepared them to be returned to Chinese villages for burial. The focus on graves was important, for if a Chinese died and his remains were uncared for and not sent back to his family grave in China, his spirit would wander forever.

Some of the societies were secret, in which case they reflected the political purposes of secret societies in China. The origins of the Hawaiian Triad Society, for example, can be traced to the late-seventeenth-century anti-Manchu activities to reestablish the Ming dynasty.[8] Some societies were district associations, with membership based on place of origin. Often they were either village or lineage village clubs. The first Hakka society was formed in 1921. Other organizations, *hangs*, were associations of craftsmen and traders, including servants in haole homes. Societies also represented members in disputes with nonmembers.

All of these Chinese societies served to keep immigrants separated from the rest of the society and to retard their assimilation. Some early Chinese viewed the societies as a means to prevent their children from becoming estranged from their heritage. Membership was all male; women did not form societies of their own, although they participated in a limited way in some of the social functions of the male societies — for example, in serving food.

One of the most famous of the Chinese immigrants to arrive in Hawaii was Sun Yat-sen, who came as a boy during the 1870s to attend Iolani School. He was, at the time, under the supervision of his elder brother, who became annoyed when his young charge wanted to be baptized as a Christian and sent him back home to China. Sun later returned to Hawaii several times as a revolutionary seeking support for his anti-Manchu activities. It was in Hawaii in 1894 that Sun organized his first secret revolutionary society, and on one of his visits he was made marshal, or Red Stick, of the Triads. And in Honolulu in 1905, he founded the Tung Meng Hui, or Kuomintang.[9] Hawaii was thus an important base for revolutionary anti-Manchu activities. During visits in 1894 and 1903, Sun toured several ethnic communities, including the Kula Chinatown on Maui, where residents still speak of him.

In December 1899, bubonic plague broke out in Chinatown in Honolulu. Authorities responded by evicting inhabitants and burning buildings. Residents were forced into detention camps. When some Chinese complained that the administrative remedy went too far, the authorities replied that the fire had gotten out of control due to a shift in the wind.[10]

A Chinese Man Speaks

The speaker is a longtime resident of Kula, Maui.

One thing I can tell you, I think the Chinese in business and in the financial world locally . . . I think they are more progressive than the others. Because originally we all came in poor, any nationality came in poor. And we got ahead in the financial world. I'm not bragging, but that's what happened. In a monetary way, they have more sense. They notice how to be successful and how to make money more. I think it's an instinct. I think it's born. God gave that talent to the Chinese. Because all the big business houses . . . Originally the Chinese start out with small little stores, huh? All through the Islands here, go back sixty years or fifty years, all the store owners are Chinese throughout the Islands, merchants. And after a while the Japanese catch on, so the Chinese yield the smaller retail outlets to the Japanese, and they went to banking. Oh, not more than forty years ago, about the end of the war. And after the Japanese go into the banking business, the Chinese go into real estate, and they're always one step ahead. Not much insurance. The Chinese didn't go much on insurance. After the small stores, they went into supermarkets. And after they make money in the supermarket, they sold them to the Japanese. Then they went into banking, and after the banking they went into the real estate and high-rises.

During the war, they were just common people, but after the war, oh, they became millionaires left and right. Many of them are millionaires today, from investments. During my father's day, seventy, eighty years ago, they weren't interested in real estate at all. I remember in my father's day they said, oh, we don't want this kind of land. The Hawaiians came to offer them a whole parcel for just a few dollars. The Chinese didn't want it. What are we gonna do with this kind of place? If we make money, we're going back to China and die. We don't want to settle here. So their mind is to come here and make a living and go back to China. The ones that made money probably all went back to China before 1920. And after that, the older ones got married and raised a family, and the bachelors, naturally, they stay here and die.

Because in those days they were addicted to opium smoking. Like up to 1930, I think they all . . . When I was young I remember that smoking. Ya, they smoked every evening. And afterwards they were prohibited. Some of them did it at home if they could afford it. Oh, just a pipe and a lamp. They go to the Chinese society — they have a regular journey over there. All the bachelors would go there. Some of them married to the natives, but not too many. Oh, you can tell when they are children of mixed blood. They don't adopt the given name from the father's side. The first name, they use the first name only. The last name is forgotten. Maybe it was illegal to smoke opium, but there were no police over here.

EDITH

Edith was born and raised in Honolulu, one of eleven children. She taught for more than thirty-eight years, was married, and had a son who died young. She has three grandsons.

In his travels, my grandfather in China took my father along to help with his work. And he learned that the returnees from the California Gold Rush had made money overseas, so he was determined to have a son go overseas to try his fortune. So he sent my father when he was in his late teenage, I think. Not exactly Hawaii, but overseas, see. So before my father left the village, his parents had him married to a bride they chose for him. And right after he got married he left China, went to Hong Kong, and got in contact with a Chinese man who represented the Hawaiian plantation owners, seeking laborers from China. So my father signed up with one of them, and that was how he got here.

He came here, and instead of working for the plantation, he went out on his own. At that time there was a big Chinese store called Wing Wo Tai on Nuuanu Street, see, and all the immigrants would contact the owner to get information, see. So my father went there and asked him about the prospect of finding a job outside the plantation. So they sent him up to Manoa, where the taro patches are. So he went to work on the taro patches for three or four years before he saved enough money. Then he went on his own, had a cabinet shop on King Street, where the Liberty Bank is now.

When he got the shop he wrote to his wife in the village, asking her to come. She didn't want to come. So my father wrote back and said, "If you're not coming, I'm going to get me another wife." Well, there was no reply, so he decided to go to the Wing Wo Tai company again that has a ship plying between Hong Kong and Honolulu with their goods. So he told the manager there to tell the captain of one of his ships to find him a wife. So the captain, when he got to Hong Kong, must have contacted my mother's foster mother. My mother was an orphan, so a lady took her and brought her up until she was about fourteen, when this captain contacted her. So that was what you would call a marriage arrangement. So she had her passage on one of the ships and came here at fourteen or fifteen, around there, and they got married in the old Chinese way, you know. She said she enjoyed the trip very well because she didn't have to do a thing. Had three meals and just sat around and chatted every day. . . . She was a little upset when she found my father's first wife was coming, but she couldn't do anything, so she said she might as well make the best of the life she has entered into. In those days, many of the men married this way through picture brides unless they lived in the village and married a village girl. But if it's from another section of China, it has to be through marriage arrangement.

Then, in the meantime, the wife in China decided to come. So she came when my mother came too, see, so my father had two wives with him . . . As usual, there was a little bickering and arguing every day. The first wife had a daughter about the same time my mother gave birth to my oldest brother, the first son. Then my mother gave birth to a daughter, and then my father's first wife decided to return to China.

Altogether there were eleven children, ten by my own mother. But she lost two in infancy — otherwise she would have had twelve.

Mother had a Chinese midwife. That's why our births were never reported to the Board of Health. Just this midwife. So afterwards, when we wanted to go to the mainland, we had to go to Immigration. So in order to get the ID to leave this island, they had to question my mother and also have two witnesses to verify our birth over here. . . . Citizens by birth, but those days they didn't believe in it because this was a territory, see. . . . We had to go to Immigration to get this ID . . . and sometimes it took months to get it. . . .

My mother was never in school — she had no education at all. She didn't have to work. She just stayed at home with the foster mother doing little house chores and things like that. She said she had a very nice life with the foster mother. Very happy life. Those days, the Chinese women were not educated — only very few of the noble class who were educated in poetry and things like that, see. Nothing to prepare them for life. Mother said sometimes she had little arguments with my father because she never had an allowance. She was never allowed a certain amount of money to spend. Well, anyway, now I can see why she doesn't need that, because my father did all the shopping and he did all the paying of bills. Everything my mother wanted, he paid or he'd buy, see. . . .

My brothers and sisters went to Chinese school, but it seems that I was the rebellious one in the family, never wanted to do what they do, you see. So I have never gone to Chinese school.

My two eldest brothers were tutored in China. See, when they were about nine or ten years old, my father's wife in China wanted to have a son. She heard that my mother had many boys, so she had somebody write a letter to my father and asked my father to send her a son. So my father asked my mother if she's willing to let the boys go. So my mother said [they could] go. So the eldest one was sent when he was about ten years old, and [my father's] wife there saw to it that he was well tutored in Chinese language and philosophy of life. Then, when he was seventeen years old, he had to come back — otherwise he would lose his citizenship.

The second son was also sent likewise, because in China if a married woman has no sons they lose face, as they say. Whether it's a son from a second wife or not, you must have a son. But my third brother was a little more Americanized, and he revolted in China. So he didn't study much, and within two or three years he wanted to come home. So he came back. Then no more after that because my father's daughter by the first wife got married and had children, so she was satisfied with some grandsons. . . .

My oldest brother finished the University of Shanghai, where English was spoken mostly, and then he came back here. One of my brothers went to the University of Peking, but he didn't like it because he didn't know enough Chinese. We all attended public school right through high school, and my older brothers attended colleges on the mainland. . . .

We spoke Chinese at home with our parents, and among ourselves we used to speak pidgin English. My father was a great believer in education. In Chinese standards, he was educated. But he was quite a philosopher and believed in the teachings of Confucius.

Well, first there's filial duty, you know — obey your father and mother. But there were times that I rebelled against some of their teaching, such as no going out with the other sex and no going out after six o'clock, no matter who. They didn't exactly make a rule, but they have talked about it so much with us that if we would go against them they would show their disapproval, you know. They would mention it, but they have never tried to punish us for it. But my mother is a little bit more broadminded because she was brought up in Hong Kong. She told us she was born in the worst section of Hong Kong, Won Chai.

She wore Chinese dress, those white top and pants. And she made me wear them, too, until I graduated from elementary school. I wore Chinese dress right through eighth grade. Even for my graduation day I wore Chinese. Then, when I went to high school, I changed into American dress. My father wore regular Chinese. He refused to wear American dress because, he said, "I can't see the need for a necktie. It's almost like tying up a dog." So he wore something like the Mao Tse-tung jacket with two big pockets, made of blue serge. He always wore blue serge. And a Panama hat. I think he was one of the early Chinese who became a citizen of the Hawaiian Kingdom. . . .

When he was working in the taro patch, somebody said, "Why don't you take the taro down to Beretania and Nuuanu and peddle the cooked taro on Sunday, when you don't have to work?" So he did, and when he went there the Hawaiian people patronized him, and he learned all the Hawaiian language. So he was able to have a piece of land to build his three-story house. . . .

When I was eight or nine years old, I used to be the holy terror of the family 'cause I rebelled against a lot of Mother's ways. And so she and I used to, well, we didn't argue, I was just contrary minded, that's all. Sometimes she threatened to whip me good and hard, and I would run away for the day, hiding myself in the mango tree for two or three hours, you know, or go under the house with a book and read for two, three hours. Then when I got back home, she forgot about the arguments we had, see.

I used to enjoy my father's companionship more than my mother's because she never went out. She was too busy taking care of the children.

During vacations, I'd go down to the fish ponds with my father. Take four books — we could check out four books at a time from the library — and stay a week or two there. Then bring back the fish on the train, get some more books, and go down for another week. There was no housework to be done — I just had a grand time there. And the meals were good. When I felt like it, I'd go out with the workmen and gather the fish for the day. Yes, it was the high point. I wish other people had that experience too. It was such a wholesome life. Nothing else was comparable, not even my marriage life. My marriage life is as usual, you know, all fine and that, but the fun part of my life is that life on the fish pond. . . .

When my father was at home in the evening, sometimes I would go with him to the opium den. Once in a while he would smoke one or two puffs, when he has rheumatism. Those days they called it rheumatism, but now it's arthritis, I think. Well, he felt that the opium would help ease the pain, see. About seven, after dinner, you know, he'll take this kerosene lantern, and we'll cut down the alley from our fence. Right next is the little opium den run by a Chinese woman. She catered to mostly the businesspeople. Just a few clients, steady clients. And so when my father felt like going, he said, "Do you want to come with me?" I said sure. He said, "Did you finish your study?" I said ya. So I would go there, and the lady would always give me some cookies, some Chinese cakes, or I would munch and talk to her, and the men would smoke their opium. Those days, no Mah-Jongg. And I really enjoyed that.

So that's how I got to know about opium, how they prepare it and so forth. They have a small, little lantern that burns — not kerosene, peanut oil. And with a little candlewick. Then they have this great pipe attached with the container that held the opium, and they pour it in the center of the hole, roll it, and then put it over the lantern, then smoke it, inhale the smoke. Then the ashes would go into this little receiver. Then when they had too much of that, the lady would scrape that clean, ready for the next time. And what they scrape out, they sell to those that cannot afford to smoke the real one, as a substitute. And they just put it in tea and drink it. That's the residue. . . .

Oh, we looked forward to New Year's because it was a seven-day thing. See, that's the time we get to wear our new clothes and shoes. And when company comes, we had to serve them tea, and they always returned with a little red paper with 10¢ or 25¢ in it, at New Year's, see. And also the different Chinese holidays, such as the Moon Festival in August. My father carried out the holidays very well. We used to have extra servings of moon cake, and we had all the special dinners for Moon Festival. Then in the evening, well, my mother has no religious expectations, so we never have to put up candles or incense sticks to worship on the moonlight night. But we had the fruits and the good times, that's all.

And my father's birthday and my mother's birthday were big occasions. We didn't do much, but we had big dinners, and the family used to gather together with friends. If it's my mother's birthday, my father would cook up a storm of special food, and vice versa. My father never drank wine — he drank only gin. That was his drink. But the ladies rarely drank, those days. Only the men. So we didn't have any liquor in our life. . . .

I and my younger sister finished up University of Hawaii here. Teaching, both of us became teachers, and we're retired now. . . . I began to teach on Maui. In those days, as soon as we finish they appoint us to go to different places to teach. And for beginners, they always put us on the outside islands. Then, after that, we would be put in the rural district of Oahu until there's a vacancy in the city. Then we move up. . . . Altogether I taught thirty-eight and a half years. . . .

I met my husband in church. At that time, when we were young, there was that Beretania church that was run by the missionary Mrs. M. And she had two Chinese missionaries from China to help her go around the Chinese community and talk to the mothers about letting their children go to Sunday school and also [to] try to convert the mothers to become Christians. That's how we got in contact with Christianity. . . . It was a Congregational church. She was one of those old-fashioned religious missionaries from Boston. She was an old Scottish woman, very nice. . . . And that's how we got to become Christians. . . .

I've changed quite a lot, quite a lot. I don't observe any more of these Chinese holidays, you know. Because I don't have that incentive, you see. And besides, our teachings are so different, our Christian teachings, see.

For a time, I had a battle with my conscience over this custom of Chinese memorial day. You know how they do it. You're supposed to take incense and things to the graveyard to worship if you have a father. That's really ancestral worship, see. Then, for a time, I saw a conflict in that ceremony with the Christian ceremony, that you shall take no other gods. So one time I asked my former minister. I said, "We Chinese all have this conflict because we have to observe our filial duty, we call it — not religious." Not religious, but whoever carries it out, we have this Taoist religious custom, see, and to show respect all the young ones have to bow to the monument, see. I said, "Isn't that against the Christian religion, you should have no other God but one?" Then this minister, who happened to be Chinese too, and he was Americanized, said, "You know, when you bow to your mother, your mother is not a god. It's just that you're showing your filial duty to her. So it wouldn't be against the Christian religion, where you have an idol that's supposed to represent God and you worship that." So after that I felt better. Because my sister-in-law observed that. She's Taoist, and she observed on memorial day for my mother, her mother-in-law, see. And she always asked us to bow to her tombstone and things, after she had all the rituals done, see. And we did that, and I also teach my grandchildren, and I tell them that this is not a god. You're just paying respect to your great-grandmother, see. So they feel a little better. Because it would be really . . . You know, this bowing to the monument can be a conflict with the Christian teaching. . . .

Yes, I want my children to know Chinese tradition, especially ethics. Be respectful to the elders, and follow some of the Chinese custom of good manners, such as when you see an elderly lady you should address her so-and-so. And try and keep up with the old Chinese custom of . . . on New Year's Day you're supposed to serve your mother with a cup of Chinese tea, see. So I usually have my son go and serve my mother a cup of tea. And I always encourage him to go and visit my mother on the way back from school, because on the way home he can stop by and talk with my mother for a while, because my mother took care of him in the early years when I had to go back to teach after maternity leave. So he was very well versed in Chinese at that time.

When he was little, my mother used to take him to Chinatown. And when English is needed, she'll ask him to translate in Chinese to her, see. I didn't speak one word of Chinese with my husband. So the Chinese my son learned was from my mother. No, my grandsons don't serve me a cup of tea on New Year's. I don't expect that from them. I say they're being Americanized.

LILLIAN

Lillian was born in Honolulu, one of nine children. She taught school and later worked as a bookkeeper. She married and had four children. As of the time we met her, she had fifteen grandchildren and nine great-grandchildren.

My father was pure Chinese, from Kwangtung. He first came in 1870, I think. After working at the Big Island for quite a while, he went back to the Orient and married my mother, who was from a well-to-do family. She had Hawaiian blood because her great-grandfather came to the Islands and married a Hawaiian woman, had two boys and two girls. One of the boys was her grandfather.

The plantation needed bookkeepers, Chinese as well as others, because most of them working there are Chinese. So my father came. He was a well-educated man so he brought a group of people to Kohala. . . . 'Course he made some money, and he bought this big farm. . . .

My father sent for a lot of brothers, and they were working on the farm. There was a big fish pond and ducks and all, and on the other side they had bananas. And then the piggery run by some of the working people. . . .

My father had a store on Beretania Street, right across from the Dillingham Building there. He also had business in Mauna Kea Street. He was quite a businessman. He had a store, and mother helped. After school we helped out.

My mother had never been to a Chinese school, but she tried to teach us to read and write in Chinese. She had five girls and four boys. But my brothers all went to Chinese school. You know how the girls have to stay home and learn to do housekeeping and everything — sewing, cooking Chinese food. We spoke Cantonese, and Hakka at home, or See Yup because of the old man that took care of the kitchen. I remember learning some of that.

My mother wasn't more partial to the boys — maybe my father was a little bit when he sent my oldest brother back to China. My older brother was the only one that went back to China. My father and mother wanted to send him back to learn Chinese, read and write Chinese and everything. He went to school in Peking somewhere. He came back here and married a Hawaiian. He was engaged the Chinese way to a Chinese girl, but he didn't marry her. When he was in school back here with this other woman, he married her, a Hawaiian. It was after my mother passed away. . . .

My father became a Christian when he came to the Islands and was baptized. . . . Mother goes to church every Sunday, and they have Holy Communion and so forth. No, I don't think my father made her become Christian. When they came here, they know it's different from China, and things like that, and even in China I don't think they were real pagans. So they learned the English way of living here more, and so they became baptized and so they were very religious. Oh yes, they were Christian when I was born. . . .

Mah-Jongg — oh, that goes back to China, to the brother that went back to China. He bought a bamboo set, how to play Mah-Jongg. And my father and mother said that's gambling, you know, when he first came back. But he said no, just for fun. We learned. And then after that my husband used to play Mah-Jongg with different groups. And I used to play with them and learned more from them. My parents didn't exactly disapprove. They said, "It's up to you folks if you want to learn." So they didn't stop us.

We spoke Hakka at home, but my parents didn't get mad if we spoke English. My father often spoke English to us, but my mother very seldom. She spoke Hawaiian fluently. . . . When I was a child, I don't think we do anything without the parents' permission.

I went to McKinley High School and a year in normal school. Then I got married and didn't go to school. No, I never regretted stopping school and getting married. I didn't, because after the talk I had with my father and my mother-in-law. . . . She butted in, and they gave me a talk and said, "You know girls are supposed to get married, and never mind about your schooling." . . . She gave me quite a lecture. . . . My father said, "You know the best thing for you to do is to get married while I'm still alive. . . . I want to see you get married in a Christian way." Then he said women are supposed to get married and bring up a family, not thinking of education. I don't think I said to him that I want to go to school, to learn, because he already told me that anytime a girl gets old and gets engaged, the best thing is for her to get married before anything happens. . . .

My husband was a very good friend of my brother. We were all about the same age going to school. And then I met his sisters, and we were in school together. We were never allowed to go out, you know, here and there. And then we and my brothers used to get permission after church, we used to go up and pick mountain apples. So that's how we got more acquainted, with a whole group of Chinese people going together. And his sister that was a schoolteacher and I were very good friends, so we were the smallest in the group. Many of them were much older. We knew each other till we were in high school, about fourteen, then he start courting me. Fourteen, fifteen years old, you see. My first memory of him was just playing with my brothers, you know. . . . My parents liked him because he was very respectable. He came to dinner sometimes with my brother, you know. . . . You know, boys have all the freedoms those days, but we don't, you see. Unless my brothers took us along. And they used to bribe us. The boys bribed us to give them the money [allowance] to go to the movies, and they can take us out. . . . And they go out working. They had a strike on the plantation, and they used to . . . they used to work for a dollar a day, and that's supposed to be good money on the plantation. . . .

He used to write me love letters, and I used to keep them for quite a while. I still have some of them somewhere, I think. He was already out of high school when he started courting me, and he was working in the bank, sugar bank. He used to work all his life, before he graduated from high school, because he was one of the main supporters of his family. . . .

One day we went to church here with my brothers and sisters. We were having a picnic. And he had a ring. He just put it on my hand. And they all laughed. But some of them knew it already, and I didn't know it. And he kissed me. I was about sixteen and a half. . . . A year later we were married. . . . It was a Western wedding and Chinese banquet afterwards, at his home.

Of course I taught school up there in Maui. Then after I came back . . . I went to Lincoln Business College, and I graduated from that and became a bookkeeper. . . . I worked as a volunteer and am past president of a lot of organizations. . . . I think I take more after my father because I do so much of helping others. . . .

My oldest married a Chinese. He had five boys and one girl. My second boy was married to a Chinese, then divorced and married a Hawaiian. My third boy was engaged to a Chinese girl, and during the war the girl ran around with somebody else, so he just ditch her. And later on he married a Japanese girl who was a schoolteacher. And my youngest daughter is married to a Chinese, you see. No, no, it's up to them who they marry. It's their life. We have already modernized. We don't believe in asking them to do this and that. It's up to them because it's their life. And my grandson, my oldest grandson, was in Vietnam, Air Force. He married a haole. And my third grandson was also in the Air Force, and he married a haole. Then my second grandson is also married to a haole. You see, whenever my children married, it's up to them. If they ask me about Chinese things, I try to teach them what I know.

Like my daughter, she's very Chinesey. She married a Chinese. She's trying to get the history of the family background, you know. If she was lucky, she would have two boys and four girls, but now she only has one boy and four girls. The second was a boy and she had a miss, you know. . . .

They know how to cook, especially my oldest son's wife. Can she cook! Real good Chinese, you know, because her parents are very strict.

To me, like any person, I just feel I'm a person and I can do what I should do, and not butting into any of my children or grandchildren or their affairs. . . .

IRMA

Irma was born in Honolulu and was raised with four brothers and four sisters. After attending normal school and college, she taught for several years before marrying a widower with three children. She then had a son of her own.

My grandfather was a Christian minister, helping the German missionaries. The family belonged to the Congregational church. My father had lost his parents when he was quite young, and there was a younger sister. He took care of her till she was older. Then she went to North Borneo to the older brother, and that left my father free, so he went to school. Then, when his teacher — that's my mother's father — went to Hong Kong, he went to Hong Kong too. So my father went to Hong Kong to study, and when this person from Hawaii went to enlist workers for the plantation, being a young man of nineteen and very adventurous, he came to Hawaii.

He was unattached. There were no interpreters here at the time. The Chinese couldn't speak Hawaiian — they could speak English. And when King Kalakaua made his trip around the world, he wanted to hire an interpreter to come here and work among the Chinese, to help the Chinese laborers here. So somehow my grandfather's younger brother, who was educated in Hong Kong, was recommended, and the king hired him, my mother's uncle. So there was communication between the two brothers, and my father went to this uncle of my mother's to get him to help out in getting her to come. Her father was my father's teacher, and he remembered her. They would exchange pictures, you know how the Chinese style is, and exchange correspondence. So she came and married him. . . .

My father came as a laborer at a plantation, and as soon as his contract was up he came to Honolulu and worked for the German consul. This was before he married. My father started as the gardener with the German consulate. I guess he saved some money, and then he started to build a store on Fort Street. And that was when he sent for my mother.

She came on a boat, and when they came to Honolulu somebody had smallpox on board the ship, so the ship couldn't land here. They had to go to San Francisco, but they couldn't land in San Francisco. When the quarantine was up, they landed here.

My mother took care of the family. . . . I remember my older brother and sister, they went to China to study. My brother went first with a group of people to Nanking, and then my sister went later. In my family, there was equal treatment of boys and girls. My parents did not show any favoritism toward the boys. . . .

We spoke Hakka, and we spoke English among ourselves. In the beginning we spoke Hakka so that we learned. I'm glad we learned now. But later on, why, we were so used to speaking English we spoke English to our parents, even. We went to the mission school, the church school. They were teaching Chinese. But after a while, when we went to high school, we didn't go. . . .

Oh, Mother disciplined us. She didn't like the idea of some of the women who would say, "Oh, wait until your dad comes home." She even ridiculed that. She would say, "If a child is naughty, I will take care of him myself. And I'll spank him myself, and I won't have to wait for his father to come home or her father to come home." She would make that statement. She would handle it herself. And we knew that she was very strict, so we had to toe the mark. Not that she was so strict that we were afraid of anything. But we had a close-knit family. We helped one another, and we helped Mother, and we did what we could. She spanked with the duster, the old duster. She would split it up. Nothing very harmful, but it would sting. With her hands, sometimes. She would advise us, and we felt we could go to her for help. Mother took care of the family, and the store too.

Mother kept very busy. We had five girls in the family and five boys. But one boy passed away, so we grew up as a family of nine children. Mother would take care of the meals, besides the store. When the older ones came back, they would help with the store. Then Mother would do sewing and other things. In those days we couldn't buy clothes, and Mother had to make all our clothes. The store was the front on the street, and the living quarters in the back. And I remember as the family grew bigger, we had a two-story home in the back. So we were always close to the store, and we had access to candy and things like that.

Like when we grew up and had to do marketing every day, we went to the fish market, and if we spoke Chinese the Chinese stall people would respect us. They would give us fresh fish. Although we were Hakka, we tried to speak Cantonese. But they were very respectful, and they gave us. And if a Chinese girl came along and spoke English to them, they would be very annoyed.

They would grumble and say, "You're Chinese and can't even speak Chinese!" My parents were very aware that we should be proud of our Chinese. They always felt that with our Chinese civilization of thousands of years, and with their contact with our grandfather, it was very patriotic. There was that deep feeling for things Chinese. . . .

Oh, in those days the Chinese New Year's festival was quite a big thing, especially when you had a store. The neighborhood would come. We had our dried lichis in big sacks and tangerines, and — to give to the children especially — candy. Oh yes, it was the Chinese New Year's and Mother would spend time making Chinese pudding. And later on, when she was retired from running the store, she learned to make puff rice. And it's quite an art, and she was very careful to sift it, get out all the sand. And even the small, little pieces of rice. And then she liked to put in a lot of peanuts, and the syrup was quite a thing to take care of, cooking the syrup. She made sure she had enough honey and sugar and other things. And she would cook the syrup at a certain temperature. But then she wanted her puff rice to be puffy and have enough sugar to hold it, and she wanted to add more peanuts than ordinary people would. She worked with a friend — they would make this puff rice together at this very good friend's home.

In fact, she and this friend grew up together in Hong Kong, and they lived here and were lifelong friends, and the families always got together. She came as a bride, too. So they would make the puff rice together, and a few weeks before Chinese New Year's, so they would have them on hand in gallon cans. Then the Chinese rice pudding, things like that. We helped, yes, we helped with the puff rice even if we had school lessons to do. The puff rice had to be done that very day, so we had to help. We'd clean the peanuts and separate them into halves.

All the Chinese festivals . . . And there was that fifth month, fifth day Dragon Boat Festival, and then they had Moon Festival time. That was another celebration, besides the Western holidays. Well, we had Chinese food, but it was mixed. Mother came in contact with the local people. She learned to cook foreign-style, with the Chinese ingredients sometimes. You know, not strictly Chinese. Our meals were more international. . . .

Mother held her own very well. She was very strong. She was very ingenious, I might say. She would do things on her own. Like when we lived in Portuguese town, the Portuguese girls dressed up very well at Holy Ghost time. That was a special festival, their festival. Holy Ghost, they called it. Like a bazaar. They all would be dressed up for church before the bazaar. And many of the girls worked for the dressmakers. They learned to sew, and they would make beautiful dresses and do nice work. When Mother saw any dress she liked, she would ask for a pattern. And the girl would cut out a pattern for her, and then she would sew our dresses.

So Christmastime, when we were growing up, we had a Christmas dress. Usually it was white or pink, but with insertion and tucks and ruffles, all done by her on her sewing machine. And when we went to church, the other mothers saw our dress. They wanted to make the same style, so Mother'd come home and cut out patterns for all the mothers. She had a lot of friends, all kinds of friends. . . .

During the summer, she would spend time making clothes for the new school year. The old school clothes would be for home, and the old church clothes would be for school. And then there would be a new set of clothes for church. Then [for] holidays she would make us special dresses, and those suits for the boys for Christmas and Easter, which were the big church holidays. And then even Chinese New Year's, the girls would have our Chinese outfits. . . .

If you go out with a boy, they earmark you with that person. So we were afraid. If we didn't like a boy, we didn't go out with him. Some of the girls did. They'd go to the beach, but we never did, my sister and I. We felt that as soon as you go out with a boy, that's your husband-to-be, that's your sweetheart. And we didn't like that, so we just didn't go. We didn't accept invitations. Mother would talk about others who would be very free to go out. And especially in the early days, they would earmark the Christian girls and say, "Oh, the Christian girls would do this, and they were not supposed to." If they would go downtown, they would be rather rowdy, and that was uncalled for, unladylike. The Chinatown people, the non-Christians, they always earmarked the Christian girls, the Christian families. So we had to be careful, as Christian girls, of our attitude and our behavior. We respected the Buddhists, but we were brought up as Christians because my great-grandfather became a Christian, and my father and my mother, see, several generations of Christians.

Of course, the Christian girls were dressed differently, more in the Western style, you know, schoolgirls — and many of the non-Christian girls did not go to school in the early days. They kept them at home to take care of the family and to take care of the business. And it was mostly the Christian families who sent their children, their girls, to school. So they could earmark the Christian girls from the non-Christian girls. We had to be careful of our behavior in the public because we didn't want the other Chinese to say that the Christian girls were not behaving well. In fact, the Christian girls became more Westernized in the early days. They went to school and mixed up with the other nationalities. The other Chinese dressed more Chinese and would be home more, and they were strict about their behavior and things like that.

We seemed to be able to mix with our neighborhood kids, although we didn't play with them all the time. They would come to the store. We would know them, and we went to school with them. They knew that we were Chinese. But they would tease others. I heard them. "Ching Ching Chinaman," they would say. But not to us. In fact, my mother said she had to discipline some of these Portuguese boys when the peddlers would go to my mother's store in the afternoon to sell vegetables along the way, and the peddler would stop in the store. And if any of the boys were naughty and would tease the peddler, my mother would get after them and scold them.

I never heard Mother complain. If she complained, we weren't at home, we were in school. We all had our chores. And we all had to study hard. Stressed education. My parents worked hard to give us an education. We all had an education [through university].

I went to McKinley High School, then I went to the Territorial Normal and Training School here, where I prepared to become a teacher. . . . When I was finishing high school, I thought I wanted to take up nursing. I couldn't decide whether to go to normal school to teach or whether I wanted to take nursing. But my father and mother suggested that if I should go to Queens' Hospital to take nursing, it would take two years. And if I went to normal school it would just take a year, and I could become a teacher, and a teacher's position would be better. With nursing, I'd have to take care of some of the unpleasant things, taking care of a sick person. . . . I took summer work [at the university], and I got my Bachelor of Arts. . . . And I got a professional certificate over and above my bachelor's. I was teaching while I was doing this university work. . . .

Dr. L. lost his wife, and then he and the children went to Amoy. Then I guess his sisters in Honolulu were concerned about his being alone without a wife, so somehow we were friends, and Auntie E. came over one day to my house and talked to me about it. I didn't know what to think of it, and I just told, "Oh, he can write to me," I said. He started to correspond with me. After some period of correspondence, then, he asked me to marry him and we made plans. Then he asked his sister to buy the engagement ring and wedding set.

He was in Shanghai waiting for me. I had met him. We were on a ship together. So, after all, it wasn't just by mail. They were family friends. . . . I went and stayed with my brother in Shanghai before the wedding. . . . The reception was Chinese, Shanghai banquet style. Shanghai banquets would have about twenty courses. I had my foreign wedding dress, then I changed to a Chinese embroidered *cheong-sam* [a dress with a high neck]. I believe Dr. L. was forty-six or forty-seven. He had three children. . . . I was thirty-seven. He was born and raised on the Big Island, went to college in Wuchang, near Hankow, and [to] Harvard-in-China Medical School. . . . He felt that China needed his services more, so he decided to return [to China]. . . . I had never married before, and I was single, and to go into a household with children, that was something, and he really appreciated that.

I married late, so I helped the family the longest. I could have married early, if I didn't think of the family. There were quite a few proposals. In fact, one person proposed three times! . . . Other girls went out, you know, to parties and things, but I just didn't want, because I didn't want to be the talk of the group. So then [when Dr. L. proposed] it seemed as though the time was right. So I thought it was time for me to marry, if I was going to marry at all. . . . But I had a profession, I was teaching, and I was earning to help the family, and many of my parents' friends knew that I was doing something for the family. They were really very respectful for that. They admired me for it. They always would praise my mother for it. I decided myself [to marry] — nobody could talk me out of it. It was my decision, finally. I thought it was high time that I should do something for myself. So I took the step. . . .

My son was a baby when the war began. When I was in the hospital, this elderly relative — her husband was Dr. D. — she came to see me. She told me not to eat anything cold, what I knew. And not to eat any fresh vegetables. . . . So when I went home, she cooked me some preserved vegetable with pork. . . . I was busy with him. . . . And other families had a baby amah for the newborn, but I didn't feel that I needed an amah. So I was the amah. Especially that my mother had written and said, "Don't leave the babies to the amahs." . . . We couldn't evacuate [to Hawaii], so we stayed on until the war was over. . . . Then we took a hospital ship back. . . .

Yes, we did come [back] to Hawaii, unexpectedly. And we were happy. The Hawaii people were able to get off here. So we went through customs and went to Immigration to clear our papers. Back home, and my mother didn't know that we were back. We just appeared on the scene, just like we fell down from Heaven! A major turning point for the good was when we came back. The children were happy to come back to Honolulu. They were born in China, but being of American parentage, they were American citizens.

When I came back, K. [her son] was small, and everything was so new to him. So I spent a whole year with him, took him to school, and all of that, just so that he could get acquainted with the new situation here. So I did not go back to teach until the following year. And I went back to teach until I retired in 1960, on early retirement.

I'd say [to the younger generation], "If you're Chinese, stick to your Chinese heritage and tradition and be proud of your Chinese heritage!"

Scottish-English

Whalers and Traders

The first Caucasian arrivals in the Sandwich Islands, another common name for what is now called Hawaii, were sailors and whalers from Norway, Germany, Russia, Spain, England, Scotland, Portugal, and New England. They began to arrive soon after Cook's voyage, when whaling ships developed the Pacific route to China. Lahaina and Honolulu became important ports of call in the thriving mid-nineteenth-century trade that took whale "oil for the lamps of China" and brought out of the Middle Kingdom tea and later "Celestials," the labor needed by the nascent sugar industry. The whalers and fur traders who stopped off in Hawaii not only took on fuel and supplies but soon discovered something equally profitable: the sandalwood growing in the uplands of the Islands. It did not take profit-seeking traders long virtually to denude the Islands of all of this precious wood, which was cut and brought to the ships by *alii*, in return for payment in goods. Five hundred whaling ships a year stopped in Honolulu and Lahaina during the trading heyday of the 1850s.[1]

Some of the sailors on the whaling and trading ships jumped ship in order to stay in the Islands they found so attractive. They introduced new languages, new ethnic strains, and, far less felicitously, a long list of diseases to which the Hawaiians had no immunity: measles, diphtheria, smallpox, scarlet fever, dengue, tuberculosis, leprosy, venereal disease, and bubonic plague (apparently from China). With the exception of the Portuguese (see Chapter V), none of these early Caucasian arrivals were followed immediately by large numbers of compatriots.

Following these early maritime immigrants, nevertheless, were other settlers from England and Scotland: engineers, craftsmen, and businessmen venturing in search of a better life. Some of them arrived via New Zealand. Many Scots settled on plantations, three-fourths of them on the Big Island, where the Hamakua Coast came to be known as

"Scotch Coast." They came for the same reasons as other immigrants before and after them: Conditions were bad at home, and they were offered jobs by others who had preceded them to Hawaii. Half were single. Some became *lunas* on the plantations; others became teachers or went into other skilled occupations.[2]

Many of these English and Scottish immigrants found the path toward political and economic power soon after their arrival. Two of the later Big Five corporate giants trace their origins to the whaling era.[3] Several of these immigrants not only became advisers to kings but married their daughters. A Welshman named Isaac Davis was given a royal appointment. An Englishman, John Young, was appointed governor of Hawaii by the king in 1804; his second wife was a niece of Kamehameha I, and his granddaughter's husband was Kamehameha IV. Archibald S. Cleghorn, who was married to Liliuokalani's sister, was the father of Princess Kaiulani.[4] Not only was the royal family no longer "pure Hawaiian," but kings were likely to listen to Englishmen. The name Beretania Street, a major artery in Honolulu, still bears witness to British influence in the nineteenth century. Had the Church of England sent missionaries in the early nineteenth century, Hawaii might have become a British territory as did Tonga and the Fiji Islands.

Missionaries

Another group of early nineteenth-century immigrants who were also of English-Scottish ancestry had an even greater impact on the Islands, an impact still being felt today. Missionaries arrived not from England, Scotland, or New Zealand, but from some of the same New England ports that sent the whaling ships. Impelled by the prospect of finding converts, the Congregational Board of Foreign Missions, operating out of Boston, sent these unpaid immigrants to Hawaii. The missionaries were dedicated to "bringing civilization to the heathens," a motivation incomprehensible to the seafaring men from the same New England towns. Their goal was to save Hawaiian souls, to bring them the benefits of a "higher civilization," and they set about "the work of God" immediately upon arrival.

The Reverend Hiram Bingham brought the first contingent aboard the *Thaddeus* in 1820; in addition to the reverend were a teacher, a printer, a skilled mechanic, a prosperous farmer, another minister (Asa

Thurston), and their wives. All were shocked at what they saw — human sacrifice, incest, polygamy, infanticide, and nakedness — and they were determined to turn the "heathens" from their "barbarous customs and habits" and to "raise the whole people to an elevated state of Christian civilization."[5] To achieve these Calvinist goals, they opened schools for girls as well as boys, and within one generation these single-minded workers peppered the Islands with white New England–style Congregational churches. Many are still in use today; others are crumbling reminders of the zealous conscience of another era.

The first challenge the missionaries faced — apart from the lack of housing and other material necessities — was the language barrier. They knew no Hawaiian, and the Hawaiians knew no English. Moreover, the Hawaiian language had never been written. Hiram Bingham and his friends romanized the language using a simplified twelve-letter alphabet. With this written language — and with the aid of two Hawaiian boys who had traveled to Connecticut aboard a whaler — Hiram Bingham began preaching, and Sybil Bingham, his bride of only a few days before departing on this venture, began teaching the Bible. Most of the early missionary brides taught the Bible.

The Women

Very few women came to Hawaii aboard the trading and whaling ships; if an occasional ship's captain brought his intrepid wife along, she, of course, left with her husband and his ship. The first female Caucasian residents were brides imbued with the same zeal as their missionary husbands. Their journey to Hawaii was arduous. Their trip was longer than the route traversed from parts of Asia — six months on sailing ships out of Boston and around Cape Horn. Crammed eight persons to a minuscule cabin, they shared their narrow bunks with their husbands, whom in most cases they had met a bare two weeks earlier. Because the Congregational Board of Foreign Missions required that the zealous young men be married before they sailed, many of the missionaries found wives just before their journey.

The Hawaii to which Scottish-English women arrived was a different place from the Hawaii that became home to later immigrants. When they first landed in Lahaina or Honolulu, they lived in grass huts with only the furniture they had brought with them. Calvinists by conviction,

Fig. 4.1. Charlotte Baldwin, of missionary lineage. *Courtesy of the Pioneer Museum, Lahaina, Maui.*

like their husbands these New England women "did the work of God." They labored to re-create in their new island homes the society and church communities they had left behind. Church was the focal point of their lives, even more than for other ethnic groups arriving before and after them. Gradually, they were able to add to their Spartan lives the amenities to which they had been accustomed.

Nurturing was central to the lives of these women. Many of the missionary brides became pregnant on their long voyage to Hawaii, and once in the Islands they continued to bear and raise large numbers of children. Within two decades of the arrival of the *Thaddeus*, twelve ships had brought a total of 184 men and 100 women from New England, but those immigrants produced many offspring, an impressive total: The Binghams had seven children, the William Richards, Dwight Baldwins, and Peter Gulicks each had eight children; and the Samuel Ruggleses had six.[6] In various ways, the missionaries began to make their mark.

These missionary women devoted much of their time — apart from raising large numbers of children — to teaching Hawaiian women to sew. Hawaiian women had been making clothes from *tapa*, a traditional Hawaiian cloth that required no stitching, and moreover, Hawaiian women often left the upper part of their bodies bare. Eager to change this situation, assiduous New England teachers taught their Hawaiian pupils to make the full-length, long-sleeved dresses known today as muumuus. Later, they added quilting to the arts they taught.

Missionary women also spent time teaching girls and women to read and write so that they would be able to read the Bible in Hawaiian transliteration. Queens and *alii* women were among their first pupils. As these Hawaiian women set the example, other women followed, and the result was the spread of literacy and of Christianity as preached by the ministers of the Congregational Board. The Hawaiian Bible became an aid for learning English and, later, Hawaiian, as one Hawaiian respondent related in her interview. The Chiefs' Children's School, Punahou School (established in 1841), St. Cross Industrial School for Girls (1865), St. Andrew's Priory (1867), and Kawaiahao Seminary (1864) were among the private schools founded through the efforts of early missionaries. Most of the teachers in these private schools were women.

Medical care and training was another field in which women were significant in the early eras of Caucasian settlement. Catholic sisters of the Third Order of St. Francis arrived in 1883 to nurse lepers in Honolulu. Three of these women went to work in the leper colony on Molokai, though they did not achieve the fame of Father Damien, who also worked and died there. Several female doctors and nurses helped to establish early training centers and schools for women in medical professions. One early public health nurse was Mabel Wilcox, the daughter of a Kauai missionary.

These women set a precedent in Hawaii for volunteer work in social welfare and the care of children and the aged, a tradition that continues today with the exceptional professional services provided by Hawaii's county offices on aging. The services provided by these offices are more advanced than those provided by most other states.

As most of the haole respondents here indicated, even when they were children, their mothers had domestic servants and also often chauffeurs and yardmen. These servants were from ethnic communities that were later arrivals in the Islands, most typically Japanese in the case of household help. Yardmen were often Filipino or Japanese. Before the beginning of the twentieth century, the descendants of the missionary women had become part of the haole colonial elite that directed the economy and polity from Merchant Street and Fort Street through controls that were totally androcentric.

Women in the prewar haole elite lived lives that would have amazed their missionary forebears. A girl upon graduating from Punahou School and then Wellesley hoped to marry another Punahou graduate, return to the Islands, and raise a family. Back in Hawaii she would enjoy the perquisites of the colonial life-style. She was not expected to enter a professional career any more than were her sisters of the same generation on the mainland. What occupied her time and attention — beyond home, family, and social obligations, such as luncheons and dinners for her husband's colleagues — was an array of volunteer and charitable endeavors, including work with Young Women's Christian Association (YWCA) groups, church organizations, the Outdoor Circle, the American Association of University Women (AAUW), and the Honolulu and other art galleries. But she had no direct or immediate role in the political and economic mechanisms that sustained her privileges. Those mechanisms were controlled by males in prewar Hawaii. Women in a variety of ways found freedom or conformity within this gender framework.

Political Influence

To better understand the lives of these Caucasian respondents, let us turn briefly to the political-economic framework within which this colonial elite operated. In Hawaii in the last decades of the nineteenth century, missionaries became advisers and ministers to kings, as had a few of their English seafaring predecessors. The Reverend Richards was appointed government interpreter, Lorrin Andrews was made high court judge, the Reverend Richard Armstrong became the minister of public instruction, and Dr. G. P. Judd became adviser and physician to the king.[7] The numbers of converts grew among royalty as well as among the common people. Kaahumanu, one of the wives of Kamehameha I, became an early royal convert; others followed. The king's missionary advisers were able to influence the direction of the kingdom's political and economic policies and were indispensable to the kingdom. Due to their positions, in the process they personally acquired political and economic power. Kings made land grants to them in gratitude for their services, gifts that turned out to be most portentous.

In 1845 G. P. Judd suggested that the king appoint a commission to investigate and determine the validity of all titles to land. He also suggested that new titles be issued and that a law be passed permitting the sale of land as permanent freehold property to Hawaiians. Aliens would not be able to purchase land as permanent freehold property, but land they had acquired before the law was passed would become theirs permanently. Traditionally, all land belonged to the king (see Chapter I). Before the Great Mahele went into effect in 1848, several insider haoles — missionaries and traders — acquired land fee simple in Manoa on Oahu and in Makawao on Maui. The December 1849 law provided that fee simple titles be granted to all native tenant claimants for lands occupied and improved by them, excluding house lots in Honolulu, Lahaina, and Hilo. The problem for the Hawaiians was that they had to present claims to the government, a practice of which they had no knowledge.

The land commission recommended in 1851 that every missionary who had served eight years in Hawaii and did not own 560 acres of land be allowed to purchase that amount at a reduced rate. This became law, and several individuals, including Charles R. Bishop — the originator of the Island-wide Bishop Trust — purchased large tracts of land for $1.45 per acre. The list of missionary purchasers includes such names as Alexander, Baldwin, Dole, and Gulick.

In 1895 a Homestead Act was passed that limited the amount of land that could be sold in a single parcel to one thousand acres. Many of the "homesteaders" were straw buyers for planters or leased land to plantations. These practices enabled the sugar planters to divert homestead lands to their own use, to accumulate enormous tracts, and to vitiate the purpose of the homestead legislation, which was to encourage independent farming and return Hawaiians to the soil.[8]

The missionaries were a mixed blessing for the Islands, neither as good nor as bad as has been claimed. Although it is undeniable that they acquired a great deal of land through purchase and gift, some also sought to defend the interests of their royal employers and of Hawaiians in general against economic and political encroachment by other Westerners.[9] Other missionary contributions to the culture of Hawaii are noted in this chapter.

The Plantation Economy

Although one result of these maneuvers with land legislation was the expropriation of lands on which the Hawaiians had lived for centuries, another was the growth of an industry that came to dominate the economy of the Islands: sugar. The availability of large tracts of land after the Great Mahele, the Reciprocity Treaty and McKinley Tariff, the Wilson-Gorman Tariff of 1894,[10] the crippling of the whaling industry during the Civil War, not to mention the Masters' and Servants' Act of 1850 — all of these factors created an environment favorable to the development of a plantation economy.

Large-scale planters came to dominate the sugar business, and earlier Portuguese and Chinese entrepreneurs were unable to compete with the haole economic and political power. All of the later Big Five corporations had their roots in the sugar industry. Whereas before the Reciprocity Treaty of 1876 sugar was a risky venture, after the treaty it became the primary route to and measure of prosperity and status.

A few families came to dominate life on each island. Several families were at the forefront on Oahu, but on Maui the Baldwins ruled supreme, and on Kauai the Rices and Wilcoxes were the social and economic arbiters. For the six decades until World War II, sugar and pineapple interests dominated Hawaiian life and formed a sharp "social barrier separating the proprietary whites from the non-white laborers on the plantation."[11]

The remaining part of the economic and political power structure — since the planters had capital and other kinds of power — was labor. In 1864 a Planters' Society was organized, and in the same year the

Bureau of Immigration was created.[12] Together, these two groups determined the policies for importing members of ethnic groups from other parts of the world as cheap labor for the plantations.

Sugar boomed. From $2 million capital invested in sugar in 1876, the capital investment jumped to over $33 million in 1891.[13] Shipping and shipbuilding also grew apace. The economic grip of the planters gradually extended beyond the plantations to banks, insurance companies, shipping lines, trust companies, railroads, and wholesale and retail outlets — most of the economy.

The members of this haole elite were confident that they were destined to rule and were certain that theirs was a benevolent rule.[14] These were the families who determined the rules and membership of the elite, who belonged and who did not. Their children went to Punahou School in Honolulu, even if the families lived on the other islands. Punahou was "The School" to attend, and it was a boarding school. After graduating from Punahou, some of the male students attended Yale, Harvard, or Princeton and then returned to Hawaii to work their way up the corporate ladder. Daughters were sent to Dana Hall, a college preparatory school in Wellesley, Massachusetts, and after that to Wellesley or Mt. Holyoke. They were expected to marry within their social class, preferably to boys they had met at Punahou. The families attended Central Union Church in Honolulu.

The plantation system created by the owners was a paternalistic one, marked by noblesse oblige toward not only the laborers but also the Hawaiians. Although land in Hawaii belonged to Hawaiians as well, it was the haoles who ruled.[15] Especially on the plantations, the haoles controlled the lives of the laborers. There the laborers lived in plantation houses, attended plantation schools, and shopped in plantation stores.

The planters followed a policy of recruiting the least educated peasants, presumably on the assumption that they would be more satisfied with plantation life. Many applicants pretended to be illiterate in order to qualify. In the case of the Ilocanos, nearly half were in fact illiterate.[16]

Hawaii's ethnic mixture was not simply a natural, spontaneous development that drew on many parts of the world. Rather, the origin of the Hawaiian "melting pot" was grounded in the sugar plantation economy and the labor policies devised by the planters.

Political-Economic Control Strategies

Numerically, the haole immigration did not keep pace with the immigration of other members of the population. From 8.3 percent of the population in the mid-1850s, the group shrank to 5.4 percent in 1900 and then grew to 12.2 percent in 1930. In 1960, the haoles numbered about 25 percent.[17] At the time of annexation, therefore, it was a small elite group — numbering only about 5 percent of the population — that controlled most positions of power and prestige.

By the mid-nineteenth century, English had become the medium for business, government, and public school education. Lawrence Fuchs remarks in *Hawaii Pono* that the controls developed and maintained by the haoles through interlocking business interests, social clubs, the press, and intermarriage were unique. "No community of comparable size on the mainland was controlled so completely by so few individuals for so long," writes Fuchs.[18] More than wealth, power, and prestige, the goal of the elite was "a way of life in which the ruling haole elite, through its ingenuity, dedication, and charity, had made Hawaii a veritable paradise on earth."[19] In achieving this goal, this elite was doubtless assisted by the relative isolation of the Islands, the single-industry economy (or dual, if pineapples are included), the idyllic climate, and the willingness of foreign labor to immigrate.

The first political goals of the elite were the overthrow of the monarchy and the annexation of Hawaii to the United States, which would ensure favorable markets for sugar. Following annexation (see Chapter I), political control by the Big Five progenitors on Merchant Street was dependent on three critical points: the governor, Hawaii's single delegate to Congress, and the territorial legislature. Because some issues were outside territorial jurisdiction and within federal purview, Washington was a critical political pivot. The federally determined issues included trade, tariff and immigration policy, military installations, and harbor facilities. The president appointed the governor for a four-year term, but the governor's prerogatives went beyond those of mainland governors. Moreover, the legislature was controlled by the Republican Party from 1902 until after World War II, and several missionary planters were elected to the legislature.[20] Robert Wilcox, who was part-Hawaiian and a candidate of the Royalist Home Rule Party, was elected Hawaii's first delegate to Congress in 1900. In 1902 Baldwin's haole group defeated Wilcox and sent Prince Kuhio to

Congress. Although Kuhio had worked to restore the queen to power when the monarchy was overthrown, he now cooperated with planter interests. He was elected as the delegate to Congress ten times before his death in 1922. The haole-Kuhio alliance meant thousands of government jobs for Hawaiians and part-Hawaiians.

The Hawaiian Sugar Planters' Association had, in effect, its own delegate to Congress: an office and lobbyists in Washington. Walter Dillingham, the gray eminence behind many governors, also kept his own representative in Washington. Kuhio was never even consulted regarding the appointment in 1903 of Governor George Carter, a former director of C. Brewer, one of the Big Five corporations. But before he died, Kuhio achieved one final contribution for Hawaiians: He pushed through Congress a Hawaiian Homes Commission bill for returning Hawaiian people to the land.[21]

Land and statehood were focal points in the Hawaiian struggle with the haole oligarchy during the 1920s and 1930s. Hawaiians favored statehood and the application of U.S. laws over monopolistic controls. The Navy, another actor in the drama, pushed for military rule after the notorious Massie case in 1931.[22] Senator Hiram Bingham, now of Connecticut — a descendant of the missionary — introduced legislation to put Hawaii under a Navy commission.[23] His efforts failed.

Chinese, Japanese, and Koreans were still disfranchised, and the Japanese and Filipinos resorted to strike tactics as their only weapon against the planters (see Chapter VI). The planters retaliated, using Hawaiians and Portuguese as strike breakers.

Education

Another critical area was the school system. The elite, as mentioned, sent their children not to public schools but to Punahou and then to college on the mainland. Most were not interested in supporting the public school system. Initially, their attitude toward public education was negative. James C. Campsie, a Scotsman, commented: "Public education beyond the fourth grade is a menace. We spend to educate them and they will destroy us." And Henry P. Baldwin, the doyen of Maui, told his haole friends in 1913 that it was within their power "to stop the expansion of schools on Maui, to model the Islands after the British colonial system by putting the brakes on education." Later, to

Baldwin's credit, he shifted his stance and advocated "education above all to make Maui a first-rate American community."[24] His wife, highly regarded by women of many ethnic groups, sponsored schools and evening classes for plantation workers. During the 1920s, new high schools and junior high schools were added to the public school system on each island.

A federal survey of education in Hawaii in 1920 led to the discussion of several key issues. Haoles advocated the abolition of foreign language schools and the grouping of students according to English language ability, and there was some discussion also of segregating students by race. Others criticized the English-standard system as undemocratic, yet English-standard schools were functioning on the Islands by the 1920s. Governor Joseph Farrington favored training students for work on plantations and in canneries rather than teaching them English literature, which, in the view of Frank Atherton, an influential businessman and educator, would not prepare them to make a living. Big Five committees were organized "to direct thousands of our Hawaiian-born children into happy service in connection with our basic industries."[25] During these years, the Kamehameha Schools for children of Hawaiian ancestry were subscribing to the vocational-technical pattern.

The seeds of educational change were planted in the 1920s and 1930s with the hiring of several dedicated teachers, some of them Hawaii-born Chinese and Japanese, others mainlanders. At McKinley High several generations of children were trained in citizenship and the meaning of democracy. One of these educators, Miles Cary, stands out as having had an enormous influence, in this regard, on students between 1922 and 1948. Students learned the Gettysburg Address and gained experience in student government through an array of sixty clubs. But another view of Hawaiian education is offered by Noel Kent, who says that the generations of Asian-Americans trained at McKinley High School gained "an individualistically oriented competitive world view exalting middle-class materialistic goals and equating success with wealth, status, and power — an education for selfishness and self-aggrandizement in the traditional American sense."[26]

Mid-Pacific Institute was a private school that closely followed McKinley's example. Teachers at these and other public schools taught students about the meaning of equal opportunity, and the discrepancy between the ideals and the reality the Hawaiians saw around them gave impetus to a democratic revolution that propelled the Democratic Party and previously disfranchised groups to power after World War II. The postwar political dispensation was also reflected in a corporate transformation that saw the rise of the tourist industry (an industry increasingly controlled overseas), the introduction of the Kaiser group's hospital and other financial interests from the mainland, and the departure of some Big Five interests to the mainland and Pacific Rim countries.[27] This was the distinctive political-economic-social milieu in which the women whose interviews follow lived their lives and found their meaning.

SAMANTHA b. 1900

Samantha was born on Kauai of Scottish-English-French ancestry. She attended Punahou, went to college on the mainland for a year, and then graduated from the University of Hawaii. She married another Punahou graduate, raised four children, and worked briefly in a library.

My grandparents were in New Zealand and married in New Zealand, because both of them came out to New Zealand in their early days. My grandmother came out to be with her brother, who had come there earlier and established in New Zealand. She had been disappointed in a love affair. Her parents had refused to grant her permission to marry. Parents don't do that these days. They don't have much to say about it. But anyway, she went out to New Zealand and lived with him.

And then my grandfather came out to New Zealand on a warship, 'cause he was a Navy officer. And I guess he left his career to be in New Zealand, and he married my grandmother. They had two sons, one of whom is my father. They stayed in New Zealand, but my father decided at the age of nineteen that there was no great opportunity for a career in New Zealand, so he came up to the Hawaiian Islands. And he certainly found a career here, though he had training as a youngster in blacksmithing in New Zealand. It always put him in good stead because he had a job on a plantation . . . I'm getting ahead of my story.

His first work in Honolulu was at the Honolulu Iron Works. Of course it was blacksmithing and designing and all of that.

My mother came up shortly afterwards with her parents. Two of her brothers had come up here earlier to look for jobs. She was born in

France, and her family came to New Zealand when she was three years old. They proceeded to forget all about France and the language and everything and never taught their children anything about it. Strove to learn English and that was it. Of course, they probably spoke it at home. Yes, they left France because of the Franco-Prussian War. They were on the Isle of Jersey at the time and decided that they would leave the area because of conscription and all that, and they weren't allowed to get into the war yet. Well, they left around the Cape of Good Hope — one hundred and one days on a sailing ship. There was typhoid on the ship, and you can well imagine. Sixty-one people died, and two of her sisters died as infants. But she had it also, typhoid, but she survived. She was a strong one. They were in the same town as my grandfather [in New Zealand] and were kind of sweethearts as young things. So she came up shortly after and they were married several years afterwards, because he [first] set himself up in this blacksmith career.

My father and mother were married three years after he became manager on the plantation, on Kauai. She came up to the Islands with her parents and sisters, but none of them stayed in the Islands except she, and she had a real attraction because she was enamored of my father and he of her. Back in New Zealand days, they were kid sweethearts. . . . So one family was up in Hawaii where her brother — my uncle — was already working on a sugar plantation as an engineer, and a couple of other families . . . I don't know where they were living at the time. But anyway, she and my father were married and set up their home on Kauai, which was natural for them because he was already engaged on the plantation. And my father learned to speak Hawaiian quite well, could converse with his native employees. They had three children — my sister and brother and I.

I never knew my grandparents or uncles or aunties except for one visit to New Zealand. My mother took me when I was three years old. . . . I have French cousins, and I have a French auntie that stayed behind in France when the other members of the family took off for New Zealand. And I went and visited those people three times. And I remember my old auntie going to bed during the dinner. She just ate soup and that's all. She was ninety-three when she died. We're a long-lived family. My mother lived to be eighty-seven, and her uncle that had come up ahead of her lived to be one hundred. . . .

My father was asked to come to Kauai to be a teacher of manual arts at a school made up of missionaries and people teaching Hawaiian boys the arts of carpentry and forging and blacksmithing and all of that, and he had quite a career at that school. He was the only man on the faculty. They were all ladies, and I mean *ladies!* He was working at the school near the Grove Farm Plantation, which was owned by the Wilcox family. But Mr. Wilcox, the owner of it, no, the manager of it . . . It was just in the beginning stages. It was a few Chinese laborers and such, and he wanted somebody to oversee it, and so he asked my father to be an overseer on the plantation, a *luna*. And a few years later he was asked to be the manager, so he went up very fast. He was manager for thirty-two years and enjoyed that career very much indeed. He made it his whole life's career, really. My father was much impressed with his work on the plantation. In those days it was "The Job." . . . Sugar was up and coming, growing like mad. He persuaded my brother to be his sugar man instead of what he wanted to be, which was an engineer. He kind of suffered from this, taking away his desires. Nowadays they would never do that.

My father was a very macho man. An Englishman, and he thought the English were it, the white race. Yes, he learned Hawaiian. He had a flair for languages. He could imitate the Irish and the Germans and everyone. . . . He could imitate the Irish and the English, and he even imitated the French. His pronunciation of words was English, and many of his expressions were English.

Mother didn't carry over much of tradition. But she was really quite a wonderful woman . . . because she became a manager's wife and had to pay attention to visiting potentates and entertain, and when you realize that she came from a household that had no servants at all, and here she landed up with a cook and a maid and a yardman and a driver. . . . She managed them all pretty well. The servants were Japanese mostly, and then we had to branch out as the population changed. We had the driver of the first automobile we had, a Portuguese man. Then we graduated — or demoted ourselves — to [a] Filipino yardman, who we were all afraid of because he could flare up with a temper, not liking to take orders from a woman. A bachelor. They [the plantation managers] had servants and didn't allow for wives. I don't know what we expected. They [the bachelor servants] lived in the servants' quarters.

I went to private school that many of the people in the town of Lihue contributed to. And there was only one teacher for six different grades. I don't know how they managed it. We had a very good teacher for the first many years that I was there. Then I went to the Kauai High

School, which I think started at the seventh, eighth, and ninth grades. When it came time for high school, I was sent to Punahou . . . 1915. I was born in 1900. My brother went to Punahou ahead of me. He was three years older than I was. My sister never did. She went to Kauai High School and always thought she missed out on a lot by not going to Punahou because she could have met so many kids that would have been friends of hers later in life. But my parents were sort of fed up with Punahou a little bit. I don't know what reason.

My high school career was involved with the man who became my husband, the boy who became my husband. We met in my freshman year, and apparently he had been casting eyes on this new girl in Punahou. He told me later, "Well, when I saw you come in chapel I said, I'm going to marry that girl." And he hadn't even met me. I guess it was mutual. Love at first sight. Well, we waited for ten years before we got married, though. Ten years from that introduction date. . . . We didn't get married when I graduated from the University of Hawaii, no. My husband was still taking his law degree. So he was still there, in New Haven. . . . In 1925 we got married. That was ten years from the day we met, which was a long haul, but in those days no college allowed their students to get married. He had a job in Honolulu before we were married. He already had an offer of a job here in a law firm before he graduated.

I wanted to be a nurse. I wanted to be a teacher. But I did none of those things. I went to the university for one year. Just took a B.A. course. Then I went to — transferred to — Barnard College for one year. My parents said, "You can go to New York for one year and that's all." Because I was going to see my boyfriend at Yale. [They were] mistrustful of New York as a place to live, but they need not have been. I was well chaperoned there. But anyway, I enjoyed that year very, very much. Endured a winter and went up to Boston for Christmas, and all in all it was a very fine year. I went to all kinds of symphonies and operas in New York City and thoroughly enjoyed it. My husband's cousin had been at Yale, all were at Yale. I had contracted with my parents to stay just one year. I went back to the University of Hawaii and graduated from there.

I worked in the library in Lihue. I was just an assistant, you know, mere neophyte. The lady who was the head of the library decided to resign for some reason. And she left before they could get somebody else to take her place. So I was the sole caretaker of the library. I was a little bit floored by that, but I had gotten into the routine by then. I knew what I was doing. But about a year after that we got married.

I guess the high point of my life was when I married the man I set out to marry, and his very loving care of me all the time. He was a devoted husband. We had four children — they all live here. One lives at Kauai, and his job is the same as my husband's. He is president of Grove Farm Plantation Company, though they don't spend their time on sugar crops as such. . . . My grandchildren are all from my sons.

FAITH

Born on Maui, Faith is descended from four sets of great-grandparents who immigrated to Hawaii. Three of those couples came as missionaries. She attended Dana Hall, married, and raised two children.

Four sets of great-grandparents came to Hawaii from New England, except one great-grandfather came from Kentucky . . . but he had lived in Connecticut when he moved up there as a young man. Three sets were missionaries when they came. There was a great surge in that part of the country which appealed to the young people — these were all in their twenties — for helping the world, helping people, and "saving the heathens." They came in the late 1820s. They came through Boston church there, all Congregationalists. And the fourth great-grandfather was a sea captain and traded with the Orient. When he married, he married a Connecticut woman and brought her out here to settle because he'd been through the Islands and thought it would be a great place to settle.

Two of the couples were on this island, over in Lahaina, and then one of them was on Kauai. There is the old house in Lahaina, and they have a collection of things and furniture. Mission people lived there, and the house is furnished. It's not supposed to go over 1850 [to have furniture made after 1850], to look like a lived-in home. It's not a museum. There is a piano. . . . The way they got their piano . . . there was a man in Lahaina, I don't know what his name was, and he left Lahaina under a cloud. All his things were auctioned off, and they bought the piano.

The fourth was a sea captain, and he went into business when he came here. His wife came from the Adams family, brother of John

Adams. I can't find any mention of Nathaniel. Nathaniel and Samuel were what they called rabble-rousers, you see, before the Revolution. But Nathaniel, our relative, didn't get much publicity.

I was born here on the island of Maui, and my father was born here. My mother was born and raised in Honolulu. Her father was a lawyer, and when the Hawaiian revolution came along Mr. Dole was president and my grandfather was the attorney general . . . that the right word? He was a wonderful grandfather. And he went to school in Amherst.

And my grandmother here on Maui . . . Wonderful! Oh, how we loved her. She was a true angel. She had six sons and two daughters. And the sons' wives all just adored her. She was born in Lahaina — Lahainaluna, above Lahaina. They lived in two, three different places on Maui, then finally they settled up in Makawao. But oh, how we used to love to go to her house. She let us do anything. Every Sunday the whole family congregated, and she had one son and his family — or two, depending on how many children they had — for lunch, and the rest would come in the afternoon. The men would all sit on the lanai, and the women inside, the children out in the yard. . . .

Grandmother would play on the piano and sing. She was noted for her sweet soprano voice. She taught the Hawaiian ladies. They would all come to the house. She taught them to sew and to sing. Of course, the first thing they had to do was to learn the language, and she taught them our hymns in Hawaiian while they sewed and made muumuus, which was a New England–style dress.

Church was a thing that all my family went to, my uncles and aunts and cousins. Everybody went. Right here, Makawao Union, although this particular church was not built then. It was built later. There was a little white church that my grandfather had a lot to do with, getting that built. No, he wasn't a minister, but that generation were children of the missionaries, you see, and they still had a lot . . . and by the time it got to me the complete missionary attitude had softened up and moved away a little bit. I won't say softened up, but changed.

My mother was happy and cheerful and energetic, and full of song and laughter. She had a good voice. My daughter had a lovely voice, and I can't sing at all.

Of the children of the original four great-grandparents, I don't know how many were ministers. Not too many actually, I don't think. They were professional people — lawyers, teachers, professors. My grandfather was the most energetic, and the most outgoing and the most full of business of any of his siblings. But there was a surveyor and a professor and a lawyer.

My father was the oldest in the family, eight children. And he went to Punahou. And when he was twelve years old, it seemed they could have their horses up on Brackett Hill above Punahou. And one very stormy night — his room was on the ground floor — he felt sorry for his horse, so he went out and put the horse in his room. He did one other bad thing. He and another boy on April Fools' Day shaved the tail of the principal's horse. And anyway, after having his horse in his room, he was called up and he was fired from Punahou. And his friend had been fired before him that same day, I guess. . . . So Grandma was so furious that her son was fired for a thing like that that, she didn't send any of her other children to Punahou. I wanted to go there very much. I longed to go there. Because I knew just a few Honolulu people . . . I was just on Maui all the time. My mother said, "No, you can't go there. The girls at Punahou are all boy-crazy." Well, my mother went there. So that's when I went away to boarding school. . . .

I wanted my daughter educated properly because I hadn't been. First my mother had governesses. My mother lost two boys, two sons. And so she got cautious with me. And then I went to Maui High School in the grammar grades, and then I went to a girls' school in Piedmont, California. I had a governess, and then I went to Maui High for a while, and then there was another period of governess, and then that boarding school. It was just all conglomerate. And I remember I had American history three years in a row because they kept changing the curriculum in Honolulu. They would say what we should have.

I was very happy to go off to school. My friends were going. The last governess . . . She had been a teacher and I loved her, but I didn't like having school alone. As soon as it was over, I would get on my horse and go down to the high school and see my friends. Two years, I think, I had a governess — before that I was at Maui High in the grammar grades.

Yes, I had my own horse. My father had horses and he rode them, and he had racehorses. He raced them Fourth of July in Kahului. Fourth of July was a big racing day.

Then I went to a girls' school in Piedmont, California — very strict, oh! Because some Honolulu friends of my mother recommended it. I was there two years, and it was very unhappy, and so different and so strict. I made one friend, who is still my best friend. . . . I was terribly unhappy, but I didn't tell my parents. I thought all boarding schools are like this and why make them worry. A lot of sad times because it was so strict. And they went on the principle you had to prove what you said, that all girls were liars, and you had to prove, and that was awful. And there were two women, Miss Ransom and Miss Bridges. Miss Ransom was the one that was terrible, Miss Bridges was very nice. She was scared of Miss Ransom. Miss Ransom was the most typical-looking — she was very homely. Pulled-back hair with a bun in the back. . . . Every night after dinner we had to count off, and she would say anything she wanted to the different girls. Just break them down. There were fifty boarders, and the rest were day pupils. At least thirty of that fifty cried themselves to sleep every night. It was a very unhappy time. And then finally, at the end of two years, I complained and they right off sent me to Dana Hall, also recommended by a Honolulu friend of my mother's.

Dana Hall is in Wellesley, near Pine Manor. Oh, and then later, when the war came, my daughter went to Dana Hall, and I lived in Wellesley a year. We couldn't get back. . . . [When I was in school] I went to Dana Hall, then to Pine Manor, which is a related school, but was sick that year. I'd had mumps and left too soon. And I was in and out of the infirmary. . . . My mother and father were in Washington, and they decided I better come home with them. I came home. I met my husband, and that ended my education, my formal education.

I didn't have very high aspirations. I wanted to get married and have a family. That was before the twenties, you see. The only thing that a woman could do would be teaching or perhaps being a secretary. And when I came home from Pine Manor, my mother put my name in as being willing to substitute teach. I had one nightmare week, because I went down to Paia School. There were no books, no list of what came next, there was nothing. And I hadn't had any of that kind of thing at Pine Manor. We learned about cooking and sewing, and I took the homemakers' course. And that week was just a horror week because those kids were . . . It was the dumb second grade, and the boys were as old as twelve and big boys. And one day they jumped out of the window and ran off. And I said let them go. I took them out for exercise because I saw other teachers doing that. Nobody helped me at all. No, I won't say that. One friend had a class not too far away. She said, "Send the naughty boys in to me," and she made them sit in the corner. No, I didn't want to teach school. . . .

I met him on a blind date. Friend of mine, they took us to a chop suey house in Chinatown, Honolulu. Upstairs, and dark and dingy . . . and all I could think of was cockroaches and I didn't know what. Anyway, neither of us liked the chop suey. We couldn't stand the look of it. Both of us just ate rice with soy on it. Then I saw him a few times, then they went to the Orient. When they came back from the Orient, he stayed over in Honolulu and got a job at the *Honolulu Advertiser*. So we became reacquainted, and my family said I could invite him up for a weekend. And he came up for a week-end. He knew he wanted to stay in the Islands a little longer. My father offered him a job, asked him if he would like to work in pineapples, because they were just beginning pineapples in this area. He was from New England, and I thought we would be living there. I had been at Dana Hall and Pine Manor, and I liked Boston very much. I wasn't worried about it. But my father offered him a job. . . . Then I got married. Everything was different after that. My family built this house for us. They lived right next door, down the hill. . . . I remember I wanted to have a big place where I could pick up all the stray dogs that I saw anywhere and take them home and we could live happily together.

EMILY

Emily was born on the island of Niihau of English-Scottish-German parentage. She married and raised three children. Her mother wrote a book of reminiscences about her ancestors' journey from New Zealand to Hawaii and life on Niihau. At the time I met Emily she was ninety-three, totally deaf, and bedridden.

My grandmother and grandfather immigrated to Hawaii from Scotland and Norway via New Zealand. The voyage took a long time. [In New Zealand] they had some adventures with Maoris, settled in Pigeon Bay. Raised a family in New Zealand and had adventures with the Maoris. Grandmother was the youngest. They had a schooner, which they procured to go down to Canterbury to get supplies and sell their produce. One time the father and eldest brother drowned. They just disappeared — this is recounted in my mother's book — and they were never heard of or seen again.

But my great-grandmother carried on. She was indomitable as a woman. And she carried on for quite a long time, until the children grew up. And she felt that Pigeon Bay was too small. So one of the sons-in-law had a ship, and they all got on board, including cows and chickens and pigs and a grand piano and I don't know what all. And they sailed off to Tahiti. But my great-grandmother didn't like that because it was too hot, so she sailed on and passed by Hawaii and went to California, but nearer to Washington State. But that was too cold, and the Indians seemed to be hostile.

So she came back to Hawaii. And they bought, eventually, the island of Niihau from the king, and they set up there and built a large house and raised sheep and cattle. They were very exclusive. They wouldn't let anybody land on the island. They wanted the natives to remain pure and to speak Hawaiian always. They're still that way now. They still own the island of Niihau.

My mother had five children, and they were all born at home. She had nurses, all were Japanese. She had servants to wait on her. No, my mother and I never did chores — we had servants. I guess my father disciplined the children more than my mother [did]. She was a soft-hearted person. I think discipline in our family was a two-way street. My husband and I disciplined the children. My father definitely disciplined the children, not my mother. I don't know anything about my grand-mother and my grandfather. But I should imagine that my grandfather was a Norwegian and he had traveled all over the world. So probably he wasn't the main disciplinarian. I don't know if I tried to model my life after my mother.

As a family, we rode horses, we went to the mountains to camp, we went to the beach and swam. Father built a pool in the backyard, and we learned to dive and swim there. But I could never learn to dive. I always belly flopped. . . .

The whole family was invited over there because I was being looked over as a possible wife for the oldest son [of the royal family]. But it didn't work. . . . I had no . . . I mean, it was simply out of the blue when he asked me to marry him. I was so surprised, I nearly fainted. If you were going to be asked to marry somebody, you should be courted. That was not done. But anyway, we had a very pleasant time then. I have a picture of my father being carried ashore from a long boat by two Hawaiians.

I have three wishes — first, I want to hear; and next, I want to walk; and third, I want to play the cello. I loved to hear it. . . . I thought

I would try to have my son learn the cello when he was about twelve. I rented a cello. One day I was listening to him, and he went squeak and again squawk to the C. . . . I said, "Bob, can't you hear that you have to change the strings?" "Oh, it all sounds the same to me." So I gave up.

I did most of the things I wanted to do. . . . We had money enough. . . . You can't think back, but just imagine ninety-three years ago. Everything has changed. You couldn't begin to say what hasn't changed — telephones, and wireless, and airplanes, and damned computers!

LYDIA

Lydia was born in San Diego to Scottish-Danish-French parents, came to Hawaii in 1920 to teach, and did so for many years. She married a part-Hawaiian and had two children.

My mother was born in Denmark and came to this country. She was in a family of five and came to this country when she was four years old. And her mother died when she was five, and the children were put out into foster homes. And her father was one of the old-time folks that didn't think that girls needed an education, you know. So she never had any formal education. Well, my father's mother was Scotch and Dutch, and my mother was half-Danish and half-French.

I was born in San Diego. . . . I just graduated from the normal school and was interested in Hawaii. I didn't have the money to leave home and go away to college. Someone suggested, "Well, why don't you go to teachers college here?" So I did, in San Diego. . . . I don't know, since I had been a child I'd had a yen to go to Hawaii and Japan. I don't know why, but I just always wanted to go. I didn't know how I was gonna get here, unless I came to teach school, so that's the way I did it.

I don't know what gave me the idea of teaching. Ever since I was old enough to know that I was going to do something as a lifework, I wanted to teach. My mother said that I've done that. She said that — I can remember, too — we lived out in the country, and being an only child I had my pets and dolls and all to play with. And I lined my dolls up for pupils, and my father made me a blackboard and put it up, and my mother said since I was old enough to know or do anything, I was always teaching school. Why, I don't know. I guess I've always had an insatiable curiosity to learn things myself and maybe think I can help other people do it. I've often wondered why it was. My father thought I'd make a good lawyer. . . .

Well, I think we've always had a pretty good educational system here, you know. It's always been a state system. And the school then, we had what they called the receiving grades — you know, before they got into the first grade. Because many of them, the Japanese, the Orientals, didn't speak English. The families didn't speak English, you see. So they needed a year to get into the English language. There were a good many Portuguese at that time, but we needed that extra year, which was really not a kindergarten setup but as I say a preschool, to teach them English. They were just the regular teachers for them. But otherwise they were just like all other children, you know, except for their language. This was before the Filipinos came in, and not many Chinese. . . . No, we didn't have many [outside activities] at that time. It was just the regular school hour. Many of our children lived up *mauka* [toward the mountains] — you know, in the homesteads — and they'd come down to school very early, and they'd have to walk home, so there wasn't much time for any extracurricular activity. And particularly in wintertime, they'd leave home far before daylight, you know.

When I was teaching I always tried to preserve the customs, you know. For instance, now with Christmas coming on, any of these holidays, we would remember them and have them bring in their cultural differences and customs, and particularly at Christmastime . . . how they celebrated Christmas or Thanksgiving or any of these other holidays. It depended, I think, on the teachers, on the families. Some families, you know, were rather reticent to reveal their ethnic customs, and of course it depended on the teachers, their attitude, and the administration. I remember some of our Filipino children that would bring in these piñatas, you know, that they make. Then their stars and decorations that they have. And the Portuguese with their baking, their bread, you know. That was one thing that they were noted for. . . . We gave operettas every year, and I used to bring in the parents and people in the community who would help us. Anybody who knew Hawaiian dances for our May Day, you know, helped us with the dances and costumes. . . . Some of them were afraid of the haole teachers, you know, but when they once found out that you were interested and wanted to share, they were fine. Oh yes, the Japanese dances, all the different ethnic dances.

I taught over a period of forty-two years. I wasn't on a regular appointment while my children were young, but I substituted, so I really was in the service for forty-two years. Elementary, everything from first grade to eighth grade. That's when we had the grades one to eight. There was special homemaking, special music. I was principal for the last fifteen years at the elementary school. I did like teaching. I still do. . . .

My husband started in down at the mill as a scale boy, weighing the cane as it came in. And he was with the plantation forty-five years, and by that time he was office manager. Lihue Plantation, owned by the company. It was company-owned — Amfac is what it is.

I met him right here in Lihue. I was teaching school. His mother was a teacher, three of his sisters were teachers. They were not all teaching at that time. He was about one-sixteenth Hawaiian. His mother was one-eighth Hawaiian. . . . I wanted to travel, I wanted to see the world, and I got to do that. Because that was a big point when my husband and I were married. He was born on this island, and he had never even been to the mainland when we were married, and he wanted to see the world, and I wanted to, and that was the aim. In '68 we took this trip, took five months and went around the world. So we had that desire satisfied.

We had a daughter and a son. Of course, the year that we lost our son, that was the tragedy of our lives. He was thirty-two years old, a fine physique and superior intelligence. When he got out of college, he took the test for cadets — Air Force cadets. He didn't want to be drafted. And he passed, one of three in the highest fifty cadets in the United States. . . . My son was killed in '62. Makes you wonder why. . . .

But it seems to me I've enjoyed every time that's gone along in a different way. I've always had sort of a happy-go-lucky disposition, I guess, my mother tells me. They call me that. My dad used to call me Hooligan, a nickname. And my mother called me Happy, Happy Hooligan. Well, I was serious, very serious-minded, and I always have been all my life . . . taken it seriously. But I don't know — I've always had a good time and enjoyed life as I went along. . . .

Some of the old Hawaiian customs . . . Well, this idea that you must never take bananas with you when you go fishing — never, never take bananas. You won't catch any fish if you do. *Aumakua* don't like it if you take bananas. . . . I was always curious, and they knew that I didn't believe them [superstitions], but I never, never . . . I was always very careful never to show any disregard for their feelings. . . . You must never put a lei around the neck of a pregnant woman. It'll strangle the child, you see. Things like that.

In the back of their mind, they're always Hawaiian. And they take the attitude of being a conquered, beaten-down person. They still feel that they must bow to the haole, that they were a conquered people. . . .

Since I have been married into the Hawaiians . . . You know, I feel the Hawaiians are quite paranoid. Have you experienced that? And they are very reticent to let you know who they are, what they are inwardly. I feel that I've been very fortunate in that I was taken in by their family as a haole. I don't know why. I wondered why it is, particularly because there were two of us girls who were teachers here at the same time. We weren't friends to begin with, but we met here. I started going with my husband. This other girl started going with his uncle, who was just a little bit older than he. I don't know, somehow I was just accepted. She never was, and why, I don't know. We went together in the same group and everything. Same family. We'd meet socially, we'd be in the group, you know. . . . His mother and sisters and all, they just seemed to treat me as one of them. One time, she said, "How come they accept you but they treat me as a stranger?" Now you see, that's the thing. Yes, it did bother her. . . . But they would say such things as "Oh, you're not a haole anymore. You're one of us." You see, that's the idea. And I have learned that when the Hawaiians do feel that way about you, alright. If they don't, they never will. And it's just something intangible that's hard to get at. . . . They just didn't seem to feel that she was one of their kind, you know. And I don't know what it is, whether it's something they feel, because . . . I couldn't see there was any reason. Even now they say, "You're a kamaaina. You're one of us. You belong to us." You know, they just feel I do. It's some kind of a kindred feeling they have. And I've noticed it with so many. There are some people that they just feel belong to them and others that don't. And they hold you off.

And it interests me, too, when some people characterize Hawaiians and say [that] underneath we feel Hawaiians are soft-natured, easygoing. But they're not. Underneath, they're tough. Well, look at the history, look at the history! I feel it a great privilege when they will take you in and accept you as one of them.

I sometimes wonder — of course, I didn't live here at that time — whether they were really oppressed by the haoles or whether the Hawaiians took it that way. They feel an oppressed, subjugated people.

. . . They have a beautiful culture, but in a way they have subjugated themselves, you know, in a way that I feel wasn't necessary. . . . That's it. Now they've turned the other way. If you're with them you'll notice that the Hawaiians will quieten down, those that I know. They won't argue about it. Of course, most of those that I know are the older ones. . . . And it's too bad, because they are a beautiful people. But they have their other side, and it's made them militant.

ISADORA

Isadora was born in Cheyenne, Wyoming, the daughter of a cowboy of Scottish-English descent. She came as a child to Kahoolawe and Maui and has identified strongly with the Islands ever since. Her interviews are quoted here at length because of her character, her memory, and her magic with words.

My grandfather went out to Wyoming in the late 1850s, and he built Cheyenne. He was from England, and he was in the cavalry. And my Uncle John, his brother, he also was a cavalry officer — major. And they built Cheyenne. Grandpa became the first contractor and builder when he got out of the cavalry in 1868, after the wars. He used to say, "Thank God I never had to kill a noble redman." He was a communications officer and used to put up poles with the wires. And they'd come and watch him. They never bothered him. He was a small boy on his father's ranch north of Cheyenne. Used to get on his pony and — he had no brothers, had two sisters — ride over to the reservation. And he'd play with the young braves there. He was like that.

My grandfather taught me [to] love all people. They're all brothers. But he'd lost everything through the darnedest thing. Anybody came to my grandfather and said, "I'm in trouble," he'd sign a note for him [from the] bank. When he died, my grandmother had to sell everything he owned to pay the bank. . . . He died in 1917, the same year the queen died. . . .

My grandmother and her sister were beautiful Scottish women out of Canada. They used to make haggis, they used to make scones, they used to make all kind of things, shortbread. No, heck, I never learned to cook until I was married, [when] we couldn't afford a servant anymore. I was a good cook. I watched my mother.

My other grandpa, he came from Scotland a little later than

Grandpa T. — probably 1858, something like that. There was a gold rush or something. He didn't find gold, but he built a ranch — Big Seville country, on Horse Creek, between Horse and Pole Creek, Wyoming.

And I was born in Camp Carlin at Fort D. A. Russell, Wyoming, north of Cheyenne, December 20, 1899. Papa and Mama were married in 1898. He was a quartermaster — went from Fort Jefferson Barracks, Missouri, to Cuba and the Philippines under General Leonard Wood and [served with] Colonel Teddy Roosevelt, the Spanish-American War. They were great friends. Then to the Boxer Rebellion under General Chafee in China. Then from there — he was still quartermaster — they sent him to Alaska. I didn't see him until I was coming four years old. He was away in the wars. Then he sold the ranch, what was left of it. They built a pretty home for my grandma out in the east end of Cheyenne. I was born in the house next to it.

Right above us about a block was the old stagecoach stables and corrals — and the stagecoach. The whips were still there. We'd sit there and crack the whips. And Mama and I took the last stagecoach trip from Shoshone to Thermopolis in 1912. And when the horses crossed the Little Bighorn, it was running kind of flooded — it was heavy. They swam, and we held up our feet, six horses. Oh, that was a wonderful thing!

When my mother divorced my father in 1910, we stayed with her father for a time. That's how come I went on the stagecoach trip. We were visiting with her father. And then I came back to Hawaii in 1915. . . .

Father and my grandfather [and the rest of] our family, during the Reformation on his side did not give up the faith. They were Earls of Shrewsbury. They left the captured ones and they went to Ireland, where one of them was a bishop. The others remained Protestant. They're still there. . . . The last thing my grandfather ever said to me when I left in 1915 was, "Remember, little girl, never give up your faith." The family has given up everything but our faith. It doesn't matter what you have, so long as you keep your faith. . . .

Mother taught me on the ranch, you know. She taught me all kind of beautiful things. I could read the *Book of Scottish Chiefs* when I was five years old. I could read it myself. She taught me to read. She and I were alone on the ranch, must be eighty miles from Cheyenne. I have a lot of her sayings written down. We made poetry together. There are poems. She wrote a good many poems. She was a very beautiful woman.

She was very staunch Catholic. She had very high ideals. She didn't care
for ranching. Anyway, she left my father — they couldn't get along. And
my sympathies went more to my father than to her for a long time,
because I'd lost my father and the ranch and my horse and everything
else. . . . Mother at the last sold my horse. And a child doesn't figure out
who's better or what. It's what affects the child.

My father never taught me anything. He didn't want me to fool
around with horses. His sisters, according to newspaper stories, were
two of the finest ranchers in Wyoming. He wanted me to be a lady. He
wanted me to play the piano. He wanted me to have all the graces of
society. He wanted me away from the ranch, he wanted me with other
people. . . . Papa went with a lot of good people — society, wealthy
people — and he wanted me to be a wonderful lady. But I wasn't. I
disappointed him horribly.

But my father wanted a son. The first time he saw me, he picked me
up, looked at me, and said, "Funny-looking little thing, isn't he?" So I
became that son. I could rope cattle as well as any of them. . . .

Oh, she was beautiful, Mama was. Then Mama met this girl, she was
in vaudeville. And I could sing, and my mother could play the piano and
she had a beautiful voice. She had studied to be an opera singer in
Seattle while my father was off to war. Oh, she wanted to be an opera
singer. Had a beautiful voice too. We were going to go on stage. Mama
was going to play the piano, and she would sing alto sometimes, but I
would sing, "Look how the moon shines tonight on pretty redwing," and
I was dressed like a little Indian girl, and I had long black hair. 'Course
it was curled. But I got a sore throat, and the doctor took out my tonsils.
And he damn near killed me — I nearly bled to death. And I can
remember waking up in bed in our room in the convent. I said, "Why
are you all praying?" So I didn't talk anymore. And my poor mother,
the tears streaming down her face. "You're not dying, you're not dying."
I didn't think I was dying — I just felt sick. . . .

Teddy Roosevelt was coming through Cheyenne in 1907, and there
was a rodeo. Mother and I sat with him. He and Papa were friends. And
E. L. of the Parker Ranch was there. He was promoting the Territory of
Hawaii. And Papa was champion roper of the world . . . and they
brought him over here. And the day we got to Moiliili Park, Uncle E.
took us up into the grandstand, and there was Queen Liliuokalani. This
was December 1907. And from then on in, oh . . . She greeted Mother
and me. I have the gifts that she gave Mother and me. Papa didn't win,

but he made a big impression. So that's how we came [to Hawaii], and then we went to Parker Ranch with Uncle E. And then we came to Maui in January 1908. Queen Liliuokalani was coming to Lahaina, so we traveled with her. And she said to me, "You will live in my land all your life. Help my people to remember aloha." And that's all I've tried to do publicly since 1936.

As a matter of fact, the queen had me at her home for my eighth birthday and gave me a doll . . . a tiny little doll, sweet little thing, Hawaiian doll. And Governor Dole and Governor Freer came to the party at the queen's home. And I had heard or read enough of history to know that Dole was the first president here. Therefore, I thought he was the queen's enemy. And when he came, I refused to shake hands. I put my hands behind me. And the queen leaned over and said, "You're being very rude to my best friends." Afterwards, she said if it hadn't been for the good that was in Governor Dole, who was the leader, that she and Prince Kuhio and some more of them might have been shot by the wild, angry mob of people. . . .

I see Waikiki as I saw it in 1907 when from Puuleahi, which is Diamond Head, along Waikiki was nothing but coconut palms, magnificent trees, people in carriages and walking and riding horseback, bicycles. Everything was beautiful, the smell of flowers and all coming from the beach. It was December, lovely green hills. We left Wyoming in the snow, this blizzard. Papa said that day as we were coming along there, seeing all this beauty . . . he said, "Child, I think we'll live here." So we did. . . .

I had Suma-san [the maid's name]. She'd come and wash my ears and get me ready for school. I would jump up in the morning, quickly clean my teeth by the tap by the door, and rush around the corner of the house in my overalls and my bare feet and my shirt, and eat breakfast with Papa and the cowboys. Every morning. One of the cowboys, he said, "I'm going to take care of this *keiki* [child]." So he took care of me. He made me my first braided rawhide rope to rope cattle with. His wife made me my first *lauhala* hat. And it had big cowboy Stetson-like pockets. She made me a lei, and she didn't make it out of breast feathers. We have peacocks here. She cut out the eye of the tail feather, and she made me a lei for this beautiful red *lauhala* hat. . . . My damn stepmother, when I went to school, took everything out of the almirah [wardrobe] in my room and put all my stuff in the tack room with nothing to protect it, and the rats and the cockroaches wrecked every-thing, including the lei. . . .

Suma-san had a baby, and it died. And there was a little cemetery above the cistern above the house. She took me by the hand one day, had a little bouquet of flowers. . . . And there was her baby's grave. And she put the flowers, and I helped her. And I said, "Suma-san, why do you have this pipe here?" "Oh, so baby get air." . . .

When I was a little girl eight years old, we had a terrible drought, and everybody was looking so sad and all. We had a stone rain god in the garden on a pedestal, and everybody was putting leis on it. . . . Anyway, he was covered with leis, and there was no rain. The sky was brazen. And I went over [and saw that] there was a little water left in the fountain, with a few goldfish locked in. We couldn't take any of it. If the fish died, we had to get more — that was all. And I thought everybody was going to die. And I picked up a handful of water, and I threw it in that face, and I said, "Now make it rain!" Then I cried because I'd lost my temper and been rude. Then I got on my pony bareback, my little black pony, and we just went and we went and we went. And we went all the way down through the lava flow. We were just going. And then we met a black dog, a big black dog, and my horse pricked up his ears, and he followed the dog. And the dog led us to the pool of water. . . . We were dyin' of thirst, we were having a dreadful drought. Cattle were droppin' dead. Well, anyway, I thanked Pele, I thanked her very much. . . .

And one day I found the entrance to a cave that might have something wonderful in it, I thought. I didn't put the reins on the ground — I just jumped off bareback and went to look in the cave. And I heard a galloping, galloping, and my pony was going back to Kihei. I chased him until I got out of breath and fell on the ground, moaning and crying and beating the earth with my fist. Oh God, I can't go home, help me! Help me! And I lay there until I was exhausted. And all of a sudden . . . You know, in Wyoming you learn from the Indians [to] listen on the ground. I was lying there listening on the ground. Maybe I could hear him someplace. And I heard hoofs. And, my gosh, it was Father Justin, my good friend, and his altar boy coming to say mass for the weekend. He had my horse. He was my hero. And after that, Father Justin was my saint. I couldn't thank him enough. I think he's one reason why I've been a very good Catholic all my life.

I graduated from Punahou and Maui High School the same year, 'cause I used to go to Punahou with my mother, and I kept it up with examinations. They'd give me oral examinations, and finally in 1918 I was graduated Maui High. I also graduated Punahou, of which I'm very proud. It's a good school, you know. . . .

When I was at school in Denver, we stayed at St. Rose's Convent for Working Girls, my mother and I. There was another girl there — her father was an Indian and her mother was a white woman. . . . Cherry Creek overflowed, and I went down to see if there was anything that ought to be put back in the water. And there was a horned toad. I had never seen one before, only photographs of them. And I picked it up and rescued it and put it in a shoe box and put in food for it, and it lived quite happily for quite a while.

I came home from school one day. School was by the church — all Franciscans, these people. I remember . . . Sister Blondina, I could have killed her. It was the first time in my life I ever hated anyone. I came in and she was standing there, and she had taken the lid off the box and she was pressing the lid on the little thing. It was on its back, and it was dead. So I had a funeral. Vera and I went out and we found a pretty place and we had a funeral.

So when it came Halloween time, I was going to have vengeance on this nun. . . . She used to sneak around the halls very soft — you couldn't hear her coming — always watching for something wrong. Well, anyway, come Halloween . . . we had gone to a burlesque show for some darn reason. You're not supposed to go there if you're ladies, you know. There were several young women there. We'd never been to one. Mama being the chaperone, we all went to this thing. And they made a pair of binoculars about this long out of cardboard. And we put them up to our eyes, like this. Anyway, somebody had a Halloween mask. It had a white skull painted on it. It was black. So [back at school] I put it on a long broomstick and put a sheet over the broom, and I lifted it up to the transom over her door. And I knocked on the door, and she looked and gave the most horrible scream and fainted. I thought that was the loveliest thing I'd ever done. My mother said, "How could you do anything like that?" And she said, "I don't blame you one bit.". . .

I went to Dana Hall in Massachusetts, in Wellesley. Was darn near expelled. I did everything I could to get expelled from Dana Hall and sent home. One day . . . I had a friend that lived across the street. She and her parents lived across the street from the tennis court. Every time, I was tennis champion there. And we beat the senior champions and became the champions. And they weren't going to put my name on the silver cup because I had got on the motorcycle of this girl's brother — a new one, and I had never seen one up close. I rushed out of the tennis court, went over to the brother and sister, and the boy said, "You wanta ride?" I said, "Sure, I'd like to ride." So okay, I get on the back seat and hang on to the thing and away we go. Instead of going around the block, he went to Redwood City and back. He was trying out his motorcycle, and I was having a whirl.

And we got back and his mother said, "Was it a good ride?" And I said, "Oh, it was beautiful!" She said, "You better get in there — you're late for lunch." So I went in. I washed my hands and did this to my hair and went in. And a few minutes later, after I seated myself, Miss L. — she was a beautiful woman, very society-style, motherly, too — [said], "It has come to our ears that one of our girls in uniform was seen riding with a boy on a motorcycle in Redwood City. Will you please stand?" So I stood. That time my mother had to come down, and the woman from across the street came in my defense. And I said, "Oh, please let me go home. I want to go home." Sure, I had all of Haleakala and Maui, and a horse, my family. So I didn't get expelled from Dana Hall. . . .

I've been a cowboy all my life. As I told you, I'm a rancher, a cowboy at heart. . . . Oh, I've done some teaching. I worked as a telephone operator at the hospital for a while. I've done some writing for the newspapers and some books of childhood memories. I have a very good memory. But all I ever wanted to be was a cowboy, a rancher like my father. Here we call it *paniolo*. I used to rope wild cattle with him and brand cattle and ship cattle and all that, so it's the only thing I ever wanted to do. I rode every trail on Maui. But unfortunately, they didn't have a chance to leave the K Ranch Company to me and the rest of us to manage. You see, the war took it away in December 1941. So I never was a cowboy after that. . . .

X.C. asked me to marry him, Y.C.'s son. . . . I loved his mother, and his father was good to me too. X.C. jilted me. We were having a New Year luau. I was always in riding clothes. I was very much a man's man, sorta thing. Roped cattle almost as well as any of them, except I wasn't quite as strong as the men. And this night, they went to a party. I didn't go, I stayed home. We were having a luau at the ranch the next day. And they say this girl R. was dressed like a peacock. And so the next day we waited and we waited, and the cowboys, the rest of us, we were all sitting around out there. And then a car drove in, and there was X.C. and R. and a friend and his girl. And we were called into the house, Papa and the rest of us. We were engaged. And without a word to me, they announced their engagement that New Year Day.

And I went out and got gloriously drunk. I was desolated. I couldn't have the ranch after all. He was mean, and he was selfish. It wasn't he I wanted. It was the ranch. In fact, R. . . . was going with somebody on the Big Island, so I thought, well, that's safe, I guess. And this day they announced their engagement.

And then one of the cowboys thought an awful lot of me, and he had had a few drinks, and I went over and sat in the car. I knew I was gettin' drunk. I leaned my head against the wheel like this for a minute and — I wasn't crying. I was so damn mad I coulda killed everybody! I had my hand on the door, and this cowboy came over and put his hand on mine. "Oh, Miss P. [Isadora], I so aloha to you." Of course, in those days a white woman didn't have anything to do with a Hawaiian cowboy. This wasn't done. I said, "Oh, go away, don't be a fool." And about that time my head went over on the horn and tooted the horn, and Papa came. Papa got into the seat, pushed me over, and they took me up to the house. And I sat on the front steps of the house. The house is still there. . . . Well, I sat on the front steps, and I was very much an Indian when I was a kid, you know. Then I came Hawaiian when I got here. The Indians and Hawaiians both, and the Scotch and Irish too . . . I howled like a wolf. Ayeee! And Papa said, "Go and get her another drink, she looks sick." So they did. I was sicker than a dog from drinkin' too much. So that was the end of my romance.

And I had to attend the wedding. I had to. And I told Papa, "Can't I get out of goin' to this funeral?" He said, "What!" I said, "I don't want to go to this wedding — it oughta be mine." "Well," he said, "You can't have everything." . . .

I met my husband in San Francisco. I was working in the City of Paris — remember that store? I started . . . I went over and got a job for the Christmas holidays and they kept me on. I came home, and then D.C. gave my husband a job as timekeeper at the ranch. . . . He had never been on a horse. He'd seen them in races in England, but he had to learn to ride. I was married in 1928, February. I had two sons, both of them pilots. Both of them were with the National Guard. The older one was a marvelous pilot. He could bring that L-19 down on only a parade ground. The younger one wanted to be a pilot and they took him to Korea, in the Korean War. . . . He's still alive. My sons went to Lahainaluna. . . .

In Hawaiian, you have God in three parts, you know. There's Kane the Creator, Lona the Sustainer of Life, and Kanaloa, who gives you the gift of death. And when Kanaloa takes your hand and leads you beyond the sunset, then you go the hidden Isles of Kane. And when you go there, there are beautiful hills and beautiful streams and everything you want. I hope my horses and dogs are over there, too, with the people I love.

I'm a Roman Catholic, sure, but I believe very much in the way of the Hawaiians. I see God in everything. I see God in other people. He created everybody and everything. . . . Over there is Kaahumanu Church . . . you look at the stones under the church. That's a *heiau,* a temple. . . . No, it's not bad luck to build a church there if you say your prayers. When you go into a *heiau,* go in like you would to a church. That's what it was. . . .

Mankind seems to want to get into groups, like. I don't know. I'd much rather be out. Haleakala [a mountain on Maui] used to be our temple. In this case, it's Hele, Heleakala — in the pathway of the sun.

V   Portuguese

Voyagers

The Portuguese were Europe's first seafaring power. By the late sixteenth century, the lure of adventure and the prospect of converts to the faith had taken them farther than any other sailors from Europe — around the Cape of Good Hope to Goa, the Straits of Malacca, and beyond, as far as Macao and Japan. The idea of venturing across the sea was thus nothing new. They had been master navigators since the fifteenth century. Moreover, for the Portuguese living in the Azores and Madeira, island life was what they knew. What they first heard of the Hawaiian Islands was appealing to them; the Islands sounded not too different from their own.

The earliest Portuguese to arrive in the Hawaiian Islands came as sailors and whalers in the 1790s. A few jumped ship and remained on the Islands, unable to resist their lure. The main migration, however, began in 1878 as a result of poor economic conditions in the Azores and Madeira. For one thing, a blight ruined the wine industry in 1876 and left many with no means to make a living. Others came to Hawaii out of a desire to evade military service. Some of them stowed away on ships and went to work on the ships when they were discovered. The Gold Rush also brought a few hundred Portuguese to California in the mid-nineteenth century. Most made their way to the West Coast via New England, where they stopped off after their voyage from the Azores.[1]

The immediate impetus for immigration to Hawaii in the late 1800s came from two sources. First, during the 1860s, a German botanist named Hillebrand, who was surveying plant life in Hawaii, was hired by sugar planters to scout for labor in Southeast Asia. He did not have much success there, but during his travels he stopped in Madeira to study tropical plants. From there he wrote to his Hawaiian friends that the climate was similar to Hawaii's and that Madeira might be an ideal place to recruit labor. Moreover, "The Portuguese," wrote Hillebrand, "would make excellent plantation laborers." He continued by writing that as they were "sober, honest, industrious and peaceable, they combine all the qualities of a good settler, and with all this, they are inured to your climate."[2]

Second, in 1876 one Pereira, a consular agent for Portugal, also urged the Hawaiian government to import labor from Madeira, where sugarcane had been successfully grown since the fifteenth century.[3] In the same year, it will be recalled, the Reciprocity Treaty with the United States was ratified, which stimulated the demand for Hawaiian sugar.

The suggestions from Hillebrand and Pereira, added to the sudden increase in the demand for sugar, inspired the Hawaiian government to sponsor contract labor from the Portuguese Islands. Moreover, the Bureau of Immigration was concerned because Chinese laborers were leaving the sugar fields and replacements were sorely needed. Hillebrand was appointed commissioner of immigration for Hawaii in the Portuguese Islands and had instructions to offer contracts providing transportation and wages of $10 a month for men and $6 to $8 for women. In November 1876, the year of the wine industry blight in Portugal, the Bureau of Immigration voted to pay passage for 200 men from Portugal — $45 for men, $50 for women, and half that for children. The bureau also guaranteed jobs, food, lodging, medical care, and garden ground for all who came.[4] The reason for paying more for women was that the government was interested in settling families rather than bachelors.

The first ship from Madeira, the *Priscilla*, landed 114 persons on October 5, 1878; the voyage had lasted 120 days. Many were farmers, but there were also mechanics, masons, and carpenters among them.[5] The second chartered ship brought 400 Portuguese the following year. In 1881 two more ships brought 800 men, women, and children.[6]

Their reception in Hawaii was enthusiastic and corroborated Hillebrand's suggestion. The *Pacific Commercial Advertiser,* in an article on October 5, 1878, praised the Portuguese with the following words: "The more we have of this sort of immigration the better. They are, as a race . . . temperate, painstaking, thrifty and law abiding people. They came here to stay, and they do not send their earnings out of the country, as do some other nationalities."[7]

The Bureau of Immigration in Honolulu was as pleased, as were the planters, with the Portuguese. The president of the bureau characterized them as a peasant people whose "education and ideas of comfort

Fig. 5.1. This mother (standing right) later died in childbirth. *Courtesy of Mrs. Laura Botilho.*

and social requirements are just low enough to make them contented with the lot of an isolated settler and its attendant privations."[8]

However, because the Portuguese brought women and children with them — the proportion of male labor was only about 30 percent — they were relatively expensive as imported labor. The immigration of Portuguese therefore declined and was temporarily discontinued in 1888. After the fall of the Portuguese monarchy in 1910, labor recruitment shifted briefly to the Portuguese mainland, and 1,652 continental Portuguese arrived in Hawaii in 1911. In 1913 the last organized group from Portugal, 228 persons, arrived in Honolulu.

Those from the continent did not adjust to plantation work as well as the Madeiran and Azorean peasants had, and many of the former left for California as soon as they were able. They were attracted to California because of its increasing wage rates, the result of the exclusion of the Chinese. Some returned to Hawaii after the fall of the Hawaiian monarchy in the 1890s.[9] But the main trend was a drift from the plantations to the cities, mainly Honolulu but also Hilo. The Punchbowl district of Honolulu became the residential center for Portuguese settlers.[10]

With the halting of Portuguese immigration after 1913, the proportion of Hawaiian-born Portuguese increased steadily. By 1920 the ratio of Hawaiian-born to Portuguese-born was four to one, an increase from the two-to-one ratio in 1900.[11] Conditions were in some respects better than at home in Portugal; there were schools on the plantations, which they did not have back home in Madeira.[12]

Women

Women were part of Portuguese-Hawaiian society from the beginning. The influx of bachelors that characterized the Chinese and Filipino immigrations did not occur with the Portuguese. The men brought their wives and children and came to stay.

The Portuguese had large families. In the 1920s, the average Portuguese family in Hawaii had at least four children. One study of five hundred Portuguese-Hawaiian men indicates that at least twenty-one of this group had twelve to seventeen children.[13] With such a high rate of childbearing, it was not uncommon for women to die during childbirth; infant mortality rates were also high.

One group of early immigrants was sent to Paia Plantation, where each family was given a cottage of two, three, or four rooms. Others were sent to the Big Island, where families lived six together in a longhouse. When they first arrived in Hawaii, there were not enough Portuguese for their own camps, so they lived in the Spanish camps. Because they lived in such close quarters, the immigrants found it necessary to share and use facilities cooperatively.

The presence of women also led the Portuguese to establish churches. Most Portuguese were Catholic, and they took their religion seriously. The calendar of religious holidays, *festas*, contoured the rhythm of their lives. Religion also played a central role in their social life. The religious and social highlight of the year was the Holy Ghost *festa* in June. The *festa* featured a high mass, a children's procession

Fig. 5.2. Baking in a Portuguese oven, ca. 1945. *Courtesy of the Alexander & Baldwin Sugar Museum, Puunene, Maui.*

around the church, and singing and dancing to guitar and ukulele music.[14] It was also a most important social event. People came to the church from miles around for a chance to meet other Portuguese, and the *festa* was the annual chance for young men and women to meet in a society that protected, if not cloistered, its girls.

Because girls were not allowed to date, courting was carried on by guitar serenades or by letter, after which the young man approached the girl's parents formally to ask for permission to meet and later to marry her. Calling on parents was a declaration of intent to marry the daughter. Because girls were outnumbered, a girl often got several proposals, and her parents then asked her to choose which suitor she would have. Young men were allowed in the girls' houses during sewing bees, where they carried on their conversations in song, in a romantic tradition transplanted from Portugal.[15] Some respondents complained during their interviews about not being allowed the freedom to date that was enjoyed by other ethnic groups; they also complained about being denied permission to go away to school.

Girls looked forward to Christmas and Easter as occasions on which they could expect new dresses. Photographs from more than half a century ago show women, especially young women, wearing starched, ruffled white dresses. Women of other ethnic communities spoke of the dresses worn by the Portuguese women as the vogue of the day, the style to be envied and emulated.

A Portuguese import central to the life-style of these immigrants was the *forno*, the domed brick oven for baking Portuguese bread. No Portuguese camp was without at least one *forno*, and ideally there was one oven for each four families. The housewives gathered once or twice a week at the *forno* to bake bread for their families and to socialize.

As a general rule, Portuguese women did not work in the fields, although some of the first-generation immigrant women did, primarily weeding. The Portuguese women had large families to care for, and when they sought to supplement the family income, it was often through dressmaking or through teaching dressmaking to women of other ethnic groups. Some respondents noted that midwives in the first generation were often Portuguese, although these early midwives assisted at child-birth, not always for money but apparently out of compassion or for barter of goods or services. Many women also worked in the pineapple canneries, both when they were in school and later as adults.

The presence of women in the camps encouraged the formation of charitable organizations. The Lusitania, established in 1882, was supported by the savings of its two thousand members and helped the poor, invalids, and orphans. An even earlier organization, the San Antonio Society, was established by whalers in 1877 to help with funeral expenses. In 1903 the San Martino was formed for purely charitable goals. Finally, in 1905 the Patria Society was organized with the primary goal of creating schools for teaching the Portuguese language.[16] By 1906 Portuguese settlers had their own language school and four newspapers.

Work

Many Madeirans and Azoreans were experienced in sugar production. A Portuguese settler may have been the first to try sugar milling on Maui. It was mainly the Portuguese who became the *lunas* on the plantations. The only other ethnic group represented significantly among the *lunas* in the early years of the sugar industry were the Hawaiians.[17] *Lunas* were given the better houses in the camps, the "front-row houses." From 1881 through 1942, the Portuguese constituted about 6 percent of all plantation workers.[18]

The first winery in Hawaii, the Serras Wine Company, began production in 1891. This was another enterprise in which the Portuguese were the pioneers. In their exodus from the plantations, some Portuguese men went into the trades as carpenters and mechanics, occupations that also attracted second-generation Portuguese.

Relations with Other Ethnic Groups

For some reason — difficult for the respondents in this study to explain and for scholars to identify — the Portuguese were not regarded as haole. It may have been because some Portuguese from the Cape Verde Islands were dark-skinned, almost black. Or it may have been because, in their role as lunas, they became more closely identified with plantation work than did other haole groups. Moreover, the sugar planters may have wished to keep the Portuguese separate from other haoles in order to keep them out of higher labor brackets. Sociologist Andrew Lind suggests that they were treated as separate from other Caucasians and regarded as such as long as they remained on the plantation.[19] Census data did not classify the Portuguese as haole or Caucasian; rather they were listed as "other Caucasians," and it was not until 1940 that they were officially recognized as Caucasian.[20]

The Portuguese intermarried in the early generations, especially with other Catholic groups. Thirty percent of all Spanish brides and grooms in the late nineteenth century married Portuguese.[21] Later, as the Portuguese moved off the plantations and into the cities, they interacted more with other Caucasian groups and came to be considered haoles themselves. Romanzo Adams wrote in 1969 that the Portuguese "tend to be indifferent to the maintenance of customs and standards that identify them as Portuguese or even to be definitely opposed to such maintenance."[22] This perception was corroborated by one of the respondents here.

TERESINHA

Teresinha was born on Maui. She hoped to become a nurse, but she was not allowed to go to Honolulu for training. Instead, she did substitute teaching and later taught kindergarten. She married another Portuguese and raised four children.

I was born in a town named Hamakuapoko — a long name, a small town — on Maui, on June 14, 1912. My mother was born on the island of Kauai. My father was an immigrant, my mother was not. Her parents came later than my father's parents . . . from Madeira, the island of Madeira.

I knew my grandparents. Mother took care of her mother, I remember. The plantation homes did not have screens in those days. I would be leaning over [the windowsill] and Mother would have this basin with the pitcher on it. That was famous for Portuguese. They called it the *jarro* and the *bacia*, basin. She'd have the hot water in the pitcher, and the basin had water, and I remember it was on a chair next to Vovó . . . means "Grandma," Vovó. I don't remember my grandpa, but Mother's mother, I remember her very, very well.

My grandfather worked in the sugar mill. He was the first sugar boiler. Then they started to have a mechanical sugar boiler. My father's father. I don't remember my mother's father. But my grandmother must have gone back to the mainland, because I don't remember her death. I remember her in the bed, such a beautiful lady, you know. But I don't remember her funeral, and that is strange because I would have.

My mother came from Kauai, like I told you. She was born there. And when the plantations found out that there was a family [already there] because different ships came in from Madeira. . . . Before the semigallow, the Azoreans came. The *Priscilla* brought them first. Then there was other ships that brought them. My mother somehow or my father's family found out that there was family over here that they knew from Madeira. So they came over here, and then Father met Mother, and that's how they got married.

Mother had nine children, and she had a baby that she lost. Babies used to die young in those days. . . . This is the baby [shows a photograph]. She was a year and about three months when Mother passed away . . . from this [other] baby she was already carrying, you see. Mother died in April, on April 26th. And Dad, imagine all these little Indians running around without a mother. When Mother died, she [the baby] had to go with my mother's brother, Uncle Manuel. Uncle Manuel kept her. He took care of her until she died. Because Father . . . It was hard with all these kids.

One would sweep house and one would mop. Like my sister Eva would sweep and I would mop, and she was one of the finicky things, you know. And I wanted to go out and play and mop that house fast, and she would keep me back. "Hurry up, Eva, hurry up. You still in here?" And I would do the mopping. . . . Helen would do the laundry. And all the rest would do the yard, the little ones. They boiled the clothes next to the oven, in the fireplace. . . .

But mother died of childbirth. And she had so many babies, so close in age. Just about one every year, just about. We're very close. Beautiful woman. The midwife came to the house. . . . We did not have a telephone in those days. Not very many people had telephones. And somebody went — one of my sisters — to tell Yamasaki to come down and take Mama to the hospital. And Mother never came home again. . . .

We didn't speak Portuguese at home. Mother spoke fluent English. But she was really good at reading and writing in Portuguese, and praying. She was a good church woman. The services were in English at the church. I don't remember the Portuguese services. That was before my time. . . .

Shrove Tuesday is Mal-assada Day, just before Easter, before Ash Wednesday. Nobody could get married during Lent. No partying. And you make *mal-assadas* for the souls. It's like doughnuts without the hole. I remember Mother making it when I was a little girl. We all had to help her as we got older, and that's how we learned to do it. It's a yeast thing, rises. I can tell you the story about the *mal-assada*. You know, there was a convent in Portugal, and the yeast for the bread would not come out. Potato yeast, that's how they used to do it. It wouldn't rise. So this nun — she must have been a rascal nun — she said, "We are not going to bake this, we are going to fry it. We're not throwing this dough away." And lo and behold, in the fat it did rise. That's the meaning of *mal-assada* — badly baked. *Mal* is bad, badly baked. Portuguese never make doughnuts with a hole in it, it's dropped. Dropped doughnuts. . . .

Oh, it's so beautiful, the Holy Ghost *festa*. Everybody waits for it. At first, the people from Kula built the church, and they said they would have a luau, because they lived so far from people. And the whole island of Maui would be invited, and they would have free lunch. We will make a luau. We all raise cattle up here, and for God to help us every year, even better. It's usually in June. In the evening before, they have a luau where you pay, with entertainment and all that. Dance if they want to after, in the Holy Name hall. They have a big high mass. Deacons now . . . everybody says a little something. People go up for the procession. They have a procession, little children with flowers. The older people sit down on benches and watch. Children with baskets of flowers, and they give it to the Blessed Mother in the church.

Holy Ghost was a time to meet, because otherwise you don't see each other. And that's how some love affairs have started. Yes, sometimes it has happened. I remember dancing at Kula, and music. Portuguese dances, always in a circle. And my husband used to play the ukulele, and we would dance. . . .

When I was a child, everybody wore hats in those days — I still remember. Not anymore. And we would volunteer and walk around the church. I love processions. Around the church on the outside, just once around the church. Of course, the priest leads the procession. There is a queen and all her attendants. They choose one, a beauty queen, for the *festa*. The Holy Ghost is for any Catholic, not only Portuguese. Each church has its own, but the Kula one is more effective. People don't have to go — it's out of the way. Ranchers would offer their cattle for the luau, you see. Everything is given. And the remains of the *lau laus* [pork cooked in ti leaves], they go to the Kula Sanatorium, where they have tuberculosis. On our island, this is the most important *festa*.

Then comes St. Anthony. This had a special intention. Give, and it shall be given unto you. Give. And people from Wailuku, all over, they go and they stay in the morning, and in the afternoon they have auctions, the cattle.

I can tell you about Christmas. We would hang stockings in the living room, on the chairs or something, or little posts, and Mother had crocheted, hanging down. I remember one Christmas my brother was a naughty boy. He got a hammer and nails without having a nice gift. But in those days we thought Santa Claus did that — he's watching us, you see. But my dad did that to punish him. But then we'd have ribbons for our hair for church. You'd see all of us with ribbons in our hair. And Mother would comb those curls out. We all had curly hair. And I remember [at] Christmastime we would have new things, maybe a pair of new shoes for Christmas. And that would last all year. In other words, that was thrifty because you're not buying all the time, you see. We walked to school without shoes those days. I couldn't see anybody playing ball with shoes on. Everybody was barefoot. We would be ready for Christmas mass in the morning. We would all go beautifully dressed with the gifts from Santa Claus. Nobody thought there was no such thing as Santa Claus in those days. Everybody just honored him so much, you know.

And I'll tell you about the box of candy. It had one layer for each child. I would eat one chocolate a day. I'd ration it. It would last about three weeks maybe, not even that. And then we'd make dolls with Mother's old clothes. You know, tie string for the elbows. And we'd make the clothes. So you see, we appreciated things. And the apples and oranges. . . . You see apples half-bitten and thrown on the road now. We ate every bit of it because we only had it at Christmastime and New Year's. Oranges and apples was a delicacy for Christmas and New Year's, not even Fourth of July. That was a specialty, and we enjoyed it immensely. To the core we'd eat it. And Mother would have all that food. So much food! Roast meat, and the Portuguese way with potatoes and everything.

In those days, they had musicians to come and serenade from the neighborhood. And they would always leave my father's house till last. And we would be up by that time 'cause they'd be here about six o'clock. And Father would give them breakfast Christmas morning, roast meat and potatoes. They would be out all night. We were neighbors to these Hawaiians. One was a policeman. I still remember he was the first motorcycle cop on Maui, and we enjoyed watching his motorcycle shining and everything. And, oh, we used to love to see him pass by with his policeman clothes and driving it, you know. We honored him as a policeman. Singing Hawaiian songs, church songs. We'd get up and watch them in our pajamas, you know. They'd say, "Be quiet, quiet in the corner." So we had good, good discipline at my home. No problems. My father did it, he was the one. He was so strict.

You know, wheat is the beginning of life. Without bread they couldn't live. And that is why the Portuguese believe in that at Christmastime. They have it in their crèche, in their little mangers, always, because it is the beginning of life. Let us remember that.

And for the funerals, Mother would spend the day until afternoon of the funeral. Then she would come home and go back for the novena.

And, of course, there was nine nights that they would have the novena, pray for the soul. And Mother would lead the prayers in Portuguese. . . . She must have been a very intelligent woman. We never questioned her. But she was just wonderful. . . .

Our home was so beautiful. We had an inside toilet. We didn't have to go out. We had a three-bedroom house with a bathroom in it. We were very comfortable. And we had a beautiful kitchen. Of course with a wood stove. I remember carrying wood. I used to hate the wood man, because he would bring the wood, father would saw it and then he would chop it, and we had to carry it to the wood house. We had a separate wood house in the back. We had everything so convenient. And the plantation man would put the clothesline so you hang your clothes up. Everything was done for us. We had nice washhouses. We had a big lanai. Country homes had them, old-fashioned things. And then a dining room. Lots of flowers in the yard. We could plant what we wanted. No, they didn't bring furniture from Portugal. They brought plants, I know. Like a grapevine for their wines and figs for their children. Sure, they used to make wine in those days. Then they had prohibition, huh? And it was all qt. . . .

Father was, shall I call him, the big wheel in those days, you know. His name was not very high as far as the job was concerned, you know. But anyway, it was a big job and responsibility that he had, to get the cane to the mill. And I remember we lived in the back of the mill. It's still there, just filled with poison ivy. Nobody has torn it down. But the houses are gone. They've planted cane there. They did away with that town. I remember living in the front row. The front row was all the big shots. [It was along] the main highway going up to the school. And in the camps we had the different ethnic groups in different sections. Not for discrimination, but for the ethnic way of living. Like the Japanese needed their *furo* [a bathtub, usually wooden]. Mama, Papa, and all the children go bathe together in this big tub. The plantation would have wood, have a special man to make that [the fire under the tub] go for them. The plantation was very good to the labor. . . .

The Portuguese had to have their *forno*, their oven to make their bread, like a kiln, you know. So it had to be in their vicinity. Because the plantation could not give every home an oven. The opening of the Portuguese oven is in front. And when they sweep the ashes, it falls into a chimney, like. Then we put a cover on it. And then if we find it's not hot enough, we take off the cover and we have more heat to finish cooking. It's cemented with bricks, the dome and all. They make the shape that they want, how high, and they know just what they want. About twenty loaves was the usual size, and they baked once a week. The bread only lasts a week. A *forno* was built for four families. If I was the first, I would have to use more wood. The second one would use less. About twenty, twenty-five minutes to bake. I used to knead all by hand. Now we have a mixer. But then, I still use my hands for the feel of the dough. . . . Round loaves. We have to have pans for health sake. We used to put it right on the bricks in the brick oven. While it's rising, you put the pan [in the oven]. Then, when you put it in the oven, you take the pan off and only the bread goes. Of course there's no thermometer in a Portuguese oven. *Forno*, we call it a *forno*. Fire under the oven. Wood . . . *keave* wood is very good, you know. When we feel it's time, then we test it with flour. We sweep the oven, then I come with the flour, and then I'll throw it in the dome. You can tell. If the flour gets brown too fast, it's not ready. . . .

When a girl was going to get married, my mother would counsel. . . . In those days, you didn't have children around — they must not hear what you say. That's why there's many things that we have lost, with the Portuguese especially. We were never allowed [to listen]. The girl would come, she'd sit on the lower step . . . and I know that she maybe is getting married. And the Portuguese, the bride does not dress herself. There's an older, responsible woman from the community or wherever, the village, and my mother would dress the bride. I still remember. Mother would spend the night. And Father had to go to work early in the morning, about four o'clock . . . to get the boys with the horses out to the fields. And everybody goes out early in the morning, whether it was rain or . . . And Mother would come and make his *kaukau* tin. You know what a *kaukau* tin is? It's a lunch can. It had two compartments, one for the rice. . . .

Primary school was public education, but the plantation just supplied the kindergarten. Baby-sitting like, you know — preparing them for school. And I walked to school. I had to walk, because I would walk with my older sisters along the street here. And I remember I was walking up so proudly because I'm no baby anymore. Big school, we called that big school. A different area, you know. . . .

I had gone every summer to the cannery to work. . . . Every summer I'd work, all of us older ones would work, and we'd get paid cash, 12 ¢ an hour when I first started. In my three high-school summers, and the fourth summer I worked again. I didn't have to save. My dad had the money. No, I didn't have to save. Three of us girls were working with my stepmother in the cannery. The younger ones stayed home and take care of the house. So then all of these envelopes . . . We'd go to the window and get our envelopes, and we'd give the envelopes. We didn't even see how much we made. We gave them to my stepmother right there. And I remember we used to ride the truck home. I didn't know what money was. We got no allowance. If my dues for a club at school was $4.95, my stepmother would give me a $5 bill. That 5¢ had to come back to her. No such thing as keep the change. I had no idea about money — she would buy what we needed and all. I had no money in my purse, even in school. . . .

Mother used to write letters for the people back home. I never asked her where she learned to read and write Portuguese. Because we weren't allowed to ask questions. I went to school through high school. Wait till I tell you about my story. My dad was so strict. I was ready to go to Queens' Hospital for nursing, and he stopped me. The younger ones had more education than I had. They were allowed to go to normal school. They went to community colleges here on Maui, and then they found jobs on the plantation offices, things like that. I wanted to go to nursing. I had biology, I had everything that I needed, you know. I corresponded with San Francisco General Hospital, and I applied there to go up, but my dad wouldn't let me go. Or Queens'. He didn't want me out of the house. He was worried about his girls. Very strict with us. The younger ones had more privileges than the older ones, though. I never had a degree, but I took workshops. I never knew I could be a teacher. Then the schools were so strict about degrees, I couldn't teach anymore, even a Catholic school, any grade. Substituting, I used to substitute. And then I got steady with kindergarten, which I loved dearly. . . .

I was a country girl, and I had to make my friends. I was the only Portuguese girl from Hamakuapoko at Maui High, you know. My friends are from every group. I've always mixed with people of other nationalities. I do eulogies for other groups at funerals.

We were never allowed within the camp, anytime. So the girls would come and visit with us. And we'd sit in the yard every Sunday. And my [later] husband had a Plymouth, I still remember. He'd pass up and down. Finally he parked it. We had a driveway, a beautiful home. Men were free. Boys were free, you know. And then he'd come in the yard to talk to us girls. And then one day . . . This is every Sunday this would happen. He'd bring boys with him in his car, and girls too. Father didn't care if it was a big bunch. Finally it was too much. And he told my stepmother, "I wonder which one Carlo" — sometimes he'd come alone — "which one Carlo is coming around here for?" And my mother said, "I don't know." She knew a little bit — she had an inkling of what was going on. But we never would hold hands or anything. It wasn't like that in those days. No. So innocent. Now that goes on through the summer.

In September I got engaged. My father was his boss in the field, with the haul-cane boys, taking the cane out or bringing the cars in, with the horses, driving horses. So he told the boys, "Gee, I have to go and ask Joe for Teresinha, for her hand, and it's killing me, boy." That Saturday night, you see, he had to come over. They worked Saturdays in those days. And he came down. I still remember a gate we had in the back there. And I went to the parlor, sitting in the rocker, and hear what was going on. And he comes down, knocks at the door. My father and my stepmother were in the kitchen. "Hello, Carlo" — I could hear that in the living room. We had a swinging door. And he said, "Come inside." And Carlo came in. I don't know what transpired. Anyway, Father opens that swinging door, and he said to me, "Teresinha, come here." And I go to the kitchen. I look at Carlo. And my stepmother, not a word. She cannot say a word. I knew it was coming, but he had to ask my father first. We talked in the yard, maybe, while the girls are there. We moved round the yard picking oranges, eating oranges . . . we had an orange tree. I told him what Father had told my stepmother. I said, "You have to do something about that." And Father said, "You want to marry Carlo?" And Carlo is so quiet standing there. I said, "I think so." "It's not I think so. You'd better *know* so." I said, "Yes, Father, I want to marry him." "Alright, Carlo, now you folks are going to be engaged. And you two behave yourselves." And that was all he said. And Carlo came with me in the living room. We had a radio then. He stayed till nine o'clock. Nine o'clock was time to go home. And then on he was allowed to come Wednesday nights. At nine o'clock my dad would be in bed. And he would say, "Carlo, it's time to go home. We work tomorrow." And he'd go like a little angel.

So the engagement was very short, because we were dying already. In six months I was married, because I was tired of being tied down. And towards the end, Carlo would like to take us to the show. So my stepmother had to go with me. I'd sit in the middle, my stepmother on the side. But it was thrilling, just sitting by him. Every Sunday night we'd go to the show. She had to go with me. He'd drive around, she would get off, I'd give him a sweet kiss, and off I'd go after her. Because Father was waiting for us. Even after I was engaged, we never had long hours. Never, never, never together. The thrilling part is fresh in my mind until today, and I loved every bit of it.

I'll tell you about our mass wedding. I had Hawaiians decorate the church with most beautiful hibiscus. And I got married at eight o'clock mass. A white gown. I bought it at New York Dress Shop — everything, veil and all. And I didn't see my husband all day. I had to come home and sweep house. That was my job. Take off your bridal clothes because the party was going to be four o'clock in the afternoon. We had our reception at the theater. So the luau was there. It was a luau that I had. We had Hawaiians do it for us. And after the mass, I didn't see my husband. He was looking around for the orchestra boys to play music. I didn't see him all day till he came down to pick me up to go to the party. I learned to dance at my shower. I never danced before in my life. He was a good man.

ANTONIA

Antonia was descended from a grandmother who arrived in Hawaii before the Priscilla. *Antonia attended McKinley High and the University of Hawaii and also got an M.A. at a mainland university. She married a non-Portuguese New Englander and worked in the Pineapple Research Institute at the University of Hawaii for most of her working life.*

My grandmother came from the Azores to visit her sister, who was married to the Portuguese consul — in Honolulu — to the Kingdom of Hawaii. The first Portuguese ship that came with immigrants was the *Priscilla*, and she always said she came before the *Mayflower*, don't you know? So she was here several years before the first Portuguese immigrants came. The Portuguese consul she was going to be staying with when she came was married to her sister. They were living out at Niu then, which was country, and they sent the hired man to the wharf to pick her up in the horse and buggy. And she was rather resentful of that fact, you see. They didn't come in person — they sent the hired man, of all things. And she ended up by marrying him, so he was my grandfather. He had been on a whaling ship and had deserted when he got to Hawaii. He liked the looks of Hawaii, so he left the ship and went to work for the Perry family. They were originally Pereiras, but transliterated the name to Perry as being easier. Practically all the Perrys, the Portuguese Perrys, in Hawaii today were originally Pereiras. And you still have both names.

My grandmother didn't know mainland Portugal at all. She lived on a volcanic island, Pico, which is the Portuguese word for peak. There was volcanic activity on her island. That was one reason Hillebrand brought the Portuguese to Hawaii, you know. Because they were from this agricultural volcanic island in the great ocean, and he thought they would be happy in Hawaii, and I think they were. I think Portuguese were happy in Hawaii, and comparatively, it's not like the Japanese and Chinese who went back to their homeland . . . finished their contracts and went back. Very few of the local Portuguese ever went back to Portugal or to the Azores. Japanese still think of the homeland and maintain ties longer with Japanese culture than the Portuguese did. Portuguese . . . after one or two generations, Portugal is for the Portuguese, you know. We are now Americans, or we are Hawaiians, and as I say, I was rather interested in recalling that my grandmother was always an alien. My mother was born a Hawaiian and became American through annexation. My father became an American through naturalization. And I was the first one born an American in American territory. You see, there are relatively few people that have had these various acquisitions of Americanism or American citizenship in their background. . . .

We lived with my grandmother. My mother, being the only daughter, had a family responsibility, you know, so we lived with my grandmother. My grandmother provided housing for the two oldest sons and their families. One married an Irish gal, and one married a part-Hawaiian. I don't think my mother finished . . . I don't think she graduated high school. And she got married at about twenty-two, and there were three of us daughters. . . .

My father came to Hawaii at age six, and he went to St. Louis. I don't think he ever lived on a plantation. If they did come as contract workers, they finished their contract and moved to town right away. He was from a large family, and they all established pretty much in and around Honolulu. There was just one girl — there were five or six boys. My father was a general auto mechanic. There's a picture of my father and mother on their fiftieth wedding anniversary . . . that picture there. It's a somewhat different-looking family.

My grandmother looked a little more Portuguese. She was a green-eyed blond, and none of us — there were three girls in my family — we always despaired that we never inherited at least the green eyes. We lived with my grandmother . . . my mother and father lived with my grandmother. After my father and mother moved to Kahuku, I stayed with my grandmother. . . . My grandmother had a complete impact, more on me than on my sisters. We used to taunt her with the idea that she was Scots — that she belonged to the Picts and the Scots — you know, that migration from northern Europe that went through the north into Spain and Portugal. And we said she had Scotch ancestors. She insisted she wasn't stingy . . . she was frugal, she was thrifty. And I remember it was fun counting the gold coins. She didn't quite believe in banks, and she had this safe. I don't know how she had acquired it, but it was a safe of which she had taught me the combination. I and my mother knew the combination, but we were the only ones beside my grandmother who knew the combination. And it was a treat to count these gold coins.

She was one of these people who did not believe in buying things on an installment plan. . . . I decided I was going to buy this radio and bought it on terms, $35. I'll never forget — $5 a month, you know, sort of thing. And she found out about it and had a fit and insisted that, immediately, "Here's the $35. You go down and pay for that radio and pay me the $5 a month." Anyway, that was a lesson. I thought I'd try it out, you know what I mean? . . . It was only after she died that I had a charge account.

At the time we thought she was a terrible martinet sort of person, you know. Because she laid down the law. We were never whipped. We were shown a hairbrush, or a Japanese slipper, you know. We were threatened, but we were never stropped. Well, she was boss. We did pretty much what she told us. Yes, pretty much. I felt sorry for my father, because he never opened his mouth, you know. He didn't assert himself, and my mother just went along. I think it rankled both of them, and I'm sure they sort of compared notes on the quiet, you know. But she was boss. We lived with her, and she was boss.

Well, I think she was very proud of me. She felt that I was able to take care of myself. That was the main thing with my family. There were three girls, and the idea was we would be able to take care of ourselves come hell or high water.

We depended on her to put up the rules, and she was boss. And we did what she wanted, we ate what she planned. Oh, life was dependent on her, and we did things according to her lights. We were all quite aware that she didn't have much respect for my father. He was just a nothing, you know. Not exactly a nothing, but he didn't dare tell us what to do. Nor did my mother. I don't know whether we were extra good kids or anything like that, whether we were in fear of our lives and just towed the mark and lived according to her lights. . . . I slept in her room. I had my own bed in her room.

Grandmother didn't always speak to us in Portuguese. She insisted that we learn English. And she tried awfully hard. She would insist that we sat and read to her, and she would follow. We didn't realize until later that she was learning herself. And we used to kid her an awful lot, because words like "knight" she always pronounced that "nigich." And we used to laugh at her for it. But we never had Portuguese intonation in our family, and she never spoke it. She never spoke English with that — what is it — a lilt? I don't know. You recognize it if you've had any dealings with Portuguese people, that there is a sort of cadence in their speech. She never had that. She didn't speak haole. You know, she was more on the Germanic side, I would say. She had more of a Germanic accent than a Portuguese accent. And she would sign her name. She would write, but she never had practice in writing. I gathered that she had not gone to school. She was very avid to learn, however, and insisted we do our lessons and tell her what we were doing, you know. We thought she was monitoring us when actually she was learning for herself, you know. She was really quite a surprising woman, when we think back now. . . .

When my father and mother were living at Kahuku, it was kind of a bad situation as I look at it now, because their house was halfway between the haole camp and the Portuguese camp. They were looked down on by the haoles and ignored completely by the Portuguese. The Portuguese have never in Hawaii been considered haole. And it's only when the tabulation is made of Caucasians . . . but very often Portuguese are included under "other Caucasians." What's the other Portuguese island? Madeira Island. There was an influx of black Portuguese that had an African admixture, and they were kinky-haired and spoke Portuguese and to all intents and purposes were members of the Portuguese community. But I think that is where the schism came into play. We always had that part of it to live down. When I was in Honolulu going to school, these haole kids . . . I associated pretty much with them, and we did our work together, and they copied my work, and you know, back and forth that way. And yet, when I went to the plantation, they ignored me completely. And it was a rather difficult situation. I didn't particularly like to go back to the plantation because, you know, I wasn't accepted by the same people that were quite friendly in town. So there was that funny thing to live down. And I didn't have the associates among the plantation Portuguese that I didn't know. I don't know to this day what their life was on the plantation. . . .

Well, there were some Protestant Portuguese, and the Catholic Portuguese looked down. There wasn't an intermingling between the two sects. As a matter of fact, there were nasty words hurled at each side, you know. And I remember there was this fellow I rather liked, and I think he kinda liked me too, but my grandmother quickly put rather an end to that. "Oh no, you don't associate with him. He belongs to such and such a church." You know, using the vernacular word. So there was that thing. But there was still unification among us Portuguese, you see. We were still all Portuguese and could fight for our rights against the other whites. But otherwise we were entirely a little group by ourselves.

The Hawaiians were sort of looked down on, at least the ones we had contact with. They were careless, they had sores, they didn't dress, you know what I mean? The kids went around with just a shirt and no diapers. We were not allowed to play with Hawaiian children because we learned bad habits from them. When I went to nursery school, I learned four-letter words the first day of school. "Where did you learn that word?" "At school, everybody says it at school." "Well, we don't say it!"

At Christmastime, I remember my grandmother used to grow wheat. You know, germinate wheat and have saucers of wheat. Then she decorated and made . . . I think it must have been a little replica of the Prince of Prague. You know, we called it Baby Jesus. And we couldn't understand why we couldn't play with that doll. But it stood on a chiffonier in my grandmother's room. And it had candles. She burned candles at specific times, and at Christmastime and various church holidays. Mother didn't carry on those traditions. . . .

I started school, went to a private . . . it was an Episcopal school for the first year. It was supposedly a preschool. But when I transferred to Central Grammar in Honolulu to the first grade, I had had enough background in that school so that I went into the second grade. There was just the one high school then, and I stayed in Honolulu with my grandmother and went to McKinley. I went to the University of Hawaii when I got through McKinley. Then I went to graduate school on the mainland and got my master's degree. I remember in high school I wanted to take journalism. I wanted to go to work for a newspaper. And when I entered college, my grandmother insisted I enroll in education. I couldn't quit in high school. I decided I wanted to quit. "No, no, no, you're not going to be like the rest of these Portugee and quit. You are going as far as we can send you." And so, when I went to the university, I had to enroll in education, because there was always teaching, don't you know? I knew that I didn't want to be a teacher. I graduated in education. In those days, there wasn't the normal school, there was the School of Education. But the job I had was more prestigious, and I was getting more money at the university than I would get teaching.

The youngest sister went to the university for the two requisite years and then to Queens' Hospital and ended up as an R.N. She has one boy, who is a school principal in Honolulu. . . .

I was a little bit annoyed at not being able to do some of the things that my contemporaries, my peers, were doing. Going to shows and dances and unchaperoned. We were brought up very religiously. Not religiously from a religious standpoint, but a manners standpoint. You didn't do things because they weren't right, you know. You just didn't do things that way. And I remember my grandmother going to dances with me. She'd just sit on the sidelines, you know, but she thought that gave me prestige because I had somebody to take care of me, somebody to watch out for me, whereas I was sort of looked down on. You know — "You can't do anything with her because her grandmother's right there." You know what I mean. And this all happened during high school days, in formative times when kids were beginning to date and wanting to go to things and school affairs and so forth. And when fellows would come and ask me to go out, she'd insist on coming, and that soon scotched that little maneuver, you know. And so I just decided that I had my own life to live. I graduated college before she died. She was so proud of that. . . .

Oh, now, there were none of the Portuguese boys that were good enough for us, don't you know. It was really funny. They were all truck drivers, and they had quit school since the sixth grade and gone to drive trucks and so forth. . . .

My husband was born in Aspen by accident of birth. Aspen, Colorado. . . . but his home was actually Connecticut. So he was a New Englander, a meat-and-potatoes New Englander if ever there was one.

Had his Ph.D. in geology and first came to Hawaii as a Bishop Museum fellow. . . .

Probably the lackadaisicalness of it [being Portuguese], but other than that, the Portuguese in general are considered kind of lazy and take-it-as-it-comes. Aside from that, I don't know. And yet there has been parallel with this a certain amount of drive. I've lived two lives, as a matter of fact. You know what I mean? There's been the haole side of me and the Portuguese side of me . . . if you have any idea of the meaning of haole in the sense I'm using it. The Portuguese side? Well, the laziness, the acceptance of things as they are, the lack of drive. I'm perfectly happy just to live each day, as a matter of fact, you know. And the haole side was what took me through school and my job . . . and a certain feeling which I retain that I want my affairs in order. I want to be sure that I can pay my own way, that I am not dependent on anybody. . . .

CORNELIA

Cornelia was born in Madeira and came to Hawaii as an infant. She married a widower with nine children, whom she raised, and she had two children of her own besides. She worked in a cannery for a time.

I was born in Madeira, 1903. I came here when I was three years old. I don't remember anything. They came to work over here because people told them that by working you get somewhere. They [first] went to Brazil. I mean the families, you know. Then, later, she [mother] met my father, and they got married in Brazil. My older brother was born there. Then there was my older sister — she passed away about five years ago. Then it was me. No, they didn't come straight over here. They went again to Madeira because my mother missed her mother and father in Madeira. Then they heard about this coming over here to Hawaii, so they came. My sister was two years older than I was. She stayed most of the time with my grandmother, in Brazil. She remembers my grandmother picking sheep wool and dying it and putting it in the sun to dry. I didn't know all those things, but she told me.

My father worked in the sugarcane, and in Brazil he was a carpenter. But because he came here — he couldn't speak English — they put him in the sugarcane. But later he had a job as a mason, working with cement and all of that. My mother always stayed at home. I had two brothers and two sisters, but my older sister passed away. My mother was taller than I am. I'm the shortest of the family. She was a good mother. I used to get a lot of spankings. Oh, yes. They didn't spare the rod in those days. Then I have children. I had a boy and a girl.

I was in sixth grade when I left school. They didn't have higher than sixth grade, so I didn't go back to school. I went to work.

Celesta's mother was a great friend of mine. And then she passed away, and Celesta's father asked to marry me. I was then working, doing housework and all. But I didn't get married right away. I waited, wondering if I could take care of that family. I was only twenty-one, and he was about eighteen years older than I was — much older than me. And I thought and thought, and I wondered if I could do it, but we got married. And the youngest one of the children was two years old, nine children. The oldest was about eighteen. How I did it, I don't know. I hardly ever spanked the children. They used to help me, not like the children of today. They were obedient. I tried the best I could to bring up the family. Some children are easy to train, but some are not. But I guess that's the way life is.

After my husband died, I went to Honolulu because I knew it was a better place to bring up my daughter. Better schools than they had here. Being that she was smart . . . I wanted her to be something else [than me]. But when they hardhead, you can't do anything. But she's very good in the radio program and in the job where she is. Every Sunday she's on the radio program, the Portuguese program.

I went to work at St. Francis Hospital. There I worked fourteen years. Warding. You know, give water to the patients and make beds, all that. Couldn't work after sixty-five. I couldn't stay any longer, because you know how the union was. I cried when they told me I couldn't work anymore. Then I came up here and got the land and I went back, worked. I make jam and jelly, but I don't sell it. You like some jam?

Well, the one thing I wanted to do was to go to Portugal. I never did. My mother had property over there. In Madeira. . . . I had a chance. I had one cousin that was working on the . . . you know . . . taking people and bringing them back. And I was pighead, and I didn't go. Well, for one thing I didn't have enough money and I hated to go on somebody else's money. . . . But I went to the mainland twice. . . . I enjoyed the mainland and all, but I didn't think that I wanted to live there.

ANGELA

Angela was born in Lisbon and came to Hawaii at age five. She was kept at home until she married. She had five children. When I met her, she was at work in the senior center and was anxious to get back to her job.

My grandmother I don't remember. I was born in Lisbon, Portugal, 1906. I was five when I came here. I was little. We got here in 1912. I remember in Honolulu, when we were in the Immigration, when we got there. Had to take off our clothes, and they had a sprinkling shower. And they had men and boys on one side and the ladies and girls, and they fumigate all the clothes. The nurses came to scrub all [of] us. We used to be three months in the boat. Then we get dressed. The clothes were all warm and the shoes were all wrinkled. I remember that. We stayed there for three days. My dad used to tell me, three days. We arrived here January 3rd, at Koloa landing. I am here from that time. They brought a small boat to bring us to the pier. From there, they used to have locomotive trains. We all came in the cars up to the . . . where the bank is now . . . used to be a plantation store. And they all bought what they needed. Back to the train and went up to the Spanish camp, where they had all the unpainted small homes. From that time till I went to the Portuguese camp . . . it was 1917. . . . A lot of people came. . . . Here was better living than Portugal. Portugal was hard.

In the camp, yeah, used to plant all kind of things. Most people had, because was all hard to get. No stores. They had stores but not like now, with all kind of vegetables. And then the money wasn't like now. Just dollar a day, $24 a month. They had a market with cheap meat, plantation market. And the meat was really good. Plantation market, way up there. Meat was cheap. I used to raise chickens and vegetables myself, for home use. I always did make bread and all for home . . . things I learn. I still do, 'cause my son wants.

I went to Catholic school, St. Patrick's Church School. Two years. But then I couldn't speak English when I got here, when I was eleven years. Then I went to grammar school. I stayed two years. I didn't graduate. . . .

When I was sixteen years old, she [mother] was working in the field too. She work that kind of weeding. And I was taking care of my brothers too. Yeah, I was older. They were already big but . . . she was working in the field too. Those days was only a dollar a day they used to pay. Yeah, my dad too. . . .

I understand now, but I don't speak Portuguese. There's nobody to speak to. My children don't speak Portuguese. My oldest son knows. My parents used to talk to him all the time. But when they [children] was little, I never used to talk Portuguese. . . .

I teach my daughters how to cook Portuguese soup. Things like that. They all crochet too. Portugal is famous for crocheting. They used to make stockings too. . . .

I like to remember Portugal. I tell them about it, my grandchildren. I have five children, eighteen grandchildren, forty great-grandchildren, four great-great-grandchildren. Like over there they used to get big well, in the water, and they used to bring up the water. And they used to wash clothes in the running rivers. They would soak it. Stone, yeah. Big flat rocks and scrub and scrub. I used to remember that. I would go with my mother, and they would hang the clothes over bushes. My son tell me, "Mom, want to go to Portugal? Let's go." I tell him I don't want to go back to Portugal. No, I don't want to go. I don't want to go even to the mainland. . . .

Now I'm a volunteer here at the senior center. I work here twelve years, five days a week, from 1970. 'Cause job is never done, you know. Always got something to do. I'm in charge of the kitchen, but I got four volunteers. That's Monday to Friday. Tomorrow we off. . . .

MABEL

Mabel was born on Kauai, the daughter of a midwife. She has worked all of her life — in a store, in a cannery, and raising nine children.

My mother was a midwife, and she came from Portugal. I don't know when she came. Only thing I know, my elder sister — she's dead now — she came at the age of ten years old to the Islands with my mother. I really don't know much about my father — it's mostly my mother. He came, but I don't know much about him. She came from San Miguel — she always said San Miguel. I don't know where my father was. She didn't talk much about my father. But later on he came to stay with us, with the family.

I was born on Kauai. It wasn't in hospital, it was in home because my mother was a midwife. We were five sisters. My mother was telling that she had boys but all died in infancy. We five sisters were raised by her. My father was a sickly man, very sickly. You know, at the time he came here they didn't have the expert doctors in the Islands. And when they came, they had all kind of herbs to cure, you know. But it didn't do any good to my father. Because I know. I was a little girl four years old, and I used to call him Papa. And my sister, she took all the burden upon herself. She came here, she became an American citizen, and she took my father with my mother to the old Queens' Hospital in Honolulu. And he was operated upon. Well, they say it was a cancer. So seven times he was operated, and he died from that. In Honolulu. So then that left my mother and us five girls. . . .

As a young girl, I used to work in my uncle's store, my Uncle Fernandes. And I used to work for $20 a month, after I was in grammar school. And this money that I used to make, I used to turn it to my mother. We were living there under the care of my Uncle Fernandes, because we had no father, and his wife was related with my father. So he brought us in to be taken care of. Well, we helped — we sisters and my mother — we helped my uncle to raise up his children. Well, he had . . . I think it was five, five boys. And his wife died from childbirth, a little girl. We stayed there. He took us more like a charity. We washed clothes for them, made their lunch and dinner and all that, my mother and I and my sisters. We all had our chance to do what my mother [was doing] — "Oh, you make breakfast this morning." That's how we were brought up without my father. And from then on, we used to wash for my uncle and iron, and then we had, you know, that brick oven. We used to bake bread, and twice a week we would have fresh bread. . . .

She worked as a midwife, but at that time they didn't pay her. She didn't want no money. I don't know why. . . . Some people knew that my mother was a midwife, and they had babies, they used to call on my mother. Many Filipinos, Portuguese, and all that. Not Japanese — they had the other side [of the camp]. My mother was midwife. She used to do everything. Take care of the lady and do her laundry and everything, and fix up. You know, the Portuguese used to put the hand on the stomach and rub it with some kind of warm oil, after the baby is born, to warm up the skin and bring all that dirt stuff that's left over, you know. And then by and by the doctor come and said, "Oh, very good, very good." And then bambye [by and by] he said, boy or girl? She couldn't tell girl — she said whatever it means girl in Portuguese. Then doctor said, "Good." No sooner she come home there was another call for her. Sometimes every two days. But they used to come and get my mother. . . .

In Lihue I went to school, the old grammar school. It's now the waterworks. My mother didn't know how to write. I went until the eighth grade, then I saw all my sisters were out married. What was my mother gonna do with all that load? She told me to quit school. When she see that [we] matured, she didn't want us to go. She wanted us to stay home. I didn't care, see. . . . My children all went to high school. Not one went to college. . . .

Her style was that, like in Portugal, they'd plant wheat, you know, wheat. She'd plant stalks of the wheat, and she had her little manger, with the tiny Christ inside the manger, and Joseph and Jesus. And she used to light a candle. Yes, we went to church, and when we came back again she'd light up the candles. And she'd say, "We're going to eat. It's Christmas morning. It's Christmas morning, so we're going to eat. And offer that to our Lord." So, being American, we thought it was odd, you know, but we had to do what she said. So we'd come home from church. We never had no drink, no wine. Only that little wheat, and she used to make lovely sweet bread. And she used to roast Portuguese roast with garlic and vinegar. And oh, how beautiful that roast used to come with the potatoes. She never knew what was salad. No salad. No vegetables. And we used to have nice hot sweet bread with butter. And with Portuguese coffee. Not much tea, but coffee and cocoa. Every Christmas it was like that.

And you know, they had before musicians. They used to come around and play Christmas Eve. They used to knock at the door, and she'd open it, and they used to play and sing. And then she'd say, "Me no more money for give you." And they said, "That's okay, Mama. Today Christmas."

She didn't like to see us cut our hair. You know, some people cut their hair. She said that's the beauty from us. We used to sit all together, but she knew we didn't like what she say. But we used to do old style, push the hair towards the ear and make a pug. That's how we used to go. And our clothing was queer, was long sleeves. Long dress, big waist. That's how it was. And when we used to go to church, she said wait [until you're properly dressed]. And our shoes, not like sandals, no, had to be . . . all your feet had to be covered. And she used to tell about Portugal. She used to tell [that] in Portugal you don't see this kind slippers, bare feet. And we bought those thick stockings, you know. Oh, those things were hot! Cotton stockings. And we used to go with hats. We never thought of hats. Fancy little turbans and all that. And we thought we looked so cute with that. She didn't like bare arms. All long sleeves. She don't believe in lipstick, oh no. She said you were born with the complexion that God gave you, and you shall be with that complexion. But you know, us modern, we know more what's own style than she know. And we all used to tell, "Funny kind, Portugal-style." . . .

We never knew nothing about babies, and we used to wonder why they come. My mother wouldn't tell. We used to tell, "Mama, why every time one man come?" She used to tell, "Oh, they ordered one nice baby and he's down the boat. And I'm gonna pick 'im up." We used to wonder. We didn't know anything about sex or babies because my mother never told us. Only she said, "That boy wants to marry you." But I was kinda scared, you know. I said, why don't she come out explain marriage, you know. I thought, my God, I no sleep with one man in one bed, and now I'm going to sleep with him, you know. I knew his family, and I knew him. And my sister and I were the first ones to get married. She married an old middle-aged man. He came to the store. I was working in the store, and he said, "Gee, you're a pretty-looking girl." But I never did listen to him. I was afraid to tell, you know. She married him.

Well, we didn't have no choice. If we stayed there, old maids, [we] were slaves. Have a man, they worked for us, we have a little money. So my mother talked to my husband-to-be and said, "You like my daughter?" In pidgin English, but he could understand. And he said ya. And then she said in Portuguese, "You wanna get married with her?" He said ya. Then she tell to me, "You like that man?" I was afraid to tell ya, that I like that man, you know. But I had no choice. I was earning $20 a month in the store. I was the only one left home. And my youngest sister sixteen, she got married. . . .

I worked in the cannery many years. I used to work in the day shift and the night. And my husband used to have the dinner ready for me when I come home. The house was all swept clean. My clothes . . . It's hard to see one man wash clothes and hang them up. He was working for the Lihue Plantation but had some differences with the bosses, you know. So he quit and went in his own business. You know the gas station down there near the beach? We leased that. He ran gasoline services and mechanic. He was a good mechanic. We made our living that way. He used to have a truck. He used to haul labor, farm, different places to go work in the cannery. And I used to work in the cannery. That's how we get our little money together. At the cannery, they didn't give no Social Security at that time, no Social Security. Then there was no more work in the cannery [so] I worked at the Ice and Soda Works, capping soda water. There too they didn't have no Social Security. Then he worked until he had a stroke. He couldn't do anymore. Then we closed the service station. He was a man that when somebody used to [ask] he used to pump kerosene. You know those Filipinos over there all used it. Kerosene lamps and kerosene stoves. But he was a man, he never did say no. He say, "How much you like?" Oh, broken English, [they said] "Me payday come pay." Some did, some did not. But he never said no. He said, "God will let me live more long." That's what he used to say.

My husband was a good provider. He had a garden, vegetable garden. Plant whatever he wanted. He planted even strawberries. Strawberries, head cabbage. That's how we lived. In the plantation he went to work for $65 a month. He was a supervisor, *luna*, was only $65. I tell you, I was having babies every two years, or one year. Yes, we got our house. That was the best living time. We had our wood free, we had our house free, we had our water free, you know. Compared with now! And land for the garden. We had our brick oven outside, all the neighbors together. This was the camp. We had free kerosene, fifteen gallons a month. And sometimes we don't use that fifteen gallons. . . .

My daughters don't speak Portuguese. I'm the only one that talks Portuguese. My husband was Portuguese, right. We talked English when they were little. My husband could talk, but not exact. My sister knows how to talk and how to write. My other sister knows how too. . . .

VI   Japanese

The Politics of Immigration

Any Japanese sailing the high seas between 1603 and 1868 did so at the risk of his life, since isolation from the rest of the world was a matter of policy in feudal Tokugawa Japan. Only an occasional Japanese fishing ship reached Hawaii during those centuries, blown off course or shipwrecked, with the sailors desperate for supplies. One or two ships were shipwrecked as early as 1804 or 1806, but these accidents happened with increasing frequency toward the middle of the century. Most famous of the shipwrecked sailors was Manjiro, later known as John Mung, who landed in Hawaii in 1841, was later educated in America, and then returned home to urge an end to Japan's policy of isolation.[1]

The first ship carrying Japanese emigrants to Hawaii arrived in 1868 and brought the celebrated *gannen mono*, the "first-year people," so called because they arrived in the first year of Meiji, the Restoration that marked the end of feudalism and the advent of Japan's modern Meiji Era. Aboard the *Scioto* were 180 persons, including 5 women and 4 samurai. The way for the journey had been paved by a letter from King Kamehameha IV to the shogun requesting Japanese workers. Although the shogun was too preoccupied with the crisis of his regime to reply, the Hawaiian government persisted and again requested workers in 1866 through the Foreign Ministry and the new Hawaiian consul in Japan.

The first arrivals came with contracts, as did immigrants from other countries. Because these first-year people were not farmers — included among them were artisans, intellectuals, criminals, and ex-samurai — they did not work well as plantation hands, nor were they well

---

This chapter is longer than the others both because the Japanese population in Hawaii is larger than that of any other ethnic group and because the level of awareness of its importance was raised with the recent centennial celebration of Japanese immigration.

well treated. In fact, because of their complaints of ill treatment in Hawaii, the workers were eventually recalled home, though some chose to remain. This debacle delayed further emigration from Japan for another two decades, despite requests from planters, who felt too dependent on Chinese laborers, known for leaving the plantations as soon as their contracts expired.[2]

Meanwhile, the Hawaiian government had become concerned about the decline in the native Hawaiian population, and King Kalakaua felt the Japanese were a kindred people who would help to reverse the downward trend. In 1881 Kalakaua made a trip around the world, and in Japan he made several proposals to the Japanese government. He suggested that Japan's Prince Komatsu marry Kalakaua's half-Scottish niece, the beautiful Princess Kaiulani. In a private session with the Meiji emperor, he also suggested the formation of a federation of Asian nations with the emperor at its head and Hawaii as a member. Kalakaua feared U.S. designs on his kingdom, and he hoped a Japanese royal marriage and such a federation would make Japan a counterweight against the United States in the international intrigue over Hawaii. Princess Kaiulani wrote to her aunt, Queen Liliuokalani, saying that she had given the proposal some thought but had decided that unless absolutely necessary, she "would very much rather not do so."[3]

Kalakaua's negotiations nevertheless bore fruit; in 1884 the Japanese government received eighteen thousand applications for six hundred places on the first official ship preparing to leave in the 1880s. The *City of Tokio*, officially sanctioned and funded by both governments, arrived in Hawaii in February 1885 with 676 men, 159 women, and 108 children aboard. The ship was met by King Kalakaua. The Royal Hawaiian Band played, police acted as tour guides, and food, shelter, and medical care were arranged. In return, the arriving Japanese and consul held a sports exhibition that featured sumo wrestling in the king's honor. King Kalakaua and his sister Liliuokalani became godparents of the first Japanese child born in Hawaii during this wave of immigration.[4]

Many Japanese immigrants thought of their contracts as an extension of *dekasegi* labor, the seasonal work that took the laborers in poorer districts in Japan off the farms during the slack winter months and returned them to the farms in time for planting and harvesting. With three-year contracts at $9 per month, they calculated they could save four hundred yen in three years and return home rich. In Japan, a silk mill worker would have to work ten years and save all of her wages to reach that goal.[5]

Reaction to information about the immigrants' wages and rumors about jobs in Hawaii resulted in *Hawaii netsu*, "Hawaii fever," in Japan. By this time several Japanese emigration companies were operating in Japan and negotiating with the planters for more favorable terms. In 1886 the Hawaiian and Japanese governments agreed upon a labor convention to regulate immigration and working conditions. The Japanese government sought guarantees of better conditions in the form of non-haole overseers, separation of Japanese and Chinese workers, and daily baths for Japanese workers. However, although the Japanese government and consul in Honolulu continued to press for improved working conditions on the plantations, their efforts met little success.[6]

In 1894 the Japanese government decided that its auspices were no longer necessary as a stimulus for emigration, and emigration was thereafter handled exclusively by private companies. Many Japanese were eager to make the journey to Tengoku, or "Heaven," as Hawaii had come to be known. The reality, however, did not always match the dream, and few workers could accumulate enough cash to return home. To return without having succeeded — even if they had enough money for passage — would have meant an intolerable loss of face.

During the 1890s, the planters had a change of heart. Immigration from Japan had been so successful and Japanese workers were now so numerous that the planters felt the need to reduce their dependency on Japanese immigrants and revert to importing labor from China. In 1896 the HSPA and the Bureau of Immigration agreed on a quota: Two-thirds of the labor recruits would be Chinese and one-third, Japanese. The Japanese no longer received a royal reception on arrival. In 1897, 480 out of 671 Japanese were rejected at quarantine and shipped back to Japan. Also in that year, Hawaiian officials denied entry to some 1,200 immigrants on the grounds that the Japanese emigration companies were evading restrictions. Moreover, in 1894 the legislature enacted a law denying entry to any immigrant unable to produce $50. Most of the Japanese arrivals could not comply.[7]

Yet another shift in government and planter attitude toward Japanese immigration occurred between 1898 and 1900. Chinese workers were leaving the plantations at a rate of nearly 50 percent. Moreover, with the passage of the Organic Act of 1900, no contract labor of any ethnic group could be hired. Equally serious for the planters, Chinese immigration was cut off by the application to Hawaii of federal anti-Chinese legislation. There was now no alternative to hiring Japanese labor. Planters approached the Japanese consul and asked that he urge Japanese workers to remain on the plantations. The consul complied, but despite his appeals to the workers in 1903 and again in 1907, many left for the mainland.[8]

By 1900, the Japanese constituted nearly 40 percent of the total population — not a majority, but a numerical plurality among ethnic minorities. Some haole writers began to question the wisdom of having so large an alien element in the population. The Japanese immigrants — the *issei* — were not citizens, though their children born in Hawaii after 1898 were. In California, anti-Japanese agitation led to the 1907 Gentlemen's Agreement, under which the Japanese government voluntarily restricted further emigration to the United States, unless the emigrants had family already there. The Japanese government issued no further passports to male workers. By this time, the Japanese population in Hawaii had reached 180,000, and by 1924, when Congress ended all Japanese immigration to the United States, 200,000 Japanese had reached Hawaii from Japan.[9]

Picture Brides

One result of the Gentlemen's Agreement and the curtailing of male emigration by the Japanese government was an influx of the famous "picture brides." Married by proxy in Japan to men in Hawaii whose families in most cases lived in the same village as they did or were known to them, these brides went by the shipload to Hawaii to be with men whom they had never seen and who were sometimes twenty years their elder. Stories are legion of the reactions of the brides and grooms when they first saw one another at the docks in Honolulu. Yet these proxy marriages were not so different from the arranged marriages customary in Japan, where the agreement was reached by the parents, with go-betweens exchanging pictures. The sentiments of the couple were not relevant.

The proxy marriages were registered in Japan and recognized by the Japanese government, but they were not recognized by the Bureau of Immigration, which required another ceremony upon arrival of the brides. Because these mass ceremonies were Christian, some Japanese leaders in Hawaii protested that they were a violation of religious freedom, and they were therefore discontinued.[10]

Before a bride could leave for Hawaii, Japanese law required that she live for six months with the groom's family. As a consequence, some brides ran away from their in-laws' homes and divorced their husbands before they even met them. Others ran away after the mass weddings at Immigration or upon seeing their husbands at the docks and could not be found by the irate grooms. It was not unheard of for an immigration official to make off with an especially attractive bride. During the height of the picture bride influx, 1912–1916, the divorce rate was more than twice what it became later. Respondents say the sobbing of the newly arrived brides could be heard in the halls of the Yamashiro Hotel, where the brides stayed with their grooms upon arrival in Honolulu.[11]

There were, nevertheless, some advantages to leaving for Hawaii as a picture bride. Escape from the tyranny of a mother-in-law, greater freedom, and a chance for adventure appealed to some young women. Others felt a sense of obligation to their parents, who arranged their marriages. Between 1907 and 1924, the span of the picture-bride immigration, some 14,000 picture brides arrived from Japan. That number includes those from Okinawa and Korea (which at the time was under Japanese jurisdiction).[12]

Women on the Plantation

Within a month of arriving in Honolulu, the Japanese women were expected to join their husbands in the fields. The early arrivals on the plantations lived in long barracklike buildings with other families and bachelors. The *issei* called these buildings *sennin goya*, "huts for a thousand people."[13] Later arrivals were provided with square, wooden houses with one or two bedrooms, an outhouse, and an outdoor kitchen. The workers were awakened by whistles blown at 4:30 A.M., and the workday lasted from 6:00 A.M. until 4:30 P.M. In order to *hoe-hana* (work in the fields) in the hot sun all day, they covered their arms, legs, and hands with clothing they fashioned expressly for this purpose. They tied straw hats onto their heads with scarves, and wore thick *tabi* (toed socks) on their feet. Even though they were so carefully attired, their hands were often blistered — the result of hoeing day after day for ten to twelve hours.

Fig. 6.1. Boys' Day, a festival celebrating the importance of a boy child, ca. 1920. *Photo by H. Iwanaga. Courtesy of the Alexander & Baldwin Sugar Museum, Puunene, Maui.*

When babies were born, mothers tied them onto their backs and took them into the fields so that they could feed and watch them during the day. To put a baby down in the fields, even with a rudimentary shelter, was to run the risk of the infant being bitten by scorpions and centipedes, or, worse, of the insects crawling into the infant's ears. When the children were old enough, they joined their parents working in the fields, often as water boys. Thus, they could not attend primary school unless they were able to stay awake for the evening English classes offered in the plantation schools.

Returning to their crowded quarters after ten hours in the fields, women had to cook, wash, clean, and care for children. If a woman had a second child, she often had to stop working in the fields in order to care for her children.[14] Without plantation wages, many turned to sewing, to operating boardinghouses or bathhouses, or to taking in laundry for bachelors to supplement the family income, as did women of other ethnic groups.

These women had large families to care for and little, if any, leisure. Yet through back-breaking work and struggle, they sought to ensure that even if they did not realize their dreams of Tengoku, their children would be better educated and have more opportunities than they themselves.

Like other immigrants, these women — and their husbands — developed ingenious strategies for survival, adapting and using whatever scant materials they had at hand. Their stoves were often five-gallon cans. Sewing by kerosene lamp, they fashioned extra thick *tabi* by dipping their needles in wax so that they would go through denim.[15]

Communal Life

Informal cooperation and mutual support were as important for the Japanese as they were for other ethnic camps. Mutual aid societies, prefectural organizations, and kin groups served these functions as well as providing means of social interaction. Most commonly represented among the Japanese were Hiroshima, Yamaguchi, Kumamoto, and Fukuoka prefectures; after 1900, Okinawa was also well represented. Some groups organized specifically as savings and loan clubs. During the 1930s, *kumi*, or associations, of fifteen to twenty-five households were common, and they often combined into *mura*, villages. These prefectural societies gathered at weddings, at funerals, and on New Year's, as kin groups would in Japan.[16]

Apart from celebrating the important New Year's and Obon festivals — the latter being the Festival of the Dead — the Japanese celebrated other holidays of their homeland: Girls' Day on March 3, Boys' Day on May 5 (when carp are hung from the roof), and sometimes Tanabata in July. New Year's was, as in Japan, the most important day in the Japanese calendar. It was a time for paying one's debts, settling quarrels, putting on one's best clothes, and visiting family and friends.

Through all these organizations and celebrations, the Japanese in Hawaii maintained a sense of continuity with their heritage. Their sense of identity as Japanese was important to these immigrants, so important that they were the only community in Hawaii that did not intermarry with other ethnic groups before World War II.[17]

Between 1885 and 1900, the ratio of Japanese men to women was four to one. One of the consequences of this imbalance was the appearance

Fig. 6.2. Children of Working Mothers at McGerrow Camp Nursery School, Puunene, Maui, ca. 1920. *Courtesy of the Alexander & Baldwin Sugar Museum, Puunene, Maui.*

of prostitution. In 1898 there were 115 Japanese prostitutes in Honolulu, and by the following year the number had nearly doubled, reaching 226. Some men even sold their wives for $100 to $200. Most of the prostitutes were teenagers who lived in boardinghouses in Honolulu. By far the largest proportion of prostitutes in Honolulu were Japanese, and they were usually controlled by their husbands/pimps.[18]

As they moved off the plantations and into urban centers, men found jobs as construction workers, plumbers, barbers, electricians, truckers, mechanics, fishermen, domestic servants, gardeners, and chauffeurs. Women became maids, cooks, food processors, and seamstresses. Some women opened small retail shops, often as family businesses. The second-generation Japanese immigrants, encouraged by parents who made their children's education their first priority, went into the professions. By 1930 there were sixty nisei doctors, fifty dentists, and twenty attorneys.[19]

Strikes

The Japanese workers, arriving later on the plantations than the

Chinese, Portuguese, and other Europeans, received lower wages (see Chapter I). In addition to the low wages, they had other grievances. They were given passbooks, which identified them and made it impossible for them to leave one plantation for another. Their wages were docked if they missed work (absences were excusable only if sanctioned by a doctor) and if they were late, even by ten minutes. They also complained of beatings by the *lunas*. On some plantations, younger, stronger men were paid more than older workers and were encouraged to set a fast pace. These motivators were sometimes the victims of beatings by workers who objected. Although many of these complaints were common to other ethnic groups too, it was the Japanese who took the lead in protesting, perhaps because they found strength in numbers.

The year 1900 was critical for both plantation owners and workers. Not only were contracts made illegal in that year — and it became necessary for planters to improve conditions in order to keep workers — but workers became aware that they had new rights and were free of their contracts. In 1900 there were twenty spontaneous local strikes in protest against specific conditions, including working conditions that led to the deaths of three mill hands in an accident. Another strike took place at Lahaina over mistreatment by *lunas*, which included the killing of one Japanese worker and the beating of others by plantation guards. The first large-scale strike occurred in Waipahu in May 1909 after workers were forced by *lunas* to buy lottery tickets. The *lunas* charged in the case were forced to resign.[20]

The first trade union movement in Hawaii began with the Higher Wage Association, an all-Japanese organization. Leadership of the union was split between those who favored confrontation with planters and those who counseled conciliation. One proponent of the latter was Sometaro Sheba of the planter-subsidized newspaper *Hawaii Shimpo*.[21] In 1908 two Japanese newspapers supported the association's demand for higher wages, *Nippu Jiji* and *Hawaii Nichi Nichi*. The planter-backed *Advertiser* and *Evening Bulletin* criticized the demands, and the HSPA continued to ignore them.[22]

On May 9, 1909, over fifteen hundred workers at Aiea Plantation participated in the Great Strike under the leadership of Makino, an English-Japanese and Negoro, a playwright. The planters hired Hawaiian, Portuguese, and Chinese strikebreakers at $1.50 a day, compared with the 69¢ they paid regular workers. The strikers at Aiea were then ordered off the plantation. Twenty-one were arrested without warrants, and the leaders were tried for conspiracy. A Japanese Christian, the Reverend Okumura, persuaded Joseph Platt Cooke, director of the HSPA, to drop the charges against the leaders, and the governor signed a pardon. Moreover, because of the strike, the HSPA promised to improve worker housing and sanitation conditions, and to pay workers according to ability rather than nationality. This strike taught workers a valuable lesson in organization and strike tactics. At the same time, many strikers were forced by lack of money to return to work.[23]

The Japanese Federation of Labor (JFL) was organized in 1919 and demanded higher wages for the Japanese plantation workers on the grounds that wages were lagging behind commodity prices. Simultaneously, the Filipino Labor Union was organized by Manlapit (see Chapter X). The two unions made contact when both had their requests for higher wages rejected. The Filipino union struck on January 17, 1920, and the Japanese federation staged a walkout on February 1.[24]

The planters ordered the strikers evicted, and about eleven thousand workers moved out and went to Honolulu, where they were housed temporarily in schools, churches, and tents. The strike was settled several months later through the mediation of a committee from Central Union Church and through negotiations between the president of the HSPA, John Waterhouse, and the Hawaii Laborers' Association, the successor to the JFL. The result was an immediate wage boost and improved working and living conditions.[25]

Temples and Language Schools

Buddhist temples and language schools were the focal points for maintaining Japanese culture and tradition in Hawaii. From the opening of the first language school in 1896 by the Protestant Reverend Okumura, the schools provided continuity and the medium of communication between the first-generation immigrants and their second-generation children. The schools also offered moral and religious training, inculcating the traditional virtues of diligence, thrift, loyalty, and filial piety in the Japanese children, who attended public school for most of the day and then ran to the Japanese schools for an extra two hours of schooling in their parents' language. Language schools also held classes all day Saturday.[26]

Language schools were opened on each island, often in conjunction with Buddhist temples, particularly the Hongwanji temples of Jodo Shinshu, the most popular sect in Japan as well as in Hawaii. Sometimes the language schools accepted boarding students and operated as full-time private schools, more often for boys than for girls. Those who could afford to do so sometimes sent their children to Japan for schooling for a few years and then brought them back to Hawaii. By 1916, 14,000 students were enrolled in 140 language schools, where they were taught by 360 teachers trained in Japan.[27]

Haoles raised questions about the language schools following World War I, and criticisms accelerated in 1924, when Japanese immigration was cut off. The Clark Bill, passed by both houses of the Hawaii legislature, called for closing the language schools. Some Japanese also supported the bill, including the Reverend Okumura and Yasutaro Soga, the editor of *Nippu Jiji*. The Hongwanji Mission opposed the bill and defended the language schools. Frederick Kinzaburo Makino, the leader of the 1909 Oahu Sugar Strike and editor of *Hawaii Hochi*, challenged the Clark Bill in the courts, and in 1927 the U.S. Supreme Court ruled the bill unconstitutional.[28] As a result of this victory, the Japanese language schools continued to operate until World War II, when they were temporarily closed.

Buddhist temples were the centers of Japanese social, religious, and cultural life on all the islands. The first Buddhist priest to arrive in Hawaii was the Reverend Gakuo Okabe of the Jodo-shu, or Pure Land Sect, in 1894. He was followed in 1897 by priests of the Jodo Shinshu, or True Pure Land Sect. Other sects — the Shingon and Zen — also sent priests. Wherever they worked, the priests were the leaders in their communities, the arbiters of social and cultural standards. Because priests often helped to settle labor and other disputes, the plantations sometimes donated land and materials for building temples. Temples were forces for stability in the eyes of the planters. Every major plantation had its temple.[29] Apart from offering language classes, temples often offered courses in flower arrangement, tea ceremony, and calligraphy.

With the waning of interest in Buddhism among the second-generation Japanese, the Reverend Imamura organized the Young Men's Buddhist Association (YMBA). (The Young Men's Christian Association [YMCA] and the YWCA were extremely active in prewar Hawaii.) He also introduced an English department in the Honpa Hongwanji, the largest Buddhist organization in Hawaii, for the purpose of teaching second- and third-generation immigrants. Buddhist Sunday schools and Sunday worship paralleled the Christian Sabbath activities. Dances, sports events, and social clubs followed. By the time of World War II, the Americanization of the Buddhist church — it had become a church rather than a temple — was virtually complete.[30]

Just prior to and during World War II, language schools and Buddhist temples came under attack for diffusing alien, then enemy, values and customs, and the language teachers and priests were sent to relocation camps in California and other western states.

TERUKO

Teruko was born in Hawaii, the daughter of a priest and an educated mother. She attended normal school and the University of Hawaii and taught for most of her adult life. She married a doctor and raised three sons. She, like her mother, is a community leader.

My father came from Fukui Prefecture, Japan. I think he arrived in 1907. He arrived as a Buddhist priest. He was not a missionary. He was a Buddhist, Hongwanji, Jodo Shinshu. My mother was a picture bride. She came from Fukui Prefecture in 1908. When she first arrived, you know, she came from Honolulu and landed on the seaport called Maku Kona, one o'clock in the morning. And then when the wave goes up, then she jumps to the wall, and that was very exciting. And about three, four hours' ride in the buggy. She reached the temple about four, five o'clock in the morning. Horse-drawn buggy. And when she saw thirty-five children . . . My father did not tell her that she has the dormitory children. Then she became the mother of these children. She was about seventeen or eighteen. Therefore, she had to take care.

It was a picture arrangement, so there was no choice. The parents made the agreement, so before she arrived to Nulii she went to my father's home in Fukui, to the temple, where she met the in-laws first. Then she came to Hawaii. But the point is, everybody says that, oh, you are a picture bride. Oh, it was difficult for you. But according to my mother, they were very happy when they became picture bride because all the in-laws were in Japan. So the picture bride became the boss. They collected the money. They paid the bills. That was really very interesting. So when the children went to school, struggled through, it was all because of the mother . . . how she handled the family life. Picture bride was just a secondary thing after they arrived here. They were the bosses when they came here.

So my mother had about thirty-five children to care for. They came to the school, to the dormitory, September. Then they went back Christmas. They even didn't go for Easter vacation because there was no transportation, so the only way they went back was New Year for two weeks' vacation. So my mother took care of them. But she had a cook. She was a doctor's daughter in Japan, so she did not know how to cook. She never went in the kitchen. In those days, you know, they had so many maids. When she married my father, there was no maid. She was so terrified of children. She didn't know how to cook, so they hired a maid who did the cooking — and at the same time she had the children too.

My mother I can remember as a mother who took care about thirty-five children. The Buddhist temples always had a dormitory because the sugar camps were so far away from the center of the plantation that they were named Camp One, Camp Two, Camp Three. And there were no other transportation, so they took their children to the Buddhist temple dormitory. So practically every Buddhist, whether it was Jodo-shu or Shinshu, or Christian, they had dormitories.

My mother was a very energetic, community-minded mother, being a minister's wife. When she first arrived, she did not know how to sew a dress. So she went to the manager's wife's home, and she like my mother very well, so she taught her how to sew dresses . . . the manager of a plantation. And there she learned how to sew, and with one pattern. She made it bigger or smaller, and everybody wore the same style. And she was the teacher to the Japanese wives of the plantation. And they all wore the same style dresses, but she was the instructor. . . . And when the plantation store got the cotton in, everybody wore the same print.

Children were going to school. When they became seven years old they went to school, but only in classrooms we spoke English. When we came out in the playground, at home . . . We all went to Japanese school [and] sometimes stay until five o'clock. So when the parents came back, the children went home, you see. So there was no delinquency. So my mother was nursery . . . not exactly the children's nursery school, but to take care of the children until six to seven years old. Taking care of the children until the parents came back. The Japanese school were places for the children to stay till the parents came back. So they were really baby-sitting. They had regular first to eighth grade. Very strict, like Japan. I told them about Peach Boy, Momotaro, and I had "Three Little Pigs" in Japanese, and they knew exactly what I was going to say, because they were learning in school. But I was telling them in Japanese, and in English they were learning English stories.

My mother went to school. In those days, very few girls went to high school in Japan, *jogakko*. But she was A student, graduated from Jogakko. Because when you are growing up, you know, we bring home A's, B's, C's, and she used to say, "Is this all you did?" and so forth. One day I asked her, "You mean to tell me you had better grades than this?" And she said yes. So later on, when I was in about eighth grade, since I was so doubtful, she wrote to her father to send all her report cards. In Japan they keep report cards. When you get married, this is very important. So my grandfather sent all the report cards from first grade through high school. All A's. Only the singing voice, singing was F.

We had Japanese school wherever I went. . . . We were transferred again to Oahu, for Waialua. Very big plantation. There my father stayed for many, many years until World War II. There we had six or seven Japanese schoolteachers. About fifteen hundred Japanese school students. . . . There was a dormitory that the plantation built, one side for boys and one side for girls. And there were about 150 dormitory students. So they had chaperones. Two teachers, who came from Japan, they were the chaperones. And the schoolteachers were teachers who came directly from Japan. Very strict Japanese teachers. Usually they came and they got married. But usually the wives came from Japan. You know, they did not choose girls from Hawaii. They were educated. They also came as picture brides, too.

I graduated from high school. Then I went to Territorial Normal School. But it was a Depression year, so they closed down the normal school, and we were all transferred to the University of Hawaii Teachers' College.

My brother, presently he is an attorney, a judge of the court of appeals. My sister graduated the University of Hawaii and she became a high school English teacher. The next one is a brother, a doctor, University of Michigan Medical School graduate. . . . Next is my sister here. . . . She went to Japan to study — then the war came. She couldn't come back, so she went to Japanese women's college in Kyoto. She graduated university there. . . . She has two beautiful children. One is now anesthesiologist. And I have another sister, second sister. Her son is also a doctor now. Then my brother who joined the 442nd Regiment and went to Italy. Came back with the GI Bill. He went to the University of Michigan . . . and became a lawyer. . . . The next is a sister. She went to the University of Michigan. She is retired from public school teaching. She became a teacher. Then my youngest brother. He is a Ph.D. doctor. . . . He became an instructor at medical school. . . . The last brother is not M.D., he is Ph.D. But the sisters all became teachers.

Eight in the family, eight children. I am the oldest. Very many responsibilities. When I was in the fourth grade, I was already helping my mother with the Sunday school. So in order to become a Sunday school teacher, my father taught me how to tell stories. And my first approach to Sunday school children, I practiced talking to a tree. Just what my father taught me . . . because, you know, according to my father, there are yellow leaves and green leaves, and all kinds of leaves. And they were the children. And they are always moving. So he referred to the leaves as the Sunday school children, and this was the way I practiced. From then on, I wanted to become a schoolteacher. This was all done in Japanese, because the children who were listening were all Japanese-speaking. They did not understand English.

After graduating teachers' college, I went to Kohala, Maui, a district elementary school, and I taught there four years before I got married. Then I taught at Kula Elementary School one year. Then I got married. . . . After Kula Elementary School, I taught at Wailuku Elementary School. The war came, so we all taught school.

Mother wanted me to be a teacher . . . because nobody [because of the language barrier] took the children to school to register them. My mother had to take them. . . . It was necessary for somebody who could speak Japanese to be the teacher — then all the parents can come. They are not afraid to register the children because the teacher can speak Japanese. They were afraid before. . . . And secondly because they had to go to work early in the morning. . . . So my ambition was to become a teacher.

I remember World War I. My mother became the leader of the community, and they knitted sweaters, scarfs, mittens, and she taught all the ladies how to knit. That was her biggest job. Then the biggest incident was one morning . . . The people went to work on a train. Then one early Monday morning that train fell in the gulch and many people died. And many were injured, and the hospital was too small, so the Japanese temple, the Korean temple, the Portuguese Catholic church became the hospitals. Then my mother, being a doctor's child, she knew how to use the bandages, how to take care of the patient. She became the assistant nurse. And really worked hard, taking care of the injured people. I remember very distinctly a German, young German doctor came to my home and offered my mother the first automobile ride. The doctor was so happy, and he had a car, so he took us on a tour to the famous place called Kipahulu now. So we rode to Kipahulu, and at the same time, I can vividly remember this young doctor giving my mother a German-made wristwatch for what she had done for the community . . . and helped him in the emergency.

I lived in the temple grounds. It was connected to the temple. It was one bedroom, one kitchen, *furo*, and later on they added another living room, bedroom. Camp houses. Plantation. About five, six steps to go into it. But the backyard was about ten steps up, because they had *furo* underneath.

Anyway, my mother was a community-minded lady, and when she was in Waialua, I was about sixth grade, able to speak because our language was Japanese. Secondary was English. I was with my mother in the manager's office, and she wanted me to tell him that she wanted to start a nursery, to take care of the little children. Day-care center. The manager was very happy about it because I don't think the plantations had day-care centers. She was about the first to start. So the plantation gave a cottage, and in the morning she was able to go. The plantation gave her two workers. The plantation paid the workers. They started it. But, you know, the mothers did not send their children to the day-care center because they were breast-feeding. They took the little ones to the cane field, you know . . . where they had centipede bites, scorpion bites, they had impetigo, all kinds. So my mother said she can have a nurse come to the day-care center. And she started it. But after about three, four months later, the mothers started to bring their children. And in no time she had about one hundred at the day-care center, so they added another house. Two houses were given. So she was the first starter of the day-care center in Waialua Sugar Plantation. . . . I think that was one of the highlights of her minister's life in the Hawaiian Islands.

So what my mother did was, every morning she got up early and put the lights in the churchyard. So the people who walked through the Japanese school yard, through the churchyard, had lights to go down the steps. That was her job.

When I recall the happiest time of my life [I think] of my childhood days spent in the plantation. . . . Because the church, the Japanese school, and my home were all in the center of the Japanese community. So I was able to help my father. You know, we didn't have theaters. So my father went to Honolulu, got those moving pictures machine, you know, and once a month we had movies. Everybody came. Japanese movies. Then, later on, the theaters were open when I was in the eighth grade, 1925. . . . So that was the entertainment for the community. My father and mother were the leaders. They made drama, Japanese plays . . . once a year. My father wrote them. Also once in three years the *shibai* [theater] people came from Honolulu to entertain. . . . When the sugar was sent out of the plantation, then the big warehouse where they kept the sugar bags on the Hana Plantation . . . it became empty, so they made a stage and that was the theater. Just once a year when the sugar bags were out. Then that whole big place became . . . like Kabuki. This is what they did on the little Hana Plantation. Just like the big time.

So many picture brides came. Practically every other week or every week we had parties because the picture brides came. . . . The go-between who wrote the letter was my father and mother, so when they came, my father and mother wrote their parents. . . . When they had a party, my mother and my father were representing the brides. Sashimi, fish, sake . . . There was homemade sake people made. The plantation people made their own sake. They made their own *koji* [mold for sake] from rice.

In those days, sixty was already old. . . . There was no old age home, senior citizen home, so they all had to stay home, and the neighbors took care. So my mother went there [to an elderly lady's house] every morning and took care of this lady. Washed her, and did a little bit of cooking. . . . She took care of this lady, and she was not the only one. Many others, here and there — she organized it. Then the plantation sent . . . they were called camp nurses. Camp nurses took over. But many times there were only one or two nurses, so my mother went in to help. This was the thing that impressed me the most. With all her growing up children, children coming up, and she still was able to take care of somebody's mother because they did not have relatives.

I think I have made up my mind that I will be like my mother and do something, many things, for the community. So the first thing I did after I retired from teaching was I organized a mentally retarded school on this island, because when I read that President Kennedy had a sister [who was developmentally handicapped] and he came out right . . . and my husband being a physician, I was introduced to poor families who had children. . . . And then when I went to university, I took up, naturally, deaf-dumb course, gifted children. Then I went to the blind school. I was interested already in this . . . and so I went to mentally retarded Waimanu Home. . . . Then I went to blind school, deaf school.

I started a school, and I had seventy-five children. No blind, this is normal . . . Okay. Then it was compulsory . . . to have nurseries, because the mothers started to work, so I volunteered myself to teach without pay. But my workers had pay — they got paid. Then this was my volunteer work for my church and my community. This was my beginning. Then I found an assistant to take my place.

So I went to the principal, I talked together. And the new kinder-garten was built in the back of the school building, so I asked if I can rent or borrow one room where nobody can see. I started my first retarded school, but it was a difficult thing to ask if you have a retarded child. Then they will ask me, "Did your husband tell you?" This is not right, see. So then there was a lady right below me here who had really a retarded child. So I asked her, "Will you please help me?" And she was an excellent secretary. So she said, "Go ahead." So we started, and about twelve or thirteen children came. They were already nine to twelve years old. Some were trainable. . . . My understanding with the parents was no mothers to come to school. They just leave their child and go home. . . . Then, after three months, I had PTA mothers' day . . . so all the mothers came. . . . They were so surprised. They started to weep. Then they organized a school. We had a permanent school. . . . The plantation was so nice when they found out that there was such a movement. They gave me a home, electricity, water, playground equip-ment, fence around. . . . So I started this movement, and I was a teacher. . . . We had a matinee movie on Shirley Temple, and we collected one thousand–something dollars . . . and we started our movement. The children increased. . . . We had buses. Parents were proud now, they were not hiding.

There are some men who can get around, you know, very sociable. But this man was so lonesome. . . . He committed suicide because nobody to take care of him. Only my mother took care of him. No money was left for the funeral. But the plantation gave the coffin, things like that. But still they had a service for him. All the people came. Then my father sent the death certificate and everything to his family in Japan — *koseki*, the family register, *o-ihai*, the records [ancestral tablets]. Yes, my father kept those — oh yes, the church. That's compulsory. The death records. During the war they burned them because all the soldiers came and checked the home. They [were] kept here. Mine was burned too, I think.

I have Butsudan [Buddhist family altar]. . . . My oldest brother, he married a Hawaiian lady, but she was a very strong Catholic, so she didn't like that shrine in the home. In those days Catholics cannot enter Buddhist churches. . . . But the second brother was a school principal. And he was a Buddhist, but his wife was Christian. So this is the religious differences. . . . So one day my brother said, "I think I better become Catholic. I will bring the Butsudan to you, you being a good Buddhist." . . . Then my husband was a Buddhist, so we married in a Buddhist temple. And my brother-in-law knew that, so he brought the shrine and the Hotoke-sama and everything, and gave it to me.

Saddest time of my life was when I found out that my father was interned. When the plane came a little before eight o'clock, just about eight o'clock, my father was going to Sunday school. [He was going] from my home, my father's home to the temple. And on the way, he saw the Japanese planes coming, because you could see the signal, the flag of Japan on the airplanes. I didn't see, my father saw. . . . We were on the north of Oahu. So my father knew way beforehand. Every night he went preaching to different camps. People didn't have cars — the minister had the car. He goes to Camp One, Camp Three, Camp Two, and that was the enjoyment of the camp. To come and chat. So that night, Sunday night, he went to one of the camps and came back, and then an FBI man came and told him that come out. So my father just wore a sweater and says, "I will be back. I'm sure I will be back right away." My mother waited. . . . Meantime, during the second year or so, she passed away. . . . The first day he was interned, he didn't come back. By then she knew that all the leaders were taken away. All the Buddhist ministers, even the Christian Japanese ministers, were taken away. Someplace in Honolulu first, then from there they were sent to New Mexico — Santa Fe, New Mexico.

They put guns on the church because the church was near the ocean. So they are on night duty, see. [It was] just about December. Therefore every temple was getting ready for the New Year festivals. . . . Those who were on night duty, they were so hungry, but there are no stores around in the plantation. So my mother has an idea . . . so she boiled the noodles and she made Japanese noodles, *saimin*. My mother became the mother, and everybody wanted the night duty. She became the most popular mother of the soldiers — [their] second mother, so she won their hearts.

KAZUKO

Kazuko was born on Maui, went to school through eighth grade, and married a fisherman. She raised six children and held responsible positions in several businesses.

I was born in Hana — that's on Maui — in 1912. My parents came from Japan in about 1900. My mother is from Yamaguchi, and my father is from Hiroshima, although they're very close, you know. They came to Honolulu, in Aiea, and lived with a sister-in-law, and later on they came to Mahiku, where they had a rubber plantation. That's very close to Hana . . . I would say about fifty miles from here. There are still rubber trees around, you know. I think my father rode on a fishing boat. I don't think he worked on a plantation in Honolulu. I'm not too sure. From what I recollect, he used to talk about fishing. I think my father went to school in Japan, but I don't think my mother did. They came from farming families.

I only knew my grandparents by writing letters to them. I didn't know them personally. [I wrote at] my mother's request, of course, because, as I say, she didn't have education, so I did quite a bit of writing to Japan.

Well, to begin with, I think she [mother] was a very strict woman. I remember many sayings, you know, the old sayings, proverbs, ya. And when I was young I didn't think anything about it — but as I grew older, had children, and associating with people, I was making great use of the proverbs. I think they did come in very handy for me to make my life brighter. Yes, for instance, I might say that my friend had bought another new shoes, you know, and then she [mother] would say, "Don't look up, look down." It's easier to look down than looking up 'cause you can't reach for the moon, though these days they do. But those days, you know, she would say, "Don't look up," because you can't reach for everything there. But if you look below, you know, you'd be a happier person. And this is the kind of thing she used to say. Or, like, she would say, "Don't do anything wrong, because if you think you're the only one know that you're doing something wrong, you're badly mistaken."

Because they say *Ten shire, ji shire, hito shire, wa shire.* Means "Heaven knows first, then earth, then the people, and you'll be the last one to know that you did something wrong." This is the proverb. *Wa shire* is *jibun,* "yourself." There's another one. When I got married and started having children she said, "Never go out on children's fights," and I find it to be very true because children, you know, when they fight, the next moment they're very good friends. But if the parents came out and had an argument, forever they'll never talk to each other. Never get into children's fights. Stay in the house. And I really find it very true. Probably she heard them from her mother, because they're the old wisdom.

Mother was working in the plantation field. This was in the sugar plantation in Hana. . . . Both my parents worked in the sugar plantation. My father was working in the sugar mill. . . . But, unfortunately, he worked out in the field, because he got an accident with the dynamite, and he lost his left eye and [could have lost] his left arm too. It was probably my mother's stubbornness. He lost his eye, and he was going to lose his arm too . . . if it wasn't for my mother's stubbornness, you know. . . . The doctor said he had to amputate the arm because otherwise, you know, he'll die. So my mother said, "What can a man do without an arm?" So she said she rather he died than live with no arm. . . . He lived, ya, he lived until about seventy-six. I give her a lot of credit, you know.

She went into the fields, and my sister took care of us. She worked a full day in the fields. And then, later on, we had this public bath — even on the plantation, which my mother took care of, and then she did laundry, you know. She did laundry for about five or six men, single men. Filipinos, mostly Filipinos. Oh, they really did work hard. My mother's life wasn't a very pleasant one because my father was like that, and my sister died when she was eighteen, then my brother had amputation of his leg when he was working on the plantation . . . in an accident. . . . Ya, the company paid some compensation. Gee, those days I think they made not even a dollar a day.

I guess I had a little more ambition than she [mother] did. It wasn't easy for her. She can't do as much as I think I did because her language was limited, for one thing. And living on the plantation, there's no way of getting up. You have to live in a city or bigger community, you know. On plantation, you just don't have the choice. But to me, I think she was an ambitious woman, only she cannot put it to use. Because I feel that she sewed her own clothes. She would take off an old clothes and, you know, she laid out on the material, and she cut it out and made her own clothes. And, I think, living on the plantation she did pretty good. I mean financially, compared to others, I think she did pretty good. . . .

My oldest sister, who was born first, died when she was eighteen, and then I had three brothers in between, and then I was born, although one died. My oldest sister died from typhoid fever. I don't know if it was an epidemic, because at that time not too many people died. But she . . . According to the doctor's report, it was typhoid.

Mother wasn't a picture bride. They came together. I'm happy about that, though. Yes, I'm happy that they came from Japan together, you know, rather than don't know what to expect and come here and . . .

Until my youngest son started going to school, I just stayed home. My husband wouldn't have me working, although I had approaches, you know, from other different places to come and work. But my husband wouldn't have it because, he said, your place is at home, while the children are young.

I only went through eighth grade in Hana, because at that time they didn't even have high school. And being first generation, my parents weren't interested in educating their children, especially not the girls. Two of my brothers went to high school. My youngest brother went to Mid-Pacific in Honolulu, and my second younger brother went to Lahainaluna. My youngest brother, being the youngest, had the chance of going to university too, in Honolulu.

I went to Japanese school until eighth grade. We went to English school in the morning, and in the afternoon to Japanese school. And at times we had to go to Japanese school first in the morning, and maybe from nine o'clock we went to English school. We had that kind of time.

Well, before I graduated eighth grade, my mother believed more in economical, you know, being practical, so she sent me in the evening [to classes] when I was about fourteen. We went to night sewing school, where they taught how to sew Japanese kimono. Because those days, they still were wearing kimono once in a while. So I learned how to make kimonos. So during the day, I went to English school, and after that to tailoring, shirts and pants, after I graduated Japanese school. I wanted to further my education, but as I said, my parents didn't believe too much in girls' education.

My children went to college. My oldest went to, I would say, junior college, because he was interested in mechanics. . . . Then my second one went to the Army, came back, and he went to business college. . . . My daughter also went to Honolulu Business College, and she's working for a wholesaler. . . . And my fourth one, daughter, went to New Mexico State College, and she's teaching at Waipahu. And then my fifth, [a] daughter, went to the University of Hawaii, and she's teaching at public elementary, and my last son went to University of Hawaii, and then he furthered his education in Chicago University, and he's a social worker. . . . That was my ambition, to educate my children . . . daughters as well as sons. It didn't make any difference to me. . . . I don't think it makes any difference in education as far as sex is concerned. My ideas are very different from my mother's. I guess we like to give our children what we didn't have. Doesn't that just keep on going, generation after generation?

My ambition was to be a businesswoman. But I regret in a way that I didn't go to school, further my education. But then again, being married to a fisherman . . . I'm married to a fisherman in Hana, and I had six children in Hana, so I'm happy, in a way, that my mother had pursued me in learning sewing. So I did some sewing — not too much because I had children early and I had one after another. So I'm glad I could stay home and do sewing for outsiders, you know.

I went into regular retail store. I opened [was the first to sell] the Chinese goods, like chests, you know. This was through a friend, said he was gonna open a Chinese store here and if I would like to manage it . . . Now I say I'm pretty brave, because without an education I said yes, I'm willing to . . . It was more luxury items, and at that time people didn't have that kind of money to spend on these goods. . . . And then, because I was interested in plants, I went into garden-supply business. It was on the same street. But the thing is, as I said, I have no knowledge about chemicals and fertilizers and things like that, so I would say I sort of self-educated myself by reading all the labels every day and bringing them home and trying it on my plants, you know. Because I don't like to tell my customers I think this is good — I would rather say I've tried it and it's very good . . . I had more handcraft, corsage supplies. So that's what they had when I bought out the store outright. So I went to the library, got out books, read on it. When I went to Honolulu, I got a corsage book and I studied it, and when I was very ready, I said I'm gonna start a class. . . . I had a class of about fifteen, twenty, you know. Oh, it was fun. I enjoyed it.

Then this Maui Dry Goods, that's a big company here . . . The manager approached me and asked me if I would manage the garden-supply shop in Kahului. . . . So I sold my business to Maui Dry Goods, and I worked for them. And I think that was a good decision I made, because from then on all these big markets came up and they all carried these kind of supplies. So who am I to compete with these big shops, you know? Yes, I think I did it at the right time. . . . And then I asked them to sell me this store, because they were selling all these small businesses. So I begged them to sell me this store. Well, they finally did, though. And then I worked — I had my own business for several years. . . . And in the meantime the Honolulu firm, they call it Gems, they came to request my selling this store to them. Well, under my condition I said, oh, as long as they take my workers, I said I'll sell it to them. And then I managed for them for one year. I'd say I worked about twenty-five years [in business]. Well, I can say this much — I'm kind of proud of myself.

You see, I was Girl Scout leader for sixteen years. And you know, you have to handle all different girls from different families. And I applied it to my children, because I felt my six children were all different. They all have their own characters. And I felt I had to cope with each child just the way I did with the Girl Scouts. I think that helped me a lot. They were all Hongwanji girls. . . . I belong to the Japanese Culture Society, and I went out teaching corsage-making, and I also had cooking classes, Chinese cooking. I went to Maui Community College to teach, and I also had Kahului Community Center. And then I also had [classes] at Hongwanji, this was a senior citizens' group that I had. And then I went to several high schools to demonstrate sushi-making.

We lived very close to the Buddhist temple, Jodo Shinshu. Japanese people went there mostly, although they did have another one called Shingon-shu. But it wasn't a temple — they had it at homes, maybe this month my home, then next month it would be another person's home. That's about the only two religions that I know of. I'm still a member. The temple is right down here. It's a walking distance. So I feel very fortunate to be living close to my temple, because I have no excuses.

As far as my children . . . When they were growing up, I spoke mostly Japanese at home, because I felt that they'd get their English education outside and their contact is more English. So in order not to lose this Japanese language, I used Japanese at home. But when the war came, the children were only too happy to bring home these banners saying "Speak English." I had no choice. We spoke English at home then. I think we were more afraid of the government, so we tried not to go against their wishes. The majority of the ministers were interned, you see, because they had contact with Japan and the consul. They were sent to the mainland.

I did watch her cooking [mother], so I think I learned quite a bit of Japanese cooking from her, because I kind of followed her cooking when I got married. . . . I think it's the same thing. They [daughters] watched how I do. Because I noticed that my daughter-in-laws are cooking what I prepared at home, because then my son would like to eat the same food that I used to prepare at home, and then I noticed that my daughter-in-law would call me up and say, "Mom, how do you prepare this?" . . .

I repeated my mother's proverbs to my children. . . . I think my daughters are repeating them to their children. I haven't really heard them do it, but, like for instance, my daughter over here would say, "Mom, you know I used to think you're terrible, always buying sale things. You know, because you did that, I always said I would not buy sale items. But, you know, I think you got me into the habit, because I'm still looking for sale things." And those are some of the things that they carry on without their parents telling them.

New Year's they pounded *mochi* [New Year's rice cakes]. We had a *mochi-tsuki* [mochi pounder]. We still do, you know, at my home. I wanted to buy machine, but my children said, "If you're going to buy machine, we don't have to have *mochi*, because the tradition is off, you see, once you get out of that." All my children and my grandchildren do it, too. We go to church New Year's Eve, and by the time we come back it's New Year's morning already, so I have my *o-zoni* [New Year's soup containing *mochi*] at that time, because then they can all have it and then they can go home and sleep as long as they want. Because they don't have *o-zoni* at their home. . . . They have it here. So I think we start out New Year pretty well. And then I prepare all my *O-shogatsu* [New Year's] dishes, you know. And they all come here in the evening, all my children and grandchildren. They make sure they come.

The life is entirely different compared to before. My children, the older ones, knows that too, because even soda we cannot afford to buy. The only time is New Year's. My husband used to go pound the *mochi*, you know, to the friend, and the friend was with the soda company, so he used to get two cases, you know. I hide that. . . . I would tell them,

"This is for New Year's Day." Because we observed New Year's Day more than Christmas, you know. My husband used to pound *mochi* until he died. We bought the stone, you know.

The neighbors, too, before was so close, you know. We feel very close [to] each other. When I go to town, I used to go to my neighbor and tell, "Oh, today I'm going over there and come back." But not anymore. And then to do things, four of our neighbors always used to do together. So for *mochi-tsuki*, we used to get together, four families. But I notice now to each his own, after the younger generation.

Japanese manners, yes, I wanted to teach my children. Honor those older people. Many things. And [my daughter] tells me, you know, whenever people give her something she always bakes in return. So I told her, "You're always doing that." "You taught us, Mom." Many things like that. That way, you don't tell them do this, do that, but they're looking at the mother and they follow you. So I guess all my children are that way. They say, "You taught us, you taught us." Well, haole way is good too, but in Japan, get so many good things.

We used to have Japanese movies in our theater, but now we don't have — but we have the TV. Channel 21 I subscribe, and from six o'clock [it] comes in. And now it's good. [At] 9:30 they have news directly from Japan, NHK.

I think the happiest moments were when my children all grew up and they had their education and they left home, and they all seem to be very happy with their choices, you know, of their mates. Because I feel that's my happiest, because I always mention to my husband that, Dad, live a good life, because the children are all happy now. They made the right choice, and so far I think this is the best time of our living.

CATHERINE

Catherine was born in Hawaii. She attended grammar school through eighth grade and then completed a year of normal school. She was married in California, lived there for six years, and raised three children. She worked in a variety of fields, including plumbing, electrical work, and teaching.

I was born in 1902, just as my mother got off the boat from Japan. I don't know how old my mother was when I was born. [As] was the custom, she hadn't seen my father before marriage. Then, in the meantime, Hawaii was looking for laborers or somebody from Japan. So my father decided to come to Hawaii. He said, "In only three years I'll come back." But at that time my mother was pregnant with me and she wouldn't dare say she was having a child, because if my grandfather should know he would never let her come to Honolulu. So she just hid herself and *gaman* (endured) and came on the boat *Kobuchiko*. They call it *Kobuchiko* in Japanese. She left Japan in February, and I don't know how many days it took. Those days it took many days. And it was a small boat. She said she suffered a lot by seasick and being pregnant and having morning sickness — she thought she'd die. [It was] 1902, and I guess they went to Ewa first.

My grandfather was a doctor in Japan. My father was the only son. He must have been a spoiled man. I don't know whether I should say or not. . . . And my grandfather got peeved with him and disowned him, so therefore he went down to Taiwan — at that time Formosa. And Japan was ruling there, so he was working for the government. And so, being the only son, the village people went to my grandfather and said, "So you must forgive him. Why don't you call him back and let him get married? And settle him down." So olden days, there was no such thing [as courtship]. They didn't even see each other, they just got married. Not even *omiai* [an arranged meeting as a preliminary to marriage] then, long, long time ago. So my mother came from Shinto family. And so they got married, in Kumamoto. When she took her *wataboshi* [bridal headgear] off, that's when she saw my father and my father saw her. Those days, they covered their face.

But my husband hasn't done any kind of farming work. He was supposed to be a doctor. He had learned some, but he only played around, played around. The family had only two, my father and my auntie. I had just one auntie. He didn't do any kind of work, so they were struggling. And the neighborhood people said, "You can't do this kind of a job. You have to go to Waipahu and start a drugstore." So that was it. I don't know if he tried to work in the cane fields at first. He didn't stay too long as a laborer.

And I was born at the time when there wasn't any midwives. No midwives. So the neighbor ladies came to help each other, and I was born. Also I was a really spoiled brat! Because they didn't know how to raise me. I would sleep daytime, cry nighttime. And she always tells me that they both took chances [turns] and put blankets around me and held me. So if they lay me down I'll just yell and cry. She always tells me that. Waipahu — I still remember the place, because I stayed till about five or six years. Right by Arakawa Store, if you go there. Right by Bigway Store. They used to have a stream, and I played, and when I was naughty, my mother would tell me, "Oh, you know where I found you? You came in a basket floating down the stream." I remember at that time I didn't like that.

My mother learned midwife from a doctor. You know, those days there's no such thing as license, anything. So she used to go around, and the doctor taught her when the leg come out first you should do this and that. This doctor was from Kumamoto, and he was a good friend of my father. So he said, "This is simple, so I'll teach you." So my mother learned. And she went around as she got older, and I was already grown up. Those days, for ten days after they give birth, you supposed to go and bathe the baby and wash the diapers and all those odds-and-end jobs.

My mother used to make *o-manju* [filled rice cakes] and things and start selling to make a living. . . . I vaguely remember the store we had — clothing store. Then we moved up to Wahiawa. And they had a store. They hired somebody. Drugstore. He [father] cannot make any kind of prescription, you know. And [it was a] candy store. I would go out and play with the children, and all the boys and girls . . . tells me to go and get some candy . . . And I always did go inside and grab a handful of candies and run away. They all told me that.

My mother, then she became a beautician and make *yomesan* [brides], you know, comb the hair in *marumage* and *shimada* [two styles] when they get married. . . . She gave up midwifery because she get backache. She had to work hard because my father didn't earn too much money.

I have a friend that's about the same age with me, and we both lived in Honolulu, and we both get together, always talking about the olden days. How Waikiki was — the duck pond was there, and Ala Moana was nothing but a dump, and all those . . . We've seen all those things. I remember our days when we were small. No such thing as water system. We had to get from the well. . . . As childhood, I used to enjoy it a lot, because I used to have friends come from town, and we would go down to the peninsula and catch crabs. . . . We were free playing. We used to enjoy it. Especially when I live in the country. You have streams — we can swim there or catch crabs, or fishing and those things.

Many years later — about 1930 when I went to Japan, I went to the grave, my grandfather's. And his grave was built by the villagers, so he had a real big monument. When I was born, they were happy, and then I was told that my grandfather wrote, "At least my first grandchild, let me name it." . . . After so many months, Grandfather died. But my father kept the promise and named him [her brother] Kotaro, just the same. . . . Grandmother was gone, too, when I went to Japan. My mother's side were gone too. Only my auntie was alive, my father's sister, and my mother's brother. . . . Only the uncle was alive. . . . So his son became a *shinkan* — you call it a Shinto priest. When I went, it was seventy-sixth generation [of Shinto priests in Japan]. My mother told me that the first one came with the emperor to Kumamoto. . . . And the emperor told him, "You better start one shrine over here." So he was the first one, and that was seventy-six generations.

My father went to Hawaii and was working at Kohala, so I had to go to a dormitory, Jodo-shu dormitory. Two years I went to school, and then he came back. That was Jodo-shu mission school. After two years, my father came back to Honolulu. But he was way up where I cannot go to school, so they put me inside Hongwanji. I was in the grammar grades yet. Then, when they moved down to Pearl City — near Pearl Harbor — that's when I started going to school from my home. And that time, country schools. Most it had was sixth grade. There wasn't such a thing as junior high then. You graduate at eighth grade. And then from there, they go on to high school, freshman and so on. So I had to come on Oahu Railway to come to school in Honolulu, and I went to Territorial Normal Training School, where teachers come and teach us. No, I didn't become a teacher. And after I finished eighth grade, then I went into freshman at normal [school]. After freshman, I quit school. That's all I've ever had [of] education.

At that time, when we were down at Pearl City, I used to go to Japanese school. We used to go early, seven o'clock, two hours, then run to English school nine o'clock, then come back two o'clock and go to Japanese school again — another two hours. Learned to read and write Nihongo, little bit, not much. But at that time they were very strict, exactly. The books were from Japan, imported from Japan, and we had geography, we had history, we had . . . something like biology, and then sewing and we had *undokai* [calisthenics]. And I remember going to school when [it was the] emperor's birthday, and was all different — we wear *hakama* [divided skirts]. But when we go to ceremonies like that, and meditation, something like that, we wear *hakama*. Real Japan!

Teachers were all from Japan, and men teachers used to have a bamboo stick. . . . But I think I enjoyed the Japanese school, too, when I was small. I still remember some of those books, the lessons that we learned, history that we learned. Even I pictured myself like the pictures that was in the book — like Toyotomi time. . . . Oh, Lord, that you have given me such a life that I have seen from the primitive days till today!

When I finished sixth grade, my father wanted me to be a telephone operator at Waipahu, 'cause they used to hire girls, you know. And all you memorized [was] the number of each person, see. But Mother says, "No, she got to have education." Mother insisted that I go to school. And my brother meantime . . . My brother and I is five years' difference, and he went to McKinley High School, then he went to normal school, and he became a teacher. . . .

Then I went to learn how to sew — sewing — and then later on I went to work for a curio store. Before the war, First World War, I mean, they had curio store [with] one department, grocery, and wholesaler, too, on top of everything, and hardware store — three departments. . . . So I worked there until I was quite big — eighteen, nineteen, like that.

After I came back from California, I taught kindergarten until wartime. . . . I was kinda old already, in my thirties, though, so I became a floor lady [supervisor]. I first worked in electricity, where they worked nothing but electric parts. When they sent me to the lumberyard . . . I learned lots about lumber. And then the third place I was sent — because they shift you around — they hired lots of women, U.S. Engineer Department. And I went to plumbing, so I know a lot about plumbing. Then, until fifty, I worked — and my daughter was already going to school. She did all the laundry, cooking. I taught her. . . . After I became fifty, I stayed home. . . . Then I took care of little children. I took one, two, three, and then two of my grandchildren until they all go to school.

Today we were sitting around and talking about how I used to see the funeral, those days — what they did with the body. No cremation, those days . . . 1910. And the Jodo Mission had a cemetery of their own on the site of the temple. And that funeral . . . I was telling those ladies, you know, they used to bring lot of charcoal and they put the casket [in the ground]. And the casket was bound with black material and covered up with charcoal and again they put the soil. It was a wooden casket. They made their own those days. I don't even know whether they had a funeral parlor. . . . All the people got together. They buried it, even the Buddhists. . . .

And I was telling where they used to have community Christmas program. Even [though] we were Buddhists we used to go. And I remember that statue of Kamehameha in the courtyard. I remember that Christmas decorations were all different from what we have today. And candles were the real candles . . . and dolls, tiny dolls. And it isn't those round [Christmas] balls. But they had tin foil . . . Christmas tree, all right.

I'm Methodist [now]. My elder son is Congregational, strong Christian now. My daughter, she goes to Baptist, I think. Her daughter is Baptist. . . . The reason why I became Christian is that I went into a Christian home. There was a member of the church that I lived together, and that family was so close family and real Christian family. It was so nice that I just became Christian. Before I came here, ya, every Sunday [I used to go] because I live near the church. I'm still a member.

YUKIKO

Yukiko was born in Japan and went to Hawaii to marry a childhood acquaintance. She worked in the fields at first, then raised five children, and became an accomplished seamstress. She still crochets professionally.

[in Japanese]

I was born in Hirukawa-machi, Fukuoka-ken, in 1898. My father had a general store, not farming. He sold everything because it was [in the] country, including sake. Fukuoka-ken. My mother's mother was from a big merchant family. She was a famous person, knew how to use the bow and arrow. My mother was raised there. She was from a good lineage. She was very skilled at sewing. At the time of local weddings, she did the sewing — and for grave visiting. She had baby-sitters and cooks, so she didn't have to cook. She was a good businesswoman. I learned to make kimono — my mother taught me to sew. My father was good at cooking.

I went to school for eight years. Then I went to a school for silkworm culture. Finance was well developed there, and the teacher taught us. We thought he was an excellent teacher. They said to go to

Jogakko, but there were no students in the countryside. So I went to the dormitory for the sericulture school. I studied there until I got a license to teach. I was there as a teacher because there were many students. I stayed there until I came to Hawaii. I was there about five years.

My parents said they didn't want to send me to Hawaii when they were approached by his [her future husband's] father. So the father came back to Japan expressly to get me. [No, it was] not his father, but his uncle came to Japan to get me. I wanted to see America, so I said I'd go. I had known him since childhood, so I said I'd marry him. So my parents agreed, leaving it to me. So they had nothing more to say after that. They didn't oppose it any longer. The uncle says it doesn't matter if you can't cook. The food there is different anyway, so there's no need to learn to cook here. I was worried because I couldn't even cook rice. I had never cooked at all. . . . I knew how to eat but not how to cook. But when I came here, I had to do everything. I didn't return [to Hawaii] with the uncle, but he returned first, then we made all kinds of preparations, and I came later. I came alone. I wasn't lonely. I knew my husband, and I was like a child wanting to see America, so I wasn't lonely. I was the only daughter, well cared for by my parents. I had two older brothers and three younger brothers. Until the age of twelve, I was the only daughter and spoiled.

I sailed from Nagasaki. It took fifteen days to Hawaii. Every morning on board I ate two soft-boiled eggs. From childhood, I always ate two soft-boiled eggs with milk. So on shipboard, the boy brought me two eggs every morning. My father had given the ship's boy the fresh eggs for my breakfast. I didn't know about it. I got special treatment. The rest of the passengers ate rice gruel. They all had brought miso with them. I didn't get seasick at all. I enjoyed the trip. I didn't have my own cabin. No, we were all together. We arrived at Waimea, Kauai. I've been here for fifty years. My husband came to Honolulu to meet me, and we got married in Honolulu. . . .

I came in 1917 to get married. It wasn't a picture-bride marriage. I knew him since childhood. We were neighbors. He came to Hawaii two years earlier, then I came. We often played together as children. We got married here in Hawaii. His father came to Hawaii about 1899. First he went to Maui, then moved to Kauai. The son came when he was seventeen.

We got married at the immigration office. After the inspection, we went to Immigration. Everyone got married there. . . . It was a large ship with lots of people on it. They were all picture brides. I don't remember how many there were. They were all happy to come to the U.S., but after they arrived and met their husbands and went to the hotel, they were all crying. I didn't have a picture of my husband and didn't say anything on the boat, but everyone else was crying. After they saw their husbands, they were all crying except for me. I knew him beforehand, so I was in a different category. In the immigration office it was still alright because the husbands couldn't come into the immigration office. But once we left there and they met their husbands, then everyone was suffering. I was in the immigration office for five days and couldn't leave. There was some kind of trouble. Three women escaped from the immigration office at night, using their obis to escape from the window. Because of that trouble, I had to stay in the immigration office for five days. Their eyes were checked at the immigration office, and if they had bad eyesight they weren't let out. . . . The people who left the immigration office that day had a joint wedding ceremony. We all got married together. We had ten days in Honolulu for our honeymoon, then on November 5th, we took the ship to Hawaii [Big Island].

When I came to Hawaii, I wanted to go to school to learn English, but I couldn't. I thought I'd earn money and return to Japan at the time. I wanted to learn English. I suffered because I didn't know how to do housework and cooking when I came as a bride.

We arrived at Waimea, and I wondered how I could live in such a place when I saw the house. It was such a small, poor house. I cried for three years — yes, I cried for three years. I told my husband I wanted to return to Japan. After my children were born, I didn't cry any longer. My father-in-law was living there, so I really suffered. The mother-in-law died early of cancer. I knew that before I married. My husband was the only son, so we lived with his father nearly thirty years. . . . There was no electricity in those days. The toilet was a community toilet far from the house, outside. We had our own *o-furo* [bath] — there was also a community one. . . . I cooked with wood — yes, it took a long time. There was no electricity in those days. We didn't even have a stove. We used a large kerosene can. . . . My husband's father went back to Japan once, but he returned. He said Hawaii is better.

I worked out in the sugarcane fields, too, for three years after arriving. Reverend Yamashita at the temple liked me and wanted me to help in teaching Japanese, but my father-in-law wouldn't allow it. When I went out of the house, I had to listen to what my husband and father-in-law said, as at home in Japan. They didn't want girls wandering around outside. I hardly ever went out. I had no baby for three years, so I worked in the fields. After three years I had a baby, so I didn't have to work in the fields anymore. I had five children. We had a Japanese midwife. All the babies were born that way, at home. We both disciplined them strictly. They had to eat everything. I taught them to reply "Hai!" in a loud voice when I called them. My husband wanted them to be educated above all. That was his first priority.

I came over the opposition of my parents, so I couldn't complain to them or go back. I couldn't write that I wanted to return. I just had to endure. I stayed home with the children and did sewing. Yes, I sewed for others and for the family, too. I sewed kimono at first, then I sewed for workers — pants and other things. Shirts, pants, dresses. I continued sewing until my children grew up. And I did housework too. I sewed in the daytime and worked in the hotel in the evening.

My husband left the sugar mill after a short time and went to work as a cook in a hotel . . . first as a waiter. . . . After the war began, my husband got angry because of what was said about the war, and he left the employ of the hotel and worked at a plantation. He worked there twenty years. He worked in the yard of the plantation manager as a yard boy. . . . I continued sewing. I did crocheting too. . . . I needed it for the children, to send them to school. . . . I'm still healthy, so I continue to work at eighty-seven. I can even use small needles.

I've worked at the hospital since a short time after my husband died. About four times a week, twenty hours. I've worked as a volunteer there over four and a half years — for care of the elderly in the hospital. I thought I'd continue the work there because of the need. As a Christian, I didn't think I could stop, so I volunteered continuously for four and a half years. Now it's ten years that I've been here.

After marriage, he [eldest son] went to the mainland and studied to be a priest, a Christian minister. My children are all Christians. I am too. My father-in-law was a Buddhist, so he opposed my going to Christian church at first. But during the war, he couldn't oppose. He allowed me to go, and I became converted in 1943. . . . My son became a minister after he returned from the war.

HANAKO

Hanako was born in Hawaii, but in her youth she went to Japan with her parents and attended school there. After higher school, she returned to Hawaii. She never married. She cared for her brothers' children and became a professional seamstress.

I was born in Pahoa, Hawaii, in 1910. Father was boss of a lumber camp of five hundred. At age six, we moved to Hiroshima to a two-story house with garden. I graduated from girls' higher school, then returned to Hawaii. Grandmother came from a samurai house. She was very strict. Three brothers came back to Hawaii. Four were born in Hawaii, three in Japan. I remained unmarried in order to care for my three brothers. They returned to Hawaii after graduating from school. Father didn't return to Hawaii — he bought a house and land in Japan. Only we children returned to Hawaii.

Grandmother emphasized manners and deportment. Mother taught me cooking and sewing, and about the family line and the value of family heirlooms, et cetera.

Mother taught me things necessary for women to learn — cooking, housework — since there was no one to help with these things in Hawaii. So she said, "Even if you go to school, you must learn these things." Grandmother spoiled me, but she was also very strict. My mother's house was *honke* [main family line] and made sake and *shoyu* [soy sauce] near Hiroshima. But they lost the land with [General Douglas] MacArthur's land reform . . . lost tenants when they got their own land. They were a samurai family but still made sake, for several generations. . . . It was a very old house though, an old name.

My three brothers all got married. . . . I lived with them until they got married, one by one. I saw my life's role as caring for my three brothers. After they married, I lived with my next brother's family and cared for his two children while the parents worked. I became the second mother. I have not regretted the decision not to marry. I moved out on my own after the second child graduated from U.H. . . . There were several proposals, but I refused them all. I was happy living with my brothers. My brothers all lived separately after marriage. I lived with the eldest. . . . When I was young, many go-betweens came, but I refused time after time. . . . My parents wanted me to marry at first, but I said no, no, no, so they eventually were resigned to the fact that I wouldn't. I felt I had an obligation to my brothers, since my parents didn't come back to Hawaii.

I graduated from Jogakko and technical school [in Japan before I] returned to Hawaii. . . . I wanted to go to English school here but I couldn't. I had to take care of my brothers. One graduated from Kyoto, one from Tokyo. Brothers' education came first. I took care of their children here in Hawaii, so I couldn't study what I wanted myself. Education of the children came first. But I couldn't study English, and I regret that. . . . I didn't need English at the Japanese school, so I used only Japanese.

After returning from Japan, I taught at the Japanese school from 1930 to September 1936, and then at Hilo Independent School until World War II. When the war began, I took a dressmaking diploma and then began dressmaking at home. In 1937 I took a diploma in tailoring and costume design from Sugita School in Honolulu. In the evening, I attended Higa Design School in Honolulu. While teaching at Japanese school, I also attended Mid-Pacific Dressmakers Association Dressmaking School in Hilo. . . . In 1947, I began the Hilo Fashion School, my own dressmaking school, and ran it until 1977. The Japanese schools went out of existence during the war, so I sewed at home. . . . From 1968 to 1978 I worked nights and weekends as cook at my younger brother's restaurant. My sister-in-law watched the restaurant during the day. I [had] worked as cook for the consul in Honolulu, so I learned there.

KIYOMI

Kiyomi was born in Hawaii and went to school through eighth grade. She married and raised seven children. She has worked as a field hand, laundrywoman, hospital aide, and dry cleaner.

I was born in Honohina, July 1908. That's on the Big Island. My mother was from Hiroshima. She passed away before my first birthday, and then I was adopted by my aunt and uncle. They came from farmers.

I went to Japanese school every day after grammar school . . . about two hours every day. We learned to read and write. The reason why I can still read and write is I just love to read Japanese books.

Magazines, books, and then I subscribe the daily *Hawaii Hochi*. Magazines — *Shufu no tomo*, we can get it. And I used to subscribe *Fujin kurabu*. . . . Then of course if you read and write . . . And in writing I'm not good, but at least [I] can. I went to school eight years, Japanese school too. And, in fact, the teacher was Reverend Motoyoshi. He even taught me simplified Chinese characters [*kuzushi*] — you know what is *kuzushi?* He was Hongwanji minister. I'm happy that I went to that school because very few children attended, so I had more attention. When I was in eighth grade, I think there were about three, that's all. Because we had another Japanese school, you know, below Hongwanji, and that was a regular Japanese school. Next to Hongwanji, that building still exists. Those days there were more Japanese here than now. And among our friends we don't speak English, you know. We always used to converse in Japanese — at home too.

You know, I wanted to go to school. And when I was in eighth grade, in fact, I was approached from one of the teachers [who said] that she heard that I cannot continue in school, so they can even help me to go. But I said, "No, no, I cannot because [of] the family situation." Father got sick and he was in the hospital, and the mother, you know, sickly too. She used to have kidney trouble. I have to work and help them out . . . after graduating from grammar school. I couldn't even have a chance to work my way to school, you know. And this person approached to me that they're going to help me, she and her sister. Too bad. . . . But I'm so thankful that my children are all nice. . . .

Even Reverend Motoyoshi from Hongwanji, you know, when I finished eighth grade, he came to the house and told my parents to send me to school. He told me to go to normal school. You know, those days you go to normal school four years, you can be one teacher . . . and then on the side go to Hongwanji Jogakko — that is the high school, Honolulu. I couldn't go. Not over here. I wasn't able to further my education. . . .

You know, I was adopted, and every year my aunt's having children and had a hard time. So I had to help. After eighth grade I worked in the fields. . . . Those days, we don't have the child labor law. So I'd go out in the field, and you know how much we used to get a month, a day? Twenty-five cents a day. . . . The train leaves at five o'clock in the morning, and four o'clock is the time we get over with the work. And in the morning, eight o'clock, fifteen minutes for breakfast. And lunch, 11:30 to 12:00, [but we often worked] right through without. Mean *luna*, you know, Portuguese. He cannot read and write. We had to eat within the time. But he was so mean, always driving us in the back. He didn't whip, though. He scolded us by name.

I got married young. I got married at sixteen. Not love marriage, you know. Match kind, *omiai*. Oh, I knew [him], but not as a boyfriend or anything. He was born in Okinawa, and he came to Hawaii eleven years old.

Well, I had seven children, and I been working right through, you know. After marriage, you cannot work in the field. After I have the children. Before I got married . . . I worked at the hospital too. Dr. Waterhouse wanted me to work there. I was also pregnant, beginning though, and I worked until I had her. And then after I had her, they wanted me to come back again, so I went back again. I went back again until I had the second one. So after that they asked me, but I said I cannot, sending the two children [to day-care] and go back to work. So I started to take in laundry. . . . [In the] hospital I did nurses' aide, because we had only one R.N., you know. No aide or anything. Plantation hospital. And then after I had my fourth one, [the rest were] kind of far apart, so they wanted me to come back when they have special cases — you know, surgery or OB [obstetrics], things like that. I used to go back. . . .

Those days, we used to have Spanish influenza. The epidemic went around. So the schools used to be closed up for a few weeks. And, in fact, they even made a bungalow outside the hospital for patients. If they were pregnant, no chance. All died, plenty died. Then, every day they take temperature at school, you know, and if you get 99 over, you sent home. Go to the doctor and then hospitalized. . . .

Laundry, oh, I used to wash for them, $2 a month. Well, beginning I used to do Filipino washing, but afterwards I used to take in other laundry, too. . . . You know those days with the small children — I often wonder, how did I ever do it? I know I used to get up early in the morning — at four o'clock we get up — and I cook lunch for my husband, and after he leaves, started to do washing or ironing. Washing all by hand, you know. Had to boil the clothes. [Only in] 1940 first, you know, we had electricity. So I said the first thing I'm going to buy is not a refrigerator but a washing machine. And then I took in another laundry, and then I said with that installment I'm going to pay . . .

My husband was a field laborer. Later on he was a track supervisor. You know, they used to lay tracks in the field. They load the cane on a car. Not machinery at all. And then the mule pulls the car till the main track that the train is waiting for.

At that time I was doing dry cleaning business. I did it for thirty years, here. . . . Fortunately, the manager of the plantation built a shop for me in the back, and I had that kind [of] presser and all. I used to press until one, two o'clock in the morning. That was during the war I started. I did it for thirty years, though. It was very hard. . . . I had the children to send to school, though. At that time it's hard to save. . . . After I couldn't do the dry cleaning — well, we have to move out from there because [my shop] became a house lot. Plantation started to sell, so was a plantation house. But I was very fortunate that the manager — I used to do his laundry, too, very good friend — and he got me the house in plantation. And when I moved there, then I had the job from the bank as a custodian, you know. Should I say custodian or janitress? — either side. I was very fortunate too. I worked until I had mastectomy surgery in 1980. I worked until then. . . . At this senior center, I'm [working] from the very beginning, and I feel this is my life here. I come every day to work.

No, I didn't speak Japanese to them [children] all the time. Sad? No. Of course I do [speak Japanese] — I used to speak but not too very much, and in the meantime we had the Second World War against Japan, so they said, "No Japanese, no Japanese." Most of the time we spoke English at home. So now the older ones tell me, "Oh, Mom, you should have spoken Japanese to us." Of course she [older daughter] went to eighth grade, you know, but she tells me I didn't speak very much Japanese at home, so they didn't learn. But I said we were forbidden from the government. We're not supposed to. And then I took citizenship too. Because getting married to the alien I lost my citizenship. So in 1943 [it was] finally granted, because 1940 I applied for it. . . .

Two were in college in the mainland, Bible college in Fort Wayne, Indiana. Her [daughter's] husband is the pastor of Missionary Church in K. . . . And my son, he graduated from Fort Wayne Bible College. . . . They're Christian, all of them. Well, I go to the Christian church too, because my son-in-law is . . . my family [is] all Christian, so . . . My daughter is minister's wife, and I do go, and I enjoy going to Christian church too on Sundays. I go to Hongwanji because I'm a member there. My family don't say anything. I'm sure they are hoping I'll be Christian someday.

SADAKO

Sadako is a friend who told me this story about her mother's life as an issei *in Hawaii.*

My mother was pregnant with her ninth child when my father died. She was thirty-nine — he was sixty-three. He had loaned people money, but she didn't get it back. She was desperate and couldn't support her kids or even speak English. The neighbor people told her, [to] give them all to the Salvation Army. She said, "No matter what, I'm going to bring up my children myself." So we were good, obedient kids.

Sometimes we got a whaling. She always said we should be extra careful or people would point their fingers at us. She did laundry for Filipino bachelors. She got up at 4:30 and boiled clothing, boiled it outside. She had mountains of laundry, and the oldest child was only thirteen. She used a charcoal iron and had one electric light bulb. I would fall asleep doing my homework, and sometimes I heard her crying, but I pretended I never heard her because she was very proud.

MIEKO

Mieko was born and educated in Japan. She came to Hawaii to marry. In Hawaii, she taught Japanese, raised two sons, worked in the family store, and became accomplished in crocheting, which she still does.

[in Japanese]

I was born in Yanai-shi, Kuga-gun, Yamaguchi-ken in Meiji 28 [1895]. My family were traders, merchants, rice wholesaling and retailing — it was quite a large operation. We accumulated rice in the *kura* [storehouse], and when the price went up, we sold it. So the house was larger than ordinary. We had about two *kura*. We had workers, and four or five young boys to handle the rice.

My parents understood children very well, and their future. When we played with the neighbor children, they had *moxa* burns. But no matter how hard we played, [our parents] never punished us with *moxa*. Father said it was very cruel to burn children when they weren't sick. So we thought our father was a very good father. Whatever we wanted to learn, they let us learn. *O-koto* [a stringed instrument], crocheting, tea ceremony, whatever we wanted to learn. So we went to the *sensei's* [teacher's] house for an hour lesson, flower arranging. So if I said I wanted to learn something, they never said no. They allowed us to learn whatever we wanted.

My grandmother complained that in a family that had been Jodoshu believers for generations, a child should not go to a church believed in by Caucasians. My father said, "Grandmother, it won't do to continue those old ways today. We don't know whom our daughter will marry. It isn't a matter of good or bad. It is good for her to learn many things when she is young. So please don't say such things." That's what he said. My father was a person who understood things well. Even if we went to church, he didn't say anything.

I became a Christian in Japan, when I was a student. I discussed it with my father first. I didn't become a believer, but my friends said, "Let's go, let's go." . . . There was a church in a house in my town. My husband was very enthusiastic about religion. The minister praised him. . . . My son went too — all his life — and my grandchildren go too.

My father died one month before I graduated from Jogakko. He had arranged for me to go to college after graduating from Jogakko. It may be strange for me to say, but I did well in school, so he let me go to school. I wanted to go, and he understood that. We had a teacher who had graduated from college very young, and we envied her. So I wanted to be a teacher like her.

At the age of twenty-one, I came to Hawaii. My husband was already here. It was a marriage of houses in Japan, not as a picture bride. I was formally accepted as a bride into the house. At the time I was in women's higher school. . . .

When I came here, my grandparents and mother bought new things for tea ceremony and the *o-koto* to bring here. We made all kinds of preparations. But Hawaii is a colony and is not a place for *o-koto* and tea ceremony, they said in a letter. So you don't need those things, they said. Then I won't go to Hawaii. Then I'll stay in Japan and teach. I passed the teachers' qualification test. I'll teach in Japan for ten yen a month. It was big money then. I don't want to go to a place where they don't learn tea ceremony, *o-koto*, and flower arrangement. I'm going to give up the idea. Mother Y. [husband's mother] said, "Please don't be unreasonable. Your passage has already been arranged, so please go for just a year." And she bowed to me and cried. "If you don't go, I'll be very troubled." "Then I'll go for a year and then come back," I said. I was raised with the *koto* and the refinements, so I thought I'd better not go to Hawaii.

We were married by Reverend Nakamura of the River Church, in Honolulu. A Christian church. My family were Jodo-shu Buddhists for generations.

I taught in the Japanese school here for about five years. It was like a small business. Then I stopped teaching and we started a small business. Of course, my husband stopped being a cook, and we started a general store. It had everything — rice, miso, shoyu, dishes, zori, *geta* [wooden clogs] . . . In those days, there were very few Japanese in business. . . . When my eldest son graduated from high school, he worked with us. . . . But he said [that] in the future this will be a shopping center here and so small stores won't survive. So he said he wanted to do wholesale business. Now my grandson is continuing that business. . . .

I liked crocheting — tablecloths, antimacassars for chairs. Mrs. B. called me and said [that] if you can do such lovely work, there will be a lot of work for you to do. Haoles will be happy and will order them, and you can sell them in the store. She showed me her book on crocheting. When I saw it, I could do it immediately. "Oh, can you do it after just glancing at the book? Can you read English?" "No, I can't read English. I can do it by looking at the pictures." So I was able to get many orders for the store, and so many that I was busy. . . . I didn't dream I could make so much money crocheting. People brought me books and asked if I could crochet things for them. . . . My friends worked at the Wilcox home as maids, and they showed my tablecloth to Mabel Wilcox. I got $7 and was so happy. This was only a month or two after I arrived here. That was a lot of money. A maid got about $4 for one month. I started the tablecloth in Japan and continued it here when I had spare time. So I don't know how long it took to make it. But I'm still crocheting today at the age of ninety. . . . I wanted to return to Japan but I never could. So I became resigned to staying here and making money.

They work about eight hours today, but there was no such thing then. People went to the mountains if they ran out of firewood. . . . They went about four [o'clock] to the mountains, when we were still sleeping. Woke us. When I went out, my husband scolded me. "You shouldn't do that. You shouldn't open the store at this hour." I thought I feel sorry for them, so I go up and opened the store. We closed the store about six at night. But the house was together with the store, so it wasn't a big chore, like a Japanese store.

When my eldest son graduated from high school he had to work. He wanted to go to college. All his friends were going to college. But he had to stay here and work because we didn't know English and needed him in the store. So we relied on him and couldn't send him to college. During the war, the FBI came to investigate the Japanese. It was a period of unrest. Our son was a citizen, so we depended on him and couldn't send him to college though we sent him through high school.

I want them [grandchildren] to continue some of the tradition while I'm alive, and I want them to go to Japanese school. I have them practice it. The one who is three is the most charming. She says, *"Obaachan, sayonara,"* *"Ashita mata aimasho, ne."* I answer, *"Mata aimasho, ne."* ["Goodbye, Grandma. We'll meet again tomorrow, won't we?" "We'll meet tomorrow."]

At the senior center, there's a woman who graduated from the same Jogakko. We made friends on the ship. We were all together. We've been friends for seventy years. When we go to a church meeting or something, we always go together. People think we are sisters.

Everyone was thinking at the Lihue Center of sending something for the immigration centenary celebration, but Lihue didn't have anything to give. So they asked me what I thought we should do. What about the leggings? At the ceremony, one person from Lihue [and] one from Kapaa went up on the stage with one of my jackets. Everyone came up afterwards and said they wanted one. "Thank you for presenting something that you made. We'll treat it carefully. Please enjoy a long life," they said. So I cried. When we came down from the stage, everyone came around to where the old people were, with *sekihan* [red rice]. They all brought *sekihan*. Young people think differently today, don't they?

VII   Okinawans

Identity

Okinawans are Japanese and have been so since 1879, when Okinawa was incorporated into Japan as a prefecture. Prior to that year, Okinawa was politically independent and looked to China in a tributary relationship and simultaneously to Japan under a system of surveillance set up by Satsuma-han on behalf of the Tokugawa shoguns. The Hawaiian Kingdom and — after Hawaii's annexation in 1898, the American government — have treated Okinawans as Japanese. The history of Okinawan immigration to Hawaii is not notably dissimilar to the immigration of other Japanese (see Chapter VI).

Yet, since their arrival in Hawaii, Okinawans have been regarded by other Japanese immigrants as a people apart. Japanese in Hawaii have insisted on the separateness of Okinawans from all other Japanese. The reasons for this insistence are many and not always easy to discern. For one thing, when the Japanese arrived in Hawaii, they were at the bottom of the plantation hierarchy in terms of pay and status. They were happy to no longer be the most recent arrivals. In addition, there were cultural distinctions between the members of the two groups. Setting them apart were the Okinawans' language, which is a dialect — an ancient one but nonetheless a dialect — of Japanese, and such cultural differences as the Okinawan's distinctive folk songs and dances, their ancient custom of tattooing women's hands and upper lips, and the predominance of pork in their diet. Hog-raising was a common occupation of Okinawans in Hawaii, as it was in Okinawa. The Naichi Japanese (those from the Japanese mainland) seized upon these differences as proofs of a distinct identity.

In Japan, the traditional target of discrimination was the pariah caste (Burakumin, or Eta), but since the Meiji Era caste distinctions were no longer legal — though in practice discrimination continued. In

Hawaii, it was easier to single out Okinawans among Japanese, and the Japanese, tired of suffering at the bottom of the plantation hierarchy, isolated the Okinawans as a separate immigrant group.

There was no ethnic distinction between the Naichi and Okinawan Japanese. The Okinawans are said to have more body hair than other Japanese, but this is not a marked distinction. The Japanese, however, are a relatively homogeneous group ethnically and culturally and are an extremely exclusive people. Minute regional differences in culture, food habits, and dialect have historically been emphasized in Japan. The emphasis and insistence on small regional differences could be seen in the prefectural societies the Japanese immigrants in Hawaii organized. All of these factors led the Japanese who arrived in Hawaii from southern Japan to discriminate in various ways against the Japanese who arrived from Okinawa somewhat later, after 1900. In their search for acceptance in Hawaii, the Naichi Japanese apparently felt the need to exclude someone, and the Okinawans were easy targets for Japanese exclusiveness.[1]

Population statistics kept by the government in Hawaii, however, made no distinction between Okinawans and other Japanese. Okinawans were simply included with the other Japanese.

One study of these intergroup sentiments suggests that Okinawans suffered more from Naichi hostility in Hawaii than they would have in Japan because there was a larger proportion of Okinawans in Hawaii and because the two groups came into closer personal contact in Hawaii than they did in Japan. In addition, the Okinawans suffered from an inferiority complex regarding their culture, whereas the Naichi Japanese felt great pride with regard to their culture — a situation that further increased hostilities.[2]

Arrival in Hawaii

Okinawans emigrated to Hawaii and California for the same reasons as other Japanese: to escape poverty, population pressure, the lack of jobs, and military conscription. Numbers of emigrants were small initially. The first 26 landed in Honolulu on January 8, 1900, followed by a second group of 40 in 1903 and a third of 262 in 1904. The numbers then jumped to 1,000 in 1905 and 4,467 in 1906, the largest

Fig. 7.1. An educated Okinawan mother. *Courtesy of Roy Yonahara.*

annual total. As a result of the Gentlemen's Agreement, the numbers dropped sharply between 1908 and 1911. In 1912, 1,678 persons arrived, predominantly picture brides. In that year, Okinawans accounted for 35 percent of the Japanese in Hawaii; they numbered more than 10,000 individuals. The ratio of Okinawans to other Japanese was consistently 20 percent. In 1980, 40,000 individuals of Okinawan descent lived in Hawaii, a number that was 15 percent of the Japanese-American community.[3]

Most Okinawan immigrants thus arrived after the abolition of contract labor. The first group of Okinawans became free immigrants six months after their arrival. Most worked on the sugar plantations — 78.9 percent of the total — as compared with 3.1 percent working in the pineapple fields.[4] Many of the first Okinawans sent money home to impoverished relatives. This proof of success in Hawaii stimulated further Okinawan immigration, and the number of Okinawans returning was small in comparison with other Japanese.

Although Okinawans had the same goal as other immigrants — to save money for three years and then return home — as with other groups, three years became five, then ten, as their families grew and they put down roots. Moreover, it was apparent to most that they were better off economically in Hawaii than they had been in Okinawa. For most, the desire to return waned with the passing years.

In Hawaii, Okinawans kept to themselves for the reasons previously mentioned. Wherever they settled in Hawaii, they formed their own prefectural and even village societies for mutual help and as a means of social interaction. Between 1907 and 1920, five all-Okinawan organizations were founded.

It became immediately apparent that Japanese from other prefectures regarded Okinawans with disrespect, even contempt. Some respondents in this study reported being hailed with "Hey, Okinawa!" or "Hey, Big Rope!" (a play on the characters forming the word "Okinawa") or with "*Okinawa ken ken, buta kau kau!*" ("Okinawans eat pigs"). Some Japanese respondents reported that their parents would not allow them to play with Okinawans when they were children. One Naichi father on Maui committed suicide because his son married an Okinawan. Naichi Japanese also referred to Okinawans as *yabanjin*, "primitives," and said they looked like Malayans or Filipinos — a comment that, from the Japanese perspective, was pejorative.[5] More recently, a nisei from

Colorado reported to me that when he asked a Japanese-American in Hawaii for a date, she replied, "There's something I have to tell you. I'm Okinawan."

Education was the key to upward mobility and respectability for the Okinawans. In 1929, a Maui boy, Edward Kushi, became the first Okinawan to graduate from the University of Hawaii. As Hawaiian-born generations have grown to maturity, people of Okinawan descent have taken their places not only in all-Japanese organizations, but also in the economy and polity of Hawaii, generally in positions of prestige. Today Hui O Laulima and other organizations seek to promote and preserve Okinawan culture.[6]

Women

Initially, women were a small proportion of the small number of Okinawan immigrants. In 1907, with the influx of picture brides, the number of women arriving jumped to 480, and in 1912, over 1,000 women came. The number dropped after 1912, then rose in 1917 to 1,308 and in 1918 to 1,403. In 1909, 62 percent of those who came were women.[7]

The proportion of women coming from Okinawa was nevertheless larger than from other prefectures. According to one author, the numbers were higher because the Okinawan government was more lenient in enforcing the regulations of the Ministry of Foreign Affairs and, in fact, wanted to encourage the emigration of women.[8]

These women suffered from the disadvantages of being both female and Okinawan. Boys were always favored over girls in being given an opportunity for education. Yet the Okinawan girls shared the aspirations, work, and much of the life-style of other Japanese women. Some Okinawan women in this study articulated their resentment at being singled out as a people apart, a minority within a minority.

This chapter is briefer than others because the Okinawans were, after all, Japanese, if a variant in the eyes of others. It will be noted that of the respondents whose interviews follow, two had attained high educational and occupational goals, and the lives of these two differed significantly from the other three.

HIROKO

Hiroko was born in a village in Okinawa, came to Hawaii as a teenager, and worked in the fields. She had an arranged marriage and raised six children.

[in Japanese]

I was born in Nakagusuku, Okinawa. I came here in 1913. At that time I was fifteen . . . or, really, fourteen. My father brought my younger brother and me. He [brother] was twelve or thirteen at the time. . . . Part of the family stayed in Okinawa. I wanted to learn more, so I came here. [Okinawa] was a small place, and there was always trouble there. I wanted to learn more languages and learn more about the world, so I was happy to come here. My father returned to Okinawa, [and] he said life was better here and he called us here. My mother stayed home in Okinawa to take care of the younger children, sisters. We also had a house there, so she stayed there. So we came without our mother, with only our father.

I went to Japanese school in Okinawa. I went to school for seven years. In Okinawa, everyone stopped after six years. I don't want to boast, but I wanted to go longer, so I went another year. Then my father came from Hawaii to take me to Hawaii. So I stopped and came here. I liked school very much. I wanted to go to school when I came here too, but I didn't know anything. There was no Japanese school here at the time. . . . I went to evening school, but I was so tired from working all day that I fell asleep when I sat down.

When I came, I thought it would have been better if I hadn't come. I cried and cried and just had to work. In Okinawa, I was just playing and going to school. At home we had a cook and a laundryman — we had everything there. I talked to my brother about how bad it was that we had come here. We went behind the house and cried. We didn't think we were going to suffer so much here, so we cried. The most difficult thing was that we didn't understand any other language. Afterwards we learned a few words.

I worked here with my father for four or five years after we came. Sugarcane field work from six A.M. to 3:30 in the afternoon. Now there are machines, so it is easy. In those days we did it all with the hoe. They didn't know about sprays in those days. There were many insects —

centipedes, scorpions — and they bit. We wore jackets, gloves, scarfs, hats — covered ourselves completely. We worked with the hoe, planted, cut the sugar . . . It was hard work. At sixteen or seventeen, it was hard work, and we were lonely.

Our friends from Okinawa or those born here were in school and knew the language. . . . My brother went to school a little. But my father was strict, and the three of us had to work. He [brother] was small, and he couldn't *hoe-hana* at first. He carried water but that was hard work too. He carried water from the fields to camp. There was only water in the fields. . . . Work is easy today, and wherever they go, they go by car.

After I got accustomed to it here, my father returned to Okinawa, after getting me married. . . . I was nineteen when I got married.

After my children were born — [a son and then] twins — I had too much work to do and didn't think about going to school anymore. In those days, we walked everywhere, carrying our babies. And I had twins, and had to walk everywhere. We had no horse. I'm afraid of horses. If we had to go very far, then we went by train, but not to work. There were no washing machines in those days — everything was done by hand . . . in a wooden barrel. It took a lot of time. But what else could we do? In the camp, we had vegetable gardens, and we planted trees in our gardens. We had meat or fish only about once a week. People came from town selling fish. It was a small camp, so we didn't have *matsuri* [festivals].

I learned to sew from someone who sewed for weddings, a cousin who came to Hawaii before us. She had a sewing machine. When I had the baby, I couldn't work in the fields, so I got a sewing machine and did sewing. So I made work clothes — pants and shirts. Stockings. Shoes. We made the shoes ourselves. We had *tabi*. The clothing was hot. We made gloves, but they got torn doing *hoe-hana*. We got blisters. People today don't know how we suffered then. No, my children don't know.

A friend took my twins to Okinawa, where my parents were, but I was sorry for them so I called them back. I cried and thought it wasn't good for them to be there, so I asked someone coming to bring them. I wanted them to go to school. I didn't want them to be unable to go to school like me, so I called them back. There was a school in the camp, so I sent them there for eight years. Since I had no education, I wanted them to go to school and acquire some education so they would know how to meet people and be able to work. All my children went for eight years. My boys went to vocational school and learned to be carpenters. The two younger boys went to high school. My mother and father did not go to school in Okinawa. They only know how to write their names.

No, no discrimination. Nothing like that. Everyone, all are friends, all are good people. They don't gossip about others here. If someone has bananas or papayas, they divide and share them. They don't accept money.

One of the twins died when he grew up, after he married. The other one is here on Maui. He comes every day to say good morning.

KAZUKO

Kazuko was born in Okinawa, married as a teenager, and immigrated to Hawaii with her husband. She raised pigs, made tofu, wove bingata fabric, and had four children.

[in Japanese]

I was born December 19, 1904, in Okinawa, Kisaba, Nakagusuku. I was married in Okinawa at seventeen and came here. We had a party here, too — a reception. He came five years earlier. I came in 1923. My parents stayed in Okinawa. Two of my brothers are in Brazil now, and one brother is here. My eldest sister returned from Hawaii to Okinawa and died there. When we first came here, we wanted to make money and return to Okinawa soon, but the children were born, and so we were not able to return. Then we decided not to go.

My father wasn't a farmer — he was an office worker. My mother did housework. I went to school in Okinawa. My teacher told me, "Please go to school." But my mother was sick with a fever, so I couldn't go to school. I graduated after [only] six years of school. The teacher from the next higher school came, but I couldn't go further in school. I graduated at twelve or thirteen. I can't forget that we played ball behind the school, boys and girls. I liked to play with the children, too. Mother lived ten more years. I sewed kimono, did that kind of work. Mother did only housework — she didn't sew, since she was ill. My father died when I was five. People who worked in the offices drank a lot. He drank too much and died from it.

When I arrived in Kailua, I had magazines — [they cost] 50¢. I learned from that because I didn't know anything. I didn't know anything when I came from Okinawa. There was a store in Kahului. Every month I bought the magazine and brought it home. After coming here, I read Okinawan newspapers and magazines, and we do even today.

When I first came, I wore kimono. We worked as hard as we could when we came to Hawaii. We lived in a small camp. . . . My husband worked in the sugar fields. There was no electricity in those days. We had kerosene. I raised pigs, pig *hana-hana* [work]. After a year, my first child was born, so I didn't go out to work. After eight years, I had four children. . . . We weighed pineapples. But no matter how much they weighed, it wasn't enough. . . . Then we did tofu-making in Kahului. And Papa [her husband] raised pigs. I made tofu. We raised pigs twice. . . . I learned how to weave in school, and I borrowed a loom and wove at home. I made *bingata*, like *kassuri* [a woven, patterned fabric], and sewed. I learned in school. . . . There was a sewing teacher here. We were taught to cut out patterns from paper. We left Paia in 1946 and came to Kahului and made tofu from then until we retired.

At the time we came there was no electricity, no icebox. Then they put in an icebox — someone came and brought it. We gradually enlarged the house. We had only one room when we first came. As the number of children grew, it got larger. The bathroom was outside. When we got to Paia, it was better. One small room and a kitchen that was open at first. After that we had a kerosene stove in the kitchen — they built a kitchen. And we had two bedrooms instead of one. Then, after three or four years, we had some money for our business. I made all their clothes myself. I made those pants. Look at the picture. I wore kimono when I first came here. . . .

I go to the Baptist church. My third son goes to the *issei* church. My parents were Buddhists. . . .

I always speak Japanese to the children. But the grandchildren and great-grandchildren can't speak it. My children and grandchildren are all married. Great-grandchildren are being born. I'm satisfied.

Human beings have all kinds of possibilities. You don't know when you'll sleep forever. So I rely on God as to whether I live or die. I always pray to Jesus, morning and night. No great changes — I'm only accumulating years. I like music. I do Okinawan folk dances, even now.

SHIZUKO

Shizuko was born on Kauai, where her father worked on a plantation. She married and had six children. In addition, she raised cows and pigs, made tofu, and operated a restaurant. She is an accomplished koto player.

I was born November 25, 1916, in Kauai. I was in Honolulu one or two years. My father worked as a gardener in a haole house. We were very, very poor. Then, at age ten, I went to Okinawa. My parents went back to Okinawa. My father had five brothers, one brother here. His mother was eighty-four or eighty-five years old, and she died. My father came to Hawaii, then called my uncle, the last one. . . . My number two brother, fifteen years old, call. Then, after, my number three brother and my mother came, and then me and my sister born Hawaii. I went back to Okinawa for ten years. I came back here when I was twenty. In Okinawa, get land and house, but still living was poor, the food and the job.

At Okinawa, the typhoon come, so I gotta take care the horse and pig. Goat get — goat [milk] for baby and sell. For two, three days, gotta make ready. All the food, three day food gotta make ready, you know. Dig the potato and the horse one [horse's food]. So that time, I no ready. The *taifu* [typhoon] come and all muddy.

Oh, I hate Okinawa. Ya, poor living that time. Ya, I wanta come back. My brother, my sister stay Hawaii. So Hawaii living, the [water] pipe, the water come. But up here [Okinawa] no more pipe. I have to carry in a barrel. Carry from my grandma house to my house. My grandma house has springs. My house never had. . . . And the wind supposed to come. If the wind no come, rain no more. Okinawa place no enough water. . . .

Grandfather time — poor. He had hard time. Nighttime he put the kerosene lamp and then *hana-hana*, working. At night, he used to work in the cane field. Then he make money and buy land in Okinawa and pay the balance. . . . But land [we] had, and my mother-in-law take care that, so we sell that, and we buy here. . . .

I like go school, but I go there learn only once. It was far to go to school. It was dark in the morning when I came down to go to school. Went to Japanese school too. It was dark when we went home after school. We had to walk. It was too far to go to school, eight miles. So we went to Honolulu. I was working. I never go long time, but I like to learn. . . . They [children] go school — they can go university. 'Come mechanic — they never go school, but they experience is more important, broke and fix. My daughter all high school, Hilo, commercial college, business school. But I like to learn. I was talking Japanese, English too. . . .

I saw my husband and liked him. He wasn't handsome, but smart. . . . I got six children — three boys, three girls. One miscarriage. One adopted out by relatives who had no children, my mother-in-law's relatives. Happiest time? What kind happy? My son born. Okinawa-style, even you marry, no born boy baby, you cannot be. No more home. My son born, blackout baby, 1944, cannot go to the Japanese hospital. . . . Baby born, I went to Dr. Yang, the Chinese doctor. The time come, I was in the store. The neck was funny, so no born . . . I go the doctor. The doctor come and see the baby. You know the bag? You know the bag gotta bust and the baby come out, but never bust, and then the baby come, so gotta open the bag. I hear if you born that kind of baby, it's good-luck baby. Dr. Yang, he said, "You got good-luck baby." I was so happy.

I worked hard — overweight. Farming good for me, shaking around, walking around, pull the grass, carry it. So I like farming. I work hard. The farm was rough. Gotta work hard. If not, cannot live. My mother taught me make tofu. I made tofu business. I marry, I do lotta business. Sell, raise cow and sell. Kill pig and sell. Restaurant. After war, Hilo, Japanese restaurant. All the Kuhio working people come to my restaurant, eat lunch and dinner. Now close up, long time ago. . . . My husband no like restaurant business. He was working as a fisherman in Oshima. . . . And my number two auntie was store. She used to make pancake, put inside something, dakin' [that kind]. I used to help sell. . . .

Yes, before was [discrimination]. But if they do to me like that, I play music and forget about. Yes, play koto. I no talk back or I no fight back or like that. Not good. Everybody misunderstand. I wrong, I tell "excuse me," enough just to get along with people. Ya, I tell [that] before was like that. . . . Okinawa people, they take care outside people, so house is after. They don't know how to clean house. So we gotta work hard to do that. After war, they make money. They are strong. If you no more money, they look down. Something like that. . . .

My brother died asthma, my cousin died asthma. So they put injection — after never helps, so I no like put injection. So I just [eat] liver soup, pork liver. Boil and come yellow, no? I drink two year and come strong. That make you strong, for kidney and everything. So I trust in liver soup, no? Sometime I catch cold, so I make liver soup and put the carrots and celery, ginger. . . . When I married, my children liked that Okinawan food — pigs' intestines, pigs' feet . . . with vegetables, *daikon* [a long white radish], carrots, *gobo* [burdock], like that.

Saddest time? I think the baby adopt one [adopted her baby out]. I didn't want, but I want to help. Funny. So you cannot get baby, I want to help. So baby come, and I go there. . . . So my son he hardly call me Mama. Only later, for telephone he call me Mama.

I like music, folk songs. I taught my granddaugher *o-koto*. My daughter plays too. Three generations learned koto. Japanese koto is really fast; Okinawan gotta be slow and nice, like that. The noise is really pretty. Come the slow one. Every day, one hour I practice, with the tape. . . . So nobody bother I stay myself . . . I sing Japanese songs. I love to sing. No, Mother didn't teach me. . . . I used to hear the record and learn. . . . I see the *shibai*, and I catch on. I catch on . . . I come home and sing myself. So I used to like the song and history, the meaning. Or something really interest. Sad place, I cry. That's good for the people, I thinking, all our Okinawan songs. Oh, ya, I dance too. Simple kind dance, Okinawan.

I went Washington, New York, South America. Japan . . . I went two times, Okinawa travel. My daughter went with me. Next year, this big koto group, she go South America and then Los Angeles and then Honolulu.

So the young people make Hui Okinawa [a club]. In Hilo, and join the Honolulu one. So that Hui Okinawa not only Okinawa people. Japanese can join. So every New Year, get entertain, the koto, dance. I no like spoil my grandchildren. Yes, everybody doing good, so I'm happy.

CHIEKO

Chieko was born on a plantation in Waipahu, one of ten children. She worked her way through high school and college. She was admitted to medical school in Philadelphia, but after a few years she left medical school and went to Columbia University, where she got an M.A. in education. She taught at McKinley High, and she also taught Peace Corps volunteers. She helped to put her brothers and sisters through school before she married.

I was born in Waipahu. I'm the third member [child] of the family, and all three girls having come in succession, my father had probably wanted a son. I'm quite sure of that. He thought I'd be the last girl, but then I had a sister following me, then four boys followed, then a girl, then the last of the boys, which makes five boys and five girls. . . .

I think some of those houses are still standing there, near the golf course. In fact, I went back there, because I went [there] to teach after so many years. I looked the place over, and I pointed out the house that we lived in. It was just about two rooms, if I recall, and a kitchen. We cooked with an open fire, and there was no electricity. I remember carrying the lantern from one room to the next one. That was on the plantation. My father and mother . . . I guess both worked in the fields, and that's about all I could remember. . . .

My mother used to come right out with everything. I understood her, I think. I used to wonder why she would be that type of person. And yet, on the other hand, I guess she had concern for the family, because she held the family together. While all the girls are away, she held those boys together and saw to it that they didn't go astray. She was the type of person who would never say anything nice about the youngsters. She said that would spoil them. Very critical. In fact, she would say, "Why would I say something nice about them? It would get them to be bullheaded." Or something like that. Oh, she was tough! She lost her mother when she was twelve years old, and so I could understand why she was the type of person she was. . . . She said, "As long as you marry a person who is not lazy, who's a good worker, who doesn't cheat people . . ." And then if she sees certain people who are not up to her standard, she would just come right out with it. She was blunt. . . . And she would say even to my brothers, "If you want to be a ballplayer, be the best ballplayer." . . .

Sometimes I disagreed with her, but if I answered back, opposed her, she would say, "If that is what education does to you . . ." Things like finances, that's where we disagreed — how to look ahead. She would always say that I would always be reasoning things out instead of trying to obey her.

I don't recall her taking care of us. I can never remember her combing my hair. My older sister used to do these things for me. She was too busy taking care of the younger ones, I guess . . . And she used to take in laundry sometimes. She forces my sister to do all the cooking, and I would take all the little kids on my back, you know. . . . I felt that I never had too much time to play — that I recall — whereas my younger sister, she was scot-free. . . . And I kind of envied that, I recall. . . .

It was a peculiar situation. She'd speak Okinawan to us and we'd understand that. But my father would speak standard Japanese. We would try to speak Japanese to her. . . . But I didn't know a word of English when I went to school. My father knew a little bit of English, but that was because of his work. He had to contract the work for the people and translate some of the things. He had to understand the plantation managers.

And then, if I recall, there was a strike that the Japanese people took part in, and my whole family moved into town, and I remember going to Moiliili. And all of us were placed in some sort of a tent or places where everybody ate together. . . . My father had a brother on the island of Hawaii, and he decided to join him there because apparently they didn't have the strike there like they did over here. And so we stayed there until I was in the seventh grade. . . . And when my older sister finished high school, my father wanted her to continue her education, and so we moved back here. . . . And there I was going to intermediate school and high school, and that's when I lived with families and worked my way through school. And I earned enough to give half of it to my family and use half of it for myself. They were white people that I worked for. . . . That was the way it happened in our family. Of course, my sister did the same that I did — she used to work for families until she finished college. And of course she would help me with the tuition part. It was $50 a semester. And I couldn't save $50 because most of my paycheck would go to myself or to the family. I felt more or less useful in helping them, just no qualms about that.

My father used to tell us, "You girls must have an education because you don't know when you'll need it." And he used to say to us, "You have to be able to help your husbands, too, when the time comes."

I think most of us went into education and nursing because during that time nobody [else] wanted a teaching job, which paid so little. So most of us didn't mind at all working in the cannery — even that was a good job. Fortunately, it provided us with a living. . . . If you wanted to improve yourself and not work in the cannery for the rest of your life, you had to get an education. That taught me a lesson, working in the cannery. That wasn't going to be what I would do for the rest of my life!

So when I finished college . . . I majored in natural and physical sciences, hoping to study medicine. Can you imagine trying to study medicine with that kind of a background? Well, anyhow, what I did after I finished university . . . I depended on my sister in New York City to help me, so I borrowed some money and went to New York City. Somehow I had more nerve, I guess. I joined them. And I was accepted at medical school in Philadelphia. . . . It was only for women. . . . My two sisters were there so I joined them. . . . One sister was studying nursing. I knew it was very difficult because she was trying to help the sister under me. I went to medical school for a couple of years, but the first year I was there, my father passed away. I can remember he died on Washington's birthday, and I cried all the way from New York City back to Philadelphia. And you know, I couldn't go back for the funeral. There wasn't money. And I guess I must have lost something. I guess I wanted to show him that I could amount to something, because he believed. . . . And I kind of worried about what was happening at home. And I found it was really difficult for them, the finances and all that sort of thing. So by the second year, I gave up. I had to go home. They were all younger than I am at home and without a father now. The youngest must have been four years old when the father passed away. He was only forty-nine, cancer. . . . We saw to it that the girl, the younger girl, and the boy go to college. Both of them did — they finished college. I decided, heck, I better find a job, quickly, so I could help them along too . . . but I knew I couldn't find a job in New York City. I tried, couldn't. The only job open to me was a nursemaid or something like that. I couldn't get teaching, because I didn't have any teaching certificate. I decided to work for a full year and earn enough tuition so that I could go to Columbia. I did it! I got my master's degree there.

Education was the key. My father never demanded that we work and help support the family. He used to tell us, "If you can find your way through, I won't ask anything of you." But he did believe in educating the girls too. . . . And I enjoyed my work at Columbia. When you are exposed to men like [Edward] Thorndike, and John Dewey, and [James B.] Conant, leaders in education in the thirties and forties, and then you get guest speakers, like Hutchins from the University of Chicago . . . They were great men. And to be exposed to minds like that! I thought it was an experience for me. I worked my way through college. . . . I did it.

I got a job at an intermediate school on the island of Hawaii. It's a godforsaken country there! Out in the sticks! . . . I felt my brother and sisters should have a chance to go to school too — like I had a chance to go to college. So I said, "When I start working one of you can start going to school, and I can help the family." . . . So my brother and I — and I got only $120 a month and he had only $130 a month working with one of the grocery stores here — the two of us managed to support the rest of the family. . . . I'll pay their insurance and things like that, see that the family is still intact. The two of us did it together, my younger brother and I. . . . He was two below me and had just finished high school. He was working as a garage mechanic, and he was paying the rent for the family, helping to hold the family together. Then the second boy was working as a mason, but then he got drafted into the Army. He was with the 100th Battalion. And I figured, good night! The next boy was just about finishing high school. So I said, "You know, I think you better head the family, so they won't take you into the Army." You know, this was the situation, and I had to work a kind of strategy out, because I'm a woman.

To make that story short, my brother was lucky — he came back from Italy. The other boy was lucky — the war had ended. So I suggested that they use the GI Bill and go to college. In the meantime, I would take care of the rest of them. I'll pay their insurance and things like that. See that the family is still intact. The two of us did it together, my younger brother and I.

The family is all independent, and that is my biggest satisfaction, having seen them through to become independent. Not a single one that I know of are dependent on other people. . . .

So I taught four years there [at the intermediate school], and then I was transferred to Kahuku, during the war years. And we would work every Friday, as a war effort, in the plantation fields, with the youngsters. But the whole point here was the plantation people realized that they couldn't control the kids. The teachers had better control of the kids, and they needed our help. I guess we felt patriotic about it! . . . I taught for one year, and then I taught at Farrington, and then one of the teachers at McKinley passed away. He happened to be a chemistry teacher, and I have a major in chemistry too, so they figured I could fit right in. I stayed there till I retired. . . . For textbook review and experimental curriculum, I went to the University of Colorado to get the newest training there. And, meantime, we carried on experimental curriculum, so I could get the reviews and whatever is necessary to carry on research. . . . I was chosen to be on the steering committee for that group. Working with people who were very astute in curriculum planning gave me some inkling of how things are done in the educational field. . . .

One of our friends introduced us. It wasn't too long — our courtship wasn't too long. We were older and I knew exactly, and all that sort of thing. Getting married, and I felt that it's time that I have a life of my own. He helped me a lot too. He would help me in many, many ways. You know, how to handle people. He would help me entertain some of the people who came here. I couldn't do it alone. . . . [I married] rather late, but I felt that all of them [brothers and sisters] were on their feet now. The two boys finished college, the girl finished medical technology. The only boy who didn't go to college was the one who helped me. And I will always have a soft spot for him because he didn't have a chance to go to college. But I thought perhaps he might be happier to be married, so I encouraged that. He's happy with his family. . . .

When I was teaching, I saw certain things on the plantation that I thought wasn't . . . It made me think. Here these plantation people are working, and then what they do, they go to the plantation store and turn everything over, buy everything there. So that all their wages would go right back to the plantation. I began to sense the inequity there. . . .

My father used to do that sort of thing, discourage people from staying on the plantation. He used to tell the younger men, "Don't stick around here too long. You get out and get your education." Of course, if the plantation managers had heard him, he'd be flying out of the plantation in no uncertain terms!

I had to ask my father, "How come they are so prejudiced against the Okinawans?" He explained to me that most of the Japanese who are here from the mainland, they come from the country and are not educated enough to understand that even Okinawans are Japanese. But because we speak a different dialect, anything that is strange is something they cannot understand. They always had some kind of prejudice.

They'd call us "Big Rope." They'd tell us we eat a lot of pork, things like that. I tell you why — because the Okinawans do eat more pork than the regular Japanese from the mainland.

Oh, I remember one time, in my chemistry class, this fellow called me, "Eh, you Okinawan!" Things like that. And then even the girls in the rest room, they don't say it directly to me, but if they were talking about some other girl, and they would just come out, "Oh, but she's Okinawan, though!" Already the distinction is there.

When I went to New York City and Philadelphia, I couldn't understand. They talked the same way about Jewish people, and I couldn't understand that one bit. And I thought, Jewish people look white to me, so why would a white person have something against another white? The same as the local Japanese would look at an Okinawan. But we were much hairier, and our eyes were much deeper set. Immediately they knew that we were Okinawans. Physically we may have looked a little different.

I used to hate it, I used to feel it. But it would be my father who would say, "Don't pay any attention to them. They don't know any better." In fact, from then on I used to come right out in class, "What have you got that's different from me?" I was pretty nervy at that time, yeah. My parents were the first ones to have girls old enough to go to college, so I'd be the only one to go to college who was an Okinawan amongst the group.

And then when I was teaching too, I saw this colored fellow who was an excellent teacher. I just couldn't help but feel that maybe he'd been going through the same thing I'm going through. And I had such sympathy for him. When I found out he was an excellent teacher, I said, "How about coming to McKinley?" I headed the department at the time. I brought him in. I felt for him, I really did.

HARUKO

Haruko was born in Okinawa, where her father was a teacher, and moved to Hawaii when she was seven. She married, raised three sons, and worked for many years as an insurance agent.

I was born in Okinawa, which is located in southern Japan. I remember my two older brothers taking me to the beach in Nago, Okinawa.

Where I was born, we had beautiful beaches, and the two brothers used to take me to the beach, so I learned to swim very early in life. . . . My father came as a contract laborer, you know, *kanyaku imin*, and he went to Kekaha, Kauai, to work. . . .

My mother was a farm lady, illiterate, but my father had taught school in Japan, Okinawa. And so he encouraged me to learn as much as I could, you know. And he was very happy that I was able to go to school. . . . His idea of learning, especially the language, [was] whatever you speak, whether it's Okinawan or Japanese or English, learn to speak well. . . . And I was known as a girl who tried to be a haole, because I tried to speak as best and naturally. . . . We had some wonderful teachers, Hawaiian teachers. And haole teachers, Polish lady. My father even asked this Polish [to] help me, invite me to her home to show me how things were done, you know, in an American family.

When I came to Hawaii, I couldn't go to Waikiki to swim, but after I started working and we were living in Kalihi, you know, I used to go to the beach every afternoon. And my mother and my mother's friends used to say, "My goodness, what kind of daughter. She goes all by herself. Young girls don't do that." So I was very different from the typical young ladies of that time.

After I came here as a little girl, you know . . . Japanese children are supposed to be quiet and you're not supposed to say very much what you think, so when I went out into the community to see my Portuguese friends and the German people and my Polish schoolteacher and found out that people here say what they think, you know — big change! It's an eye-opener. Oh, I couldn't get over it. It was so different, and imagine telling your friends what you really think about it. . . . So that was very surprising. . . . The Polish or Germans, you know, and Portuguese and Hawaiians, they would say, "Well let's do so and so," — and, oh, I spent all my allowance. I have no money, you know. Japanese having no money is shame. Why should he be shame? So that's one of the first things I taught my boys. Don't be afraid to say, "I can't afford it. I don't have any money." I don't know why Orientals feel that way.

Hawaii is America, isn't it? The freedom to ask questions, the freedom to go and find out if you want to, and there was nobody to stop you, you know? That was amazing. And the freedom to come for help. Over here, if you want to go to school in the worst way, you can find a way. Because they will help. Not everyone, but there is a way. And in

Japan, if you don't have the money, if you don't have the influence, you can't do anything.

We went to Kauai, and he [father] didn't last too long [working in the fields] because he wasn't used to working in the hot sun. So the *luna*, overseer, that time was kind enough to give him a job of a water boy. Distributed water to all the workers. . . . After a couple of years, he came back to Honolulu. His goal was always to have some kind of a business, so he opened a grocery store, a store that had little groceries and little dry goods, and he did okay. . . .

My father had died by the time I was in eighth grade, and one younger brother died shortly after that in an accident, so one brother in particular I thought I had to support. . . . So I thought the shortest way to getting a job was business school, so I went to Phillips Commercial. Business courses, English and related subjects. I went two years, and then I got a job. I got different jobs. Before that was kindergarten — I taught kindergarten. Kindergarten was after I was married.

My mother was very much against my marriage. When I got married to my husband, she was very much worried and against it because she said he didn't finish his high school. Almost finished, but he didn't quite finish it, and he had no parents here. They had gone to Okinawa after working here for a while. He had no job, no money. He had a job, but she couldn't see the future of him. I was idealist, and is he a good man, an honest man, willing to work and learn? What's wrong with that, you know? It was very different those days, because people didn't go off and get married to somebody [just anybody]. . . .

You see, there was this very sad, very bad parting that was on my mind. I left my brother, my younger brother, with my mother, and he was to write to me, how things were with mother, you know. Mother was a widow then. And so my brother wrote to me that mother was kind of ill. So I told my husband I must see my mother. So he said, "Okay, why don't you take the next boat?" No plane those days. . . . And I found out that by the time we went there, my mother had died. . . . And my family, my relatives, all thought I was terrible not to have come, and to have caused Mother's heartache and worry, you know. So that was the beginning of blaming myself, of my nightmare. . . . I couldn't sleep, and so when Miss L. discovered me, she said, "Gee, I don't know why, but you look terrible." . . . Doctor after doctor, we found nothing was wrong. . . .

Funny, at one time you're more American, and then as you grow older you revert back to your roots. But I was very, very Americanized in my relationship with my children, with my friends. But my relation to my husband was [as a] Japanese wife. Yeah, very submissive. . . . The happiest time was when the children, one by one, finished their college, my goal. I had happy times.

I taught kindergarten. I had an interview. And Miss B. says, "You don't have college degree and you don't have any experience, and all you have is a business office experience," and she was kind of reluctant. But Miss L. says, "She could learn," so I went to university on my own time to take up courses in child education and preschool basics, you know. And I taught there seven years. Was interesting. I had to brush up on my Japanese because a lot of mothers didn't understand English. They were first generation, you see. . . .

In Depression days, we didn't have money for the rent, so I thought about my income and educating the boys and saving money for a house and all those things, you know. And I said, "Gee, I can stay here for another ten years, and the most I could get was maybe $50 or $60."

So I was thinking about it, and I discussed this with several of my friends. And what can I go into, you know, at my age and my limited education? And one friend said, "How about some kind of sales?" I said, "I like sales, but what?" "Oh, how 'bout things like insurance?" . . . So I didn't resign, but I asked for an interview at this company and got into insurance. I knew that I could make $150 to $200 a month minimal. I had to learn how to get organized and manage, you know. So it [working] does teach you, because those are requirements. . . . My husband had quit service station, and he was in sales, too. Appliance sales. But he wasn't as motivated as I was, so he didn't do too well. But enough. . . . Going into insurance was the biggest decision, 'cause it was a time when I was able to plan what I wanted to do and . . . This job of mine has helped me to do a lot of things that I never dreamed was possible. I wouldn't have had the chance. . . . We go to conventions in Chicago. I was the only woman in the group of about twenty-five or thirty young people.

I felt a little bit of that [discrimination], but I was the type that disregarded that, you know. And in the end, people got to know me and they didn't . . . I didn't experience that discrimination. Probably I knew it and I disregarded it intentionally. . . . Personally, as I told you, I wasn't discriminated that much, but I was made to feel that Okinawa was inferior for some reason or another. "There's no value in their music or dance," you know. I have a brother in California who is well educated. He has studied Okinawan history and poetry and the music and everything. He plays the *samisen* [a three-stringed instrument]. So I asked him, "Is it true that Okinawan culture has no value? In the historical sense?" He says, "Oh yes? Whoever told you that? Have you ever listened to Okinawan music? The words?" He says, "I told you there was music and dance and that Okinawan culture is something that you could really be proud of." So my idea was changing.

My mother sang and she danced. They were beautiful. You know, in Okinawa there's a dance called *kachashi*. This is different from the formal historical dances they had, you know. . . . There are beautiful dances of Okinawa, the modern and the ancient ones. In the *kachashi*, everybody participates individually, together. How you perform is up to you. It's all individual. And my mother was a beautiful *kachashi* dancer. So as a little girl, I asked her one day how to be able to dance like [her]. And she said, "Child, *kachashi* is something that nobody can teach you because it's a dance from your heart." Your heart dances with it, you know. The movement is according to the rhythm. The other part is your heart.

VIII   Koreans

The Politics of Immigration

Korean immigration to Hawaii occurred within a single decade, 1896–1905, and movement was more strongly tied to international political and diplomatic issues than was immigration from other areas. Sino-Japanese relations, Russo-Japanese relations, the halting of Chinese immigration to the United States, and the Japanese colonial occupation of Korea all figured importantly in the story of Korean immigration.

The story began in 1876, when Japan signed a treaty opening the Hermit Kingdom, as Korea was called, to begin diplomatic relations with the rest of the world. At that time, Korea was in a tributary relationship with China, and Chinese Foreign Minister Li Hung-Chang — to counter the Japanese influence in Korea — mediated immigration negotiations between Korea and the United States. The resulting Treaty of Amity and Commerce, signed in 1882, provided that Koreans who visited the United States "shall be permitted to reside and to rent premises, purchase land, or to construct residences or warehouses in all parts of the country."[1] This treaty paved the way for Korean immigration to the United States and thus to Hawaii, after it became a U.S. territory. No immigration occurred for several years, however, for international political events intervened.

Sino-Japanese rivalry in Korea erupted in warfare in 1894–1895, and although Japan defeated China in Korea, it had difficulty consolidating its control there. One problem was the increasing influence of Russia in Korea. The instability arising from the international rivalry and fighting caused numerous internal and domestic problems for Koreans, and the uprooting of the populace also led many Koreans to move to port cities in search of work. Because of the unrest, they were attracted by the appeals of Hawaiian planters for immigrants to Hawaii. Another precondition for Korean emigration was poverty and a prolonged drought and famine in 1901. The endeavors of Christian missionaries in Korea provided still further impetus for emigration.[2]

The planters were generally happy with Chinese labor, but by the 1890s, they had become concerned that Chinese laborers were leaving the plantations as soon as their contracts were completed. Moreover, by 1897 planters had begun to realize that annexation was impending and that with it would come an end to Chinese immigration. Japanese workers, in addition, were already making demands of the planters and causing more trouble than the planters had bargained for. Once again it seemed that the planters would have to turn elsewhere for a source of cheap labor for the cane fields.

In November 1896, Frederick Hackfield of H. Hackfield & Co. — the German forerunner of American Factors — proposed to President Dole, members of his cabinet, and the president of the Bureau of Immigration that Koreans be imported as a substitute for Chinese and Japanese laborers. The following year, the Hawaiian government rejected Hackfield's proposal to import Koreans for reasons having more to do with international rivalries at play in Korea than with the merits of the case.[3]

The final condition necessary for the Korean immigration was recruitment by planters' agents. While Puerto Ricans were seen as a possible solution to the labor shortage that followed the prohibition of Chinese immigration, the use of Puerto Rican labor was criticized by some as "a hasty and poorly planned move (see Chapter IX)."[4] Thus, the Hawaiian Sugar Planters' Association turned once more to the idea of importing Korean labor.

The planters found that most Koreans could not afford the $50 steamship fare to Hawaii, but at the same time, contract labor was illegal following annexation and the HSPA could not legally advance transportation costs directly. The HSPA therefore hired an agent, David Deshler, and instructed him to establish a bank at Inchon that would loan immigrants money for passage. Through the East-West Development Company, he hired a staff and began recruiting laborers in the port cities. His efforts were facilitated by Methodist missionaries such as George Heber Jones, who advised his parishioners to emigrate to Hawaii. Other Americans in Korea, both diplomats and missionaries, joined the effort to encourage Korean emigration.[5]

The arrival of the first Koreans on the plantations in 1902 pleased the HSPA. One report to the HSPA noted that the immigrants had been

Fig. 8.1. A picture bride, ca. 1910. *Courtesy of Mrs. Rachel Lee.*

in a starving condition in Korea and "seem to be just what our plantations need." The Korean laborers were described in a 1903 report as "a
steady lot of men, accustomed to farm work. They begin well and appear
contented and willing."[6]

The Decade in Hawaii

Because of the economic distress in Korea, the Korean government
also decided to encourage emigration, and in November 1902 it established an emigration office for that purpose. The following month, the
first shipload of Koreans left for Hawaii. Those on board were from
many occupations: One-seventh were peasants; others were coolies,
servants, ex-soldiers, students, and housewives. According to their
Confucian beliefs, the emigrants considered leaving their families un-
ethical; they either took their familes with them or sent money for their
livelihood. Approximately 65 percent of the Korean emigrants were
illiterate.[7]

The first ship to leave was not a passenger ship but a freighter.
Women were put in the same cabins with men. For Confucian-trained
people from a society in which not even a seven-year-old boy and girl
would sit together, the experience was strange, if not shocking.[8]

There is no consensus on the numbers of Koreans who immigrated
to Hawaii during the decade in question. One source lists a total of
7,226 immigrants: 6,048 men, 637 women, and 541 children. Another
report puts the total at 7,394, of which 735 were women and 447 were
children under the age of fourteen. In both cases, the ratio of men to
women was ten to one. The total, whatever the source, was approximately 7,500.[9]

The Korean immigration to Hawaii stopped in 1905, as abruptly as
it began. The reason is to be found in Japanese colonial control of
Korea. The Japanese minister to Seoul notified the Korean government
that Korean emigration to Hawaii was interfering with Japanese emigration, and he told the government that he regarded that as unfriendly.
This Japanese pressure on the Korean government effectively ended
Korean emigration.[10]

Fig. 8.2. Girls wearing Korean costume. *Photo by L. E. Edgeworth. No. CD25227. Courtesy of the Bishop Museum, Honolulu, Hawaii.*

Societies

The first organization to spring up among the Koreans in Hawaii was the church, which became the focal point of the social and political activities of the community. Approximately 40 percent of Korean immigrants were Christians when they arrived;[11] others converted after their arrival. Between December 1904 and September 1907, over twenty Korean organizations were founded in Hawaii. Each of these organizations included among its purposes resistance to Japanese colonial policy and the achievement of political independence for Korea. In 1907, these societies came together for greater strength, and the United Korean Society was formed.[12]

Koreans in Hawaii also organized self-governing bodies on all plantations. In May 1905, the Korean community requested a Korean consul in Hawaii. The response of the Korean government — no doubt influenced by Japanese pressure — was to appoint the Japanese consul as an honorary Korean consul. Japan had just defeated Russia in the Russo-Japanese War and had established a protectorate over Korea. The Korean community, however, did not accept the Japanese consul and continued to appeal directly to the Korean government.[13]

Like the Chinese and Japanese, the Koreans established language schools to maintain continuity of language and culture. Language classes were often taught in Korean churches. Because of a lack of other texts, the Bible was used for teaching students to read and write in Korean. Church bulletins also functioned as newspapers for the Korean community, one of the most important being the *Honolulu Korean Church Bulletin* published by the Korean Methodist Church.[14]

Women

The gender disparity in immigration during this decade — ten men to one woman — was partly alleviated by the importation of picture brides following the enactment of the Gentlemen's Agreement. However, the total number of women to emigrate from Korea did not exceed 1,000 (see Chapter VI).

The obvious value of these early female immigrants in terms of the ratio of men to women was superseded by the Confucian precepts to which the Korean immigrants adhered. Confucianism determined the construction of gender relations between Korean men and women in Hawaii. The Christian faith of these women did not relieve them of the heavy burden of Confucian filial piety, and at times they displayed an overriding sense of duty to family in disregard of personal interests. Bound by the strictures of the Confucian ethic and its androcentric social consequences, these women worked first for their families and only secondarily for individual interests. Like their sisters from other parts of Asia, these women often did double or triple duty, working not only for the welfare and survival of their families but also cooking and doing laundry for bachelors from the old country on the same plantation.

If these women aspired to have an education — even a high school education — they often had to earn their way by working as domestic help for haole families. This was a common pattern in the life course of Japanese girls as well.

From the stories of these respondents, we see a picture of a uterine Korean family, with the husband or father playing a marginal role, often more concerned with concubines, gambling, and drinking than with the welfare of his family. Ruth's story is a particularly poignant example. The women whose interviews follow all took considerable pride in the educational achievements of their children and grandchildren and saw in them some realization of their own aspirations.

Korean women, like their Okinawan sisters, were in a sense triply colonized. Being female and belonging to a people already colonized by Japan, they were thrust into yet another colonial setting. The vestiges of Japanese colonial attitudes persisted in the new Hawaiian setting.

YOUNG HEE

Young Hee was born in Korea in 1900 and came to Hawaii as a teenage picture bride. She had no formal schooling and on arrival did construction work. She later learned tailoring, which enabled her to support five children after her husband deserted the family.

I was born Korea, 1900. I came to Hawaii at sixteen, picture bride. Now eighty-five years old. Born in Ulsan, South Korea. Country girl.

Very poor family, a small family. My father passed away. My mother took care of me, and my uncle helped — my father's brother. All the family gathered to help, Oriental. My mother, after a while, moved away to Pusan. You know Pusan? She wanted to take me to Pusan, but my uncle, Oriental-style, he didn't want me to go to Pusan. He said, "If you go to another place, to Pusan, you won't have money, and I won't be able to help. Why do you want to go to Pusan? Better stay in Ulsan, better to stay in the family, not marry outside and cause shame to the family." Oriental style was very hard, you know. We couldn't change our minds in the olden days. But my mother was very young, and she took me and went away. In olden days, you couldn't go to another man's house, and it was my father's brother's house, so I supposed to stay in it. You have enough to eat, you don't have to go to another house. My uncle came, and he took me back. "My niece is my daughter," he said.

My mother changed her mind and wanted to get married again. It was alright — she was still very young, you know. But in old Korean style, once you marry, you don't marry again if you're a respectable lady. That was the style in China and Korea. I don't know about Japan. She was supposed to stay with her husband's brother, but she didn't want to. She worked very hard in the rice fields and bean fields, and I think she had no fun. Now I understand. But at that time I didn't understand. My mother was pregnant, and she wanted to get married again. My uncle came and said, "I'm going to take my daughter back" — me. My mother said no. I was six or seven years old at the time. My uncle said she couldn't keep me. My mother couldn't do anything. He took me back to Ulsan. So I grew up in my uncle's family.

But I was very sad, I cried a lot. But I was so young I couldn't do anything. . . . No, I couldn't run away back to Pusan. So just cried a lot. My mother and I walked at night, without train or car, all the way to Pusan. We stayed at a woman friend's house in Pusan. Then my uncle came and said, "You can't keep her. I'll keep her myself." My mother couldn't do nothing. In Oriental style, women could do nothing — they were not independent. He said, "You come with your uncle. . . . You are my brother's girl. I'll raise you. When you grow up, you'll marry." So I was raised at my uncle's house.

My uncle taught me to read Korean a bit. At that time, girls didn't go to school in Korea. There were no local schools. Only Seoul had schools at that time. So my uncle taught me to read. In those days, not many women went to school. Country people said it was not good for girls to go to school in those days. So I learned to read a little.

Every year my mother came to see me — about once a year she came. She brought candy and cookies, Japanese-style, and came to see me. And when I saw her, I cried and cried. Then my auntie held me so I wouldn't follow my mother. Every year for three or four years my mother came to see me. After four years, I didn't cry anymore. She just brought me something to eat. I didn't love her anymore after four years — it was just gone after four years. She loved me, but I didn't have any feeling for her anymore. I wasn't happy. I loved my auntie instead. Now I preferred my auntie instead. My mother always came every year, but I didn't cry anymore, nothing.

When I was about fifteen she came, and I was already grown. I was very tall, you know. . . . She said, "I have something to discuss with you." Every time she came, she couldn't come to the house, you know. My uncle wouldn't like that. But I wasn't happy to see her — it was just that she was my mother. She gave me candy and something always. My auntie said, "It's better if you don't come because every time you come, she cries." Oriental style was very hard in the olden days, not like American style. Independence is good, huh? Very good. . . .

I didn't know my husband, didn't love him. My mother very young and made the arrangement. She was a widow. I don't know how old my mother was, but she was very young. . . . One day when I was fifteen, she [mother] came again, and my neighbor called, my mother's old friend. My mother said, "Say, I found a good place for you to go to." She said, "Here at your uncle's house, you'll only end up working as a farmer." This is hard work, in the rice fields. We had to work in the rice fields with the men, the women too. "If you stay here, you'll have to work very hard. You go to America. There, the women don't work," she said. My mother was no liar. I came here at seventeen and I went to work at Captain W.'s house in Honolulu. I went to take care of the baby. . . . She had only one baby but she didn't work . . . take care of the baby. She was really nice to me, and my husband was the cook there. . . .

When my mother suggested I come to America, yes, I wanted to come. I could read and write even though I had never been to school. I thought I was lucky to have come to America. I like it here. I got used to it. I can be independent here. In Korea, in the old style, women couldn't be independent. I never, never wanted to return to Korea. I couldn't go anyway. I had my children. . . .

My husband was from Seoul, not Ulsan, and he went to America. He wasn't a farmer, but an educated man. In Seoul everybody went to school. I don't know how many years, but he could write. My husband was a smart man. I saw the picture [before she married him] but I didn't know him, I didn't love him. Nothing — I was only sixteen and didn't know anything about men. But my mother said, "You go. You won't be a farmer, you won't have to work hard." She said, "It's just like Heaven!"

. . . For one year I didn't work. I stayed at home the first year. At that time, every time a boat came in — a Japanese boat — when I heard the horn I quickly went inside and cried. My husband was happy, but I wasn't happy. I didn't love my husband, you see. I didn't like it at night. It was alright in the daytime, but when nighttime came I wasn't happy. . . . Olden days, I was a country girl. Let him go, I thought, I'll just take care of the babies. I didn't scold him. . . . My husband was eighteen years older than me. He was happy to have children, and everything was alright in our living. . . . Two or three years after coming to Hawaii, I had a baby. I had four sons and one daughter. My children are all good children. . . .

We went to a pineapple plantation [for] two or three years. Always on the move. The store where my husband worked went broke, so we had to leave. Customers didn't pay cash. It was a credit system. So the store went broke because people couldn't pay. Koreans were very poor. So he took a truck and tried to sell in the countryside after the store went broke. Korean staples, dried peas come from Korea.

[At Captain W.'s house] I got paid $13 a month for taking care of a haole baby. . . . I learned how to make cake. She was so nice to me [haole housewife]. It was easy work and very nice. . . . We didn't clean the house. I worked there two or three years taking care of the baby. I was just eighteen. Then the captain had to go away to war, and his wife cried. I thought of her as if she were my mother.

And my husband found a job working with the boats at Pier Fourteen. I did the laundry for the boat captain. I think my husband worked there eleven or twelve years. Then the war was over and the Depression hit. Orientals lost all their good jobs, you know. At that time, my husband had $50 a month, so we had no worries. . . . It was big money. Soldiers came back from the war to face Depression. . . . There were no jobs, so it was worse for Koreans. Even American citizens had no jobs, returning soldiers. So my husband lost his job.

So we moved to Hilo. So I tried my hand at a small laundry . . . but I couldn't make money at it. After a while, I found a tailor. I asked my husband, "What are you going to do? I don't have a job, you don't have a job." . . . So he said, "I think we have to go to a sugar plantation." I said, "No, I don't want to go to a sugar plantation. I want to learn to do tailoring," I told my husband. So he said, "Alright, go and talk to a tailor." . . . I asked, "How much do you pay?" He said, "You work for three months without pay and after that I'll pay you." But I already had two babies. What could I do for three months? I wanted to learn tailoring, better. I could sit down, do clean work — better than washing clothes. That was my idea. My husband said, "How can you learn tailoring? We better go to the sugar plantation." . . . We were so poor then, we didn't have enough to eat. . . .

So my husband went to find a job on the plantation. My husband was a smart man. On payday, they had to count the money in those days. The pay came in a big bag, not in checks the way it does today. At that time, people with no education couldn't count, you see. So the Japanese camp and Korean camp called my husband. They called my husband on payday to count, forty or fifty workers. He used the *soroban* [abacus] and could count quickly. He was paid for that . . . worked for all the Korean people for that kind of work, the uneducated people. Japanese workers on plantations had no education too — the ones that came to Hawaii. His pay was alright then.

I learned tailoring for three months then, without pay. Actually, after the first month, he gave me $20 for the second month. "You're a smart lady," he said, "You can keep $20." So every month I got $20 and could buy rice. At that time rent was cheap — $15 or $16 [for] one bedroom, community toilet.

I raised my children with my tailoring work. I stayed on the plantation. They said, "You're a good lady. You're not wrong, but your husband is wrong." So they let me stay. I cooked, too, for people on the plantation, you know. Boarding cook. I was a pattern tailor, too — made patterns. I made coats too. That kind of work. I took care of my children all by myself. No divorce, no. Never remarried.

We separated when I was thirty-one, yes. Something was a little bit wrong with my husband. He had some trouble. Smoking opium. The government knew about it, so he went into hiding. He always took a little bit of money for the opium. He knows it was no good and thought nobody knew, but someone found out. . . . He was in jail one year, then went back to Korea.

He was in Korea ten years — then there was the Korean War. There was an American ambassador in Korea. He [her husband] went to talk to him. He said he could speak English, and he talked to the ambassador. The ambassador said, "Okay, I'll give you a letter. Your children are American citizens." A letter came to me asking me to help him with money. My heart was already broken. Why would I help him? I was angry! It was over ten years since I had seen him, going on twenty years. What he did was wrong. How many times have you wronged me? It's better if we are separated. I'm alright. . . . My husband went to Korea, and he found my mother. I think he stayed at my mother's house. My mother was very kind. He scolded me for not having money. I worked hard and made money, and he used it and scolded. I didn't want to give him money. I said, "You leave here."

Even if he had stayed here, I would have wanted to divorce him. He went to Korea and didn't come back. He was smart — that's why he went to the ambassador and said how many children he had, American citizens. Children! He didn't take care of them, I did. God helped me to raise them. He was deported because he broke the law. He dealt in opium from Hilo to Honolulu via post office. . . .

The hardest job I did was in Hilo, construction. The other women were small and couldn't do that kind of work with men, but I'm tall and I could do it. It was very hard work. Almost two years, during the war when the young men were all gone to war. That's why I got the job. . . . I worked with men in construction. I wasn't scared to work with the men, nothing. I talked with the men. Women are the same as men. I wasn't scared of anything. . . .

I married in the Methodist church. I go to church on Sunday, every Sunday, sometimes on Wednesdays, too. There were two Methodist churches in Honolulu at the time. . . . My husband didn't go to church. If I talked to him about it, he said, "I no savvy people Christian." That kind of person can't hear what they say in church. I always prayed to God for my children. I wanted my daughter to be well educated. That's what I hoped for her. She became a schoolteacher. . . . God helped me, always God helped me. I pray every day. . . . I enjoy church. Sometimes I enjoy going to another church, too. Sometimes I go to Syngman Rhee church when somebody comes from Korea and talks. I don't miss whenever someone comes from Korea and talks at one of the Korean churches. . . . God has blessed me. My daughter had two sons. One is married, the other will graduate from the university. They are both educated men.

ANNA

Anna was born on a plantation on Oahu. She worked her way through McKinley High School and was awarded a one-year scholarship to college in Ohio. She took her mother back to Korea, became a prisoner of war of the Japanese, and after the war worked for U.S. Army occupation forces. She married an American and had two children.

I was born on Oahu, on a plantation. March 1, 1909. My parents are both from Korea, immigrants. Came in 1901, I think. They are the first immigrants from Korea. . . .

When I was small I had, I think, three brothers and two sisters. Quite a few died in infancy. They died when they was small. . . . [She lived in a] plantation house. The living room was separated from the kitchen and latrine. We had kerosene lamps, a charcoal iron, and logs for firewood. For transportation, we walked, used the plantation railroad, or horse and buggy.

Father worked on the plantation. When he was in Korea he was a scholar. Not a teacher — he just studied. He didn't like the work here, so it was kind of hard for him. He's not that kind of laborer. My mother supported the family. [She did] everything. She can do all kinds of sewing at that time. She sewed for other people. She did laundry. . . . So my mother had to wear the apron strings, you know.

Mother was a beautiful, intelligent, industrious, ambitious, hard-working lady. She was a wonderful cook and all-around seamstress. She was a good Christian and a good businesswoman. My mother hauled firewood on her head from the mountains and carried buckets of water on her head. She was very strict, shrewd, and old-fashioned. She cooked, washed, and ironed for the plantation bachelors. And she took care of the community bathhouse. Her daily work was never done. She worked hard and supported the family. She taught us how to speak and to respect our elders. We were forbidden to talk with boys, after six years old.

Mother got up early in the morning, I don't know what time, but before four o'clock, because she did the cooking for the bachelors, immigrant bachelors. But then in those days, she had to go to the hill . . . mountain — they call [it] the Molokai Koala Mountain Range — and that's where she goes up and picks all the branches of trees and put it on her head — carried it on her head — and bring it down to the kitchen that she was working. That was firewood. And later on, they had firewood company. And during the daytime, all day, washing the laundry. People pay, bachelors, yes, all Korean. And she had to iron and patch up clothing. In the evening, she had to go to the separate wash bath, you know. She had to fill the tub up with water from their well. And she carried the water from the well and she pour it, and she burn the fire and make it warm up. That is all for the bachelors. And work hard like that. In the evening, cooking. She had no help at all. I was too small at that time. I'm the youngest. My oldest sister helped her but not very much. . . .

I worked my way through high school. I did housework and, for the families, baby-sitting in Honolulu. I worked for a haole family. I help my mother . . . whatever money I earned, you know.

I went to Waialua School. I was there when I was in elementary school. Then I came to Honolulu and went to . . . secondary school. I went to McKinley High School. Graduated from there, 1928. . . . Then I found my way, and I went to a college in Ohio. I had friends in Michigan, American friends there in a church. They helped me to get a scholarship. I guess they give for one year. That's all, because I couldn't afford. Mother wanted me to come back home because she was sick. I came back to Hawaii. At that time, I had a married sister who was helping too. We scraped up and tried to do everything what we can.

And I had an opportunity to go to Michigan, and [I] lived with my uncle. He got me a job as a secretary in a small firm, food catering. I worked there as a bookkeeper.

After I came back from Michigan, my parents both wanted to go back to their homeland because they were getting old. My father came first because he was paralyzed that time, and in Korea I had relatives who could take care of him. But later on, my mother thought that as a wife she should be with him, so she wanted to go to Korea. And my sister helped us out, and she and I both got together, and I went to Korea with my mother . . . 'cause my mother was blind. She could see a little bit, but . . . So she want to go back to my father, and I brought her back to Korea . . . and got the family together. . . .

So I brought my mother back to Korea. . . . I stayed there and found a job working for the missionary institute. I got a job working for Chosun Christian College. It was a Presbyterian missionary school for boys. And I worked there until the war broke out — world war. During the wartime, I was taken by the Japanese as a prisoner of war because I was working for the American missionaries. . . . So I was a prisoner of war for about two years, I think. I was a house prisoner. . . . All kinds of mistreatment. . . . I have trouble with my hearing because the Japanese slapped me all the time. . . . I'm suffering with lots of this mistreatment. I was in jail several months. . . . Just enough food to keep you alive. Rice and a little cabbage pickle. . . .

My father died during the war. I came back right after. Occupation troops came, and I was working for the federal government as a War Department worker for Korea. . . . So I got married to my husband in Korea. . . . I married an American. He was a civilian working for the War Department. And he got into an accident. I had two daughters. One was born in Seoul, Korea, and the other was born in Honolulu. My husband deserted us a long time, because you know how men are — fickle. They just run around. . . .

I came back to Hawaii. I was living a hard life with my two children. By that time, my husband deserted us. He didn't come back. He went back to the mainland. He went to see my mother-in-law, and she live in mainland, Minnesota. That's where she was living. And she wanted me to stay with her with the little girl I had at that time. I was pregnant at that time, pregnant with the second one. She wanted me to live with her, but I didn't want to stay there. I wanted to get out. People there were strangers to me, so I wanted to come back to Hawaii because I had an older sister living here at that time. . . . Later on, with the second daughter, I found a place to live by myself, in Honolulu.

Later on I went to the Kaneohe Library. I worked for the State Department in Kaneohe. Then I was transferred to the Washington Intermediate School in Honolulu. . . . So at that time I got hold of my husband, and he was trying to help us. I lived like that for many years. He never did come back. . . . I gave my daughters whatever they wanted . . . As much as possible — but I think I gave them too much freedom. But, anyway, I had hard time with them. . . . I had hard time to train my children to be old-fashioned and to follow the old-fashioned ways, but they wouldn't listen. They don't even eat Korean food. They like bad food. . . .

My sister is a Jehovah Witness. And you know how Jehovah Witnesses are — very strict. They don't associate with outsiders very well. She wanted to convert me to Jehovah Witness. Follow her ways, she said, and all that. But I couldn't follow her ways. . . . I'm a Methodist, but I was hired by the Presbyterians. I used to go to church but not now. Nowadays I don't go to church because I'm hard of hearing.

HELEN

Helen was born on Maui. She attended McKinley High and normal school and taught for several years before marrying a professor and raising four sons.

Actually my parents arrived from Korea in 1903, you see, and I never had a grandmother because my granddad had concubines only. . . . He left all his concubines back in Korea. Three generations arrived here. . . . My father was supposed to come by himself because he'd heard that in this place called America the streets were paved with gold, so within a few years you'd become a millionaire and you'd go home, see. So he was coming by himself. Later he told me this story. "Your mother did not say one word. She walked into the *ahn pang* — *ahn* is inner, *pang* is room — so she walked into the inner room and started packing. Didn't say a thing." And my granddad did the same thing, only he said something. . . . Well, anyhow, three generations arrived, and I was born. Three generations arrived — my grandfather, my paternal grandfather, my mother and father, and their two surviving sons. They had already lost five sons from infant mortality. I believe when my mother left the country, when she left the homeland, she left definitely with the idea this is for good. I'm sure in her heart that she knew she was never going to return to Korea. . . . And it happened to be the first group of Koreans that Emperor Yi agreed to let leave the Hermit Kingdom. . . .

They came as laborers, you see, but the saddest part of it was that my father was an absolute great scholar. I did not realize that until long after he died. . . .

See, my parents were the leaders of this group that came on the SS *Mongolia,* and so they were always kept intact. They were sent immediately to central Maui.

The reason they came was famine in Korea. And one of grandfather's concubines set fire to the ginseng fields or something. . . . I don't think my father intended to go back, because when I think of the things they brought with them, like that chest for example . . . I'm sure they yearned — they must have had yearnings — because they did send my oldest brother back. He had consumption. . . .

Central Maui — that's where sugarcane is raised by irrigation. But the point was [that] over in east Maui in Hana there's lots of rain, so they don't need to irrigate. So that's when they started the Kipahulu Sugar Plantation. They sent this whole group, with my parents as leaders. They gave them lumber. They told them to go and choose a spot they wanted, you see. And there was Hana, the big city, and a smaller city. Then two and a half miles away, toward the mountains, they found a choice spot with a stream running, so that's where they built the house. . . . They built their own homes, plantation buildings. The plantation gave them the lumber for the buildings. When the world war broke out, I remember they told us we could move, and they gave us the whole Japanese language school. . . .

Four rooms, and then there was a big dining room and a kitchen behind there, and then my grandfather's room was right there. He had a room of his own. Every morning we would go to see him, and we would bow and ask him in Korean, "Did you sleep peacefully during the night?" Every morning we would kneel and greet him. He had a moustache and beard. I used to braid his beard. . . . I'm forever grateful for him. . . . My granddad said he would last ten more years after coming here, but he lasted twenty years. And for someone brought up in those famine days in Korea, to live that long is wonderful. . . .

Grandfather was a Buddhist, you see. My father became a Christian with my mother, definitely. She became a Christian very early in Korea. Oh yes . . . my mother went to Syngman Rhee's church, the Korean Christian Church. You see, he started it way back, because they were all Methodists to begin with, remember. But the Methodists don't allow you to own your own property. That's the reason Syngman Rhee left the Methodists, because he wanted Koreans to establish themselves, and you have a piece of the good earth to establish yourself. That's why he left the Methodists and started the Korean Christian Church. . . . His statue was placed up there at the Korean Christian Church at Liliha Street. . . . We learned all the hymns, and we used to walk five miles to go to church on a Wednesday evening in Hana. . . .

She [mother] could not speak one word of English. We spoke Korean at home, oh yes. . . . My bridal costume was Korean bridal dress. . . . I borrowed it from the Art Academy to please my mother. . . . No, I didn't speak Korean to my children. . . . Everything I knew, I wanted to teach them, you see, so that they would revere the Korean culture. . . . Even my sons, because they were living in that culture when the idea was [that] if you're an American you speak English. I remember. Even my parents told me that.

When I was a child, we sat, we shared what happened, and we would sing Korean folk melodies, folk songs. This particular one I sang is about "My mother sends me up into the mountains in springtime to dig for the *toraji* root," which is a favorite root, an edible root, and you dig it only in the springtime. And the song says, "Mother sends me up to dig for those, but instead I find a lovely little stream, and I wade in it and finally fall asleep. And sometimes there's a road that leads to the stream and another road that leads to the circus. Sometimes I go to the stream, sometimes I go to the circus." . . .

I remember particularly the prayer meetings we went to when Japan was trying to take over Korea. . . . I remember how we sat up — we had to keep a vigil to pray that the Lord must not let the Japanese take Korea. And we walked from camp five, six, seven miles, all the way down with the kerosene lanterns. There was one Korean church. I have a picture of that church in Hana.

Well, I graduated from eighth grade, you see. And Hana School had a reunion — Hana School graduates from the year 1907 to 1978. Of course there was nobody there from the 1907. Of course I went, for goodness sakes. . . . I went to tell them the story about Hana School graduating class of 1923, because the earliest class that reported was 1954. I think I talked at least two hours. I didn't need a microphone. Oh yes, the whole story of the ten people in the graduating class of 1923. I remembered every single one of them. Two Portuguese sisters, two Chinese-Hawaiian brothers, a brother and sister team, and, of course, my brother and I, Korean. My brother and I went to school together, same grade right from the start. Because they couldn't keep me. When he went to school for the first time, I followed him. I remember going to that school and just thrilled pink to see the desks in a row, and I remember putting my hand on either side and skipping along the rows. And there was one Filipino, yes. I kinda wondered if he were still living. Boy, I would love to see him again!

Then my parents decided that I would go to Kawaiahao Seminary because it's a boarding school. You can stay there. I said no. I made up my mind to go to the biggest school here — that's the high school. "Well, you can't do that," [they said]. The biggest school is a public school, and they don't have dorms. I said, "In a city like this? You can't find a dormitory? There must be." So I went to the library, and the librarian told me about Kaiulani Home. So I went to see. Kaiulani Home was run by two ladies. Miss Flood and Mrs. Warren. And even in my young mind, I felt that maybe Miss Flood wouldn't understand the problems of a little girl. So I asked for Mrs. Warren. And I told her my story. So they let me stay. . . .

I wrote to my father, "You know, there is not a single Korean in this high school. You know, it's a big school. . . ." And the gist of my letter was, "Gee whiz, if I don't meet somebody who speaks Korean, I may forget to speak Korean myself." And you know what his answer was, to show what a scholar and philosopher he was? Still it's in my mind. "Don't worry, the fact that you're Korean will never disappear. You cannot, because it's your face. You are an American, but you are not white. . . . Your face is nonwhite, non-Caucasian." But you know what his advice was? You learn to speak English better than an Englishman. That was his advice. And I swore that I would.

My mother said, "You're going to be a teacher!" She promised God. She had seven sons in a row. "Dear Lord, if you give me a daughter she is going to become a teacher, and she's going to follow in the footsteps of Jesus Christ." . . .

Just about that time, we had no teachers' college here. It was a territorial normal and training school, see? I graduated from McKinley High School in 1927 and I was ready after years of normal and training school. I was ready to teach. . . . And I had a degree from Colorado State Teachers College. This was in Greeley. It's the University of Northern Colorado now. . . .

So I became a teacher, and I did not get married for six years. . . . In those days, everybody who graduated from normal [school] spent at least ten years in the outside islands before they were sent to teach in the city, which was ridiculous. But anyway, that was the way it was at the time, you know. But I wanted to go! I wanted to go. . . . Mrs. F. came to see me during my student teaching and she asked me to teach in her school, so I said I'm going to teach in Paia School, and then I can go to Hana, you see, to see my birthplace. . . . What happened was, I did not go to Hana, see. . . . They sent me as an experiment to this place, the Kawananakoa Experimental School, that was being run according to the precepts of John Dewey. It's still there. . . . Today it's an intermediate school. So the idea was, we were going to experiment. We're not going to send you to the outside islands. We're going to let you go right there to Kawananakoa Experimental School. . . . I was scared stiff. . . . But they said, "You can do it." So I stayed. I had everything packed to go to teach at Paia School. I never did have a chance to go to the country to teach. I wanted so badly to go, really I did. I wanted the experience going back to Maui. Then I got a scholarship after teaching a year at Kawananakoa, and I studied a year and a half and came right back and taught. . . . I've been with the university since 1946, thirty-eight years, something like that. . . . Then I started a business offering professional education services, and I actually had a business for five years.

I never wanted to be anything but a teacher. I didn't even want to get married. No man was good enough for me, believe it or not. And yet I was not an egotistical person. . . .

That's another beautiful story. You know, Hawaii's such a little place, plus the Koreans are a minority. But he didn't know I was alive. I didn't know he was alive until we met one Saturday night. I had come home with my degree, and friends gave me a coming-home party. And whom should I meet but J. Ya, and gee whiz, I thought he was a traveling salesman because he was so articulate! Gee, he was a handsome fellow, too! And he had a little moustache, you know. I just laughed at the moustache, so the next . . . after two dates he cut it off. . . . It's funny — it's such a small place and we never met until long after. He taught at the university. . . .

I went to Korea sixty-two years after my parents left Korea. I remember thinking, you know, funny, I had read as much as I could and I had read about what a poor country Korea was, that the forest was just denuded of all its trees. . . . But I looked, and it was beautiful. The tears just began flowing, you know. It was beautiful. I said, gee! Because I had expected, you know, a very poor, poor country. . . . This is a universal feeling. It's not just me, you see, as a Korean-American woman. It's a universal feeling that you have even centuries after your family has left the homeland. You feel that your roots started there, you see.

RUTH

Ruth was born on the Big Island, attended business school, and, after losing her mother at sixteen, supported six younger sisters and a brother. She worked at several jobs and then went to nursing school.

My parents both came from Korea — they married there and came here in 1903. Due to poverty in Korea. My sister was born 1905, I was born 1908, on Ewa Plantation. . . .

We didn't stay in camp too long. Father and many friends went up to Oahu Country Club area. Gardening. My father planted flowers and vegetables for family use. I don't know how he took them to market. . . . [Maybe] horse and buggy. We lived way up in Nuuanu. . . .

Then we moved to Kalihi and they worked in a dry cleaners. We thanked him for not staying on the plantation. Then he decided to move to Kaiulani School area. Another clothes cleaners. We all helped mother in the cleaners. . . .

As soon as they came to Honolulu, we belonged to St. Luke's Church. Mrs. W., a missionary from England, was organist at St. Elizabeth's. She bought clothes for the children at rummage sales. And she helped my brother buy a car.

I was on my way to McKinley High School to become a teacher. When I reached Fort Street, I went up Fort Street instead of down. My body turned up and I saw Honolulu Business College. I looked up and saw a sign that said "Keep climbing up." So I walked up, and the receptionist said, "What do you want?" I said, "I want to see the principal." She said, "The girls come to study typing, shorthand. Those who pay in advance pay $75 a year. Those who pay by the month pay $8 a month." So I walked home and told my mother, "This school, you have to pay money." Mother asked, how much? "Almost $8." So my mother was able to find just enough to see that I registered. All my friends had signed up at McKinley. I walked every morning to school. Then in June, summer vacation, I worked at Libby McNeill, stenciling department. Twelve cents an hour, and I bought cafeteria lunch. When summer was over, my mother says, "Go back to school and finish." But the principal said there are jobs all over the city, so it's better to go to work now. . . .

After eighth grade, I worked at Dole, 8 ¢ an hour, 64¢ a day. Eight hours. I gave a small manila envelope with my paycheck to Mother. She kept on putting it away. . . . I worked at Libby McNeill summer vacation. Stenciling department, 12¢. . . . After business school, I got a job in a manufacturing agent and stayed there a while. . . . I went to multigraphing school, then got a job at Inter-Island Steamship Company, my first secretarial job at Inter-Island Steamship. . . .

My mother was a perfect mother, perfect angel, beautiful and sweet and kind to her children. . . . My mother never complained. She raised eight children there. Seven girls — the boy was after me, one older sister. . . . We all helped Mother in the dry cleaners. . . . Then mother got sick. She had too many children. Kidney ailment. The doctor recommended she go to hospital. I carried her to photographer's shop, and they took her to Queens' Hospital. They said they had to do surgery. I was only about sixteen. I left her at Queens' Hospital. She didn't come out of anesthesia. She breathed louder and louder. She wanted to see my brother graduate. It was very serious, so I went to get my brother and father, but she passed away Easter Sunday. She must have had some premonition, because she told me [that] in an orange crate she kept money for her funeral expenses. Being the oldest, I said, "Let's go to the hospital." Then, when she died, I took the money to the mortuary. On the day of the funeral I don't know who came, I was so saddened. My older sister couldn't come. She was pregnant and we didn't let her know. I took the brunt of all the worry.

My father told me to give all the kids away. "They're only girls," he said. I didn't want to. I earned $50 a month, 12¢ an hour at Libby. Now at the Inter-Island Steamship Company in 1924 I got my first secretarial job. I had six kids with me. I took the youngest with me to work, two and a half years old and four. Father refused to work for us. . . . What can you do? . . . Then at Palama Settlement I heard I could do multigraphing, typesetting. . . . They asked me to work for them. . . . I had six kids with me and I took the youngest to work with me. . . . Every day for the next three years I took my sister to work with me. . . . The head worker hired me there. They paid $50 a month to start. It was near home . . . I went home at noon to cook lunch for my father. I paid $20 for rent and had $30 left for food and clothing. . . .

My brother finished community college. Our parents worshipped boys, you see. We helped him shine shoes growing up. And he delivered the *Advertiser* for three years on his bicycle. He never complained. He worked so hard delivering papers. We had no time for recreation.

At lunch hour they let me do switchboard [at Palama Settlement], and the nurses would talk to me. I had eight mouths to feed. They said, "You better take up nursing. You can earn $75 a month the third year." So I put $10 in the bank each month. I said, "I think I better see if I can get into nursing school." . . . One of the women there bought clothes from rummage sales for my sisters. I'm very proud that I raised my sisters. I don't tell them my hardships. . . . My little sister slept on a table and I fed her. Every day I took four of my sisters and told them to come to the settlement house at four P.M. I would give them a hot tub bath. And we walked home together. I did the laundry in the bathtub. I was seventeen. I went home to cook lunch for my father. I did the cooking and marketing, besides working.

After four years, I told my brother, "Looks like you got to take over." I wanted to go to nursing school on the mainland. He never offered to contribute. I never asked him. . . . One of my friends said, "Ruth, why don't you go to St. Luke's Hospital, study nursing?" I said

I'd try to get into a school that will pay a little more. I wasn't keen to go to Queens'. I decided to go to San Francisco, so I applied and made arrangements. I always wonder what made me walk up the hill to the commercial school instead of to McKinley. If I went to McKinley, what kind of job could I get? I had no clothes, but two girls from the mainland gave me their two-piece suits. . . . I told my father I'm leaving for St. Luke's. My brother drove me to the pier. My father just played cards with his old fogies every day. . . .

I stayed in San Francisco thirty months. I was twenty, and I had no high school diploma. So I went to night school. . . . I had to get my R.N. . . . We took the exam in San Francisco. Nurses worked hard for their degrees. . . .

So after nursing school I got my R.N. We decided to go to private-duty nursing in Honolulu. Then I got a message from Kula San[atorium]. I caught the next boat and came to Maui and started. It was heavenly, nice surrounding. I got $150 a month.

Then my brother sends a wire — "Father killed accident." I went to the head nurse. I said I got sad news. . . . If I could borrow $300 to bury my father? I did it all myself. My brother didn't help. I had started to send my sister $75 a month. Instead of buying food for our sisters, she was spending it on her clothes. I went to the mortuary, and I got a cemetery plot. I don't know who came to the funeral. Each month I paid back the hospital. To this day my brother and my sisters don't know where the money came from. They don't know what I went through, to this day. . . .

I worked long hours in nursing. I worked at Baldwin High during the war. I was glad to get into high school with lively kids. I worked at Puunene Plantation. They hired me. Then I began insurance and sold products. Women were happy to get the products, and I had so much fun . . . Then this insurance man caught me. My husband said, "Why don't you take a try?" We studied and passed the [insurance] test together.

I met my husband at Kula. A Boy Scout man. The happiest time was getting married to my husband. It made up for all the sad years.

IX   Puerto Ricans

The Politics of Immigration

Two events in Puerto Rico in 1898 and 1899 precipitated the flow of emigration to Hawaii. The first was the Spanish-American War and the resulting dislocation of Puerto Ricans. The second event was even more disastrous: the great hurricane of August 8, 1899, which destroyed the subsistence crops of the majority of the population as well as much of the coffee crop. Following the annexation of Hawaii and then of Puerto Rico in 1900, delegates to Congress from the two new possessions proposed the recruitment of laborers in Puerto Rico for the cane fields in Hawaii as a means of solving mutual economic problems.[1]

Contract labor had just become illegal, so it was not possible for the planters to guarantee passage or provide contractual guarantees for individual workers. The HSPA, nevertheless, sent scouts to Puerto Rico, who reported that workers there were "industrious, moral and law abiding." Some were workers experienced on sugar haciendas, and others had worked in the coffee country, coffee being the major Puerto Rican export.[2] In view of the problems the planters were experiencing with Chinese and Japanese labor, Puerto Ricans, like Koreans, appeared to the HSPA an attractive and feasible alternative.

In Puerto Rico the issue of emigration was debated in the press. Some advocated it as a solution to overpopulation and to the lack of jobs and poverty; others feared that an exodus might threaten the economy or that the workers would be exploited. Charles Allen, the governor newly appointed by President William McKinley, sought to assuage such fears.[3]

For the Puerto Rican peasant, there were not many ways to survive the 1899 economic plight. The great hurricane had caused 3,369 deaths. Many people saw their palm-leaf huts destroyed, their vegetable and fruit crops ruined. The plantations — sugar, coffee, and tobacco —

had suffered such damage that there were no longer jobs. Day laborers were impoverished, and the peso was depressed.[4]

Several decades earlier, in the 1870s, the economic plight of the worker had already stimulated emigration to other islands in the Caribbean and to Central and South America. Therefore, when agents appeared in Puerto Rico in 1900 on behalf of the HSPA, recruits were willing. One especially successful recruiter was Alberto E. Minville, the son of a Puerto Rican mother and an American father. He concentrated his efforts on the coffee-growing areas of the southwest.[5]

Although individual contracts were illegal, HSPA agents in April 1901 posted an agreement for employment that offered free passage, housing, schooling, medical care, and wages for men of $15 per month the first year, rising to $16 the second and $17 the third year. Smaller daily rates were posted for women and children.[6] To most Puerto Ricans, the offer was impressive. To some, it was irresistible.

The first group of immigrants came on board the SS *City of Rio de Janeiro*. Though their final destination was the Pioneer Mill Company in Lahaina, the scene of the recent Japanese strike, the ship docked at New Orleans and the group then traveled overland to San Francisco. During the journey, some of the immigrants left the group to pursue other opportunities. The size of the group had decreased from 114 persons to 56 by the time the immigrants reached Lahaina on December 23, 1900. Within a few months of the arrival, a total of 5,200 people — a number that Governor Allen said was one half of 1 percent of the total population and scarcely a cause for alarm — had arrived in Hawaii aboard several ships, including 2,869 men and boys over the age of twelve. On October 14, 1901, the trustees of the HSPA decided to discontinue immigration from Puerto Rico in accordance with their original plan to import 5,000, and the first phase of immigration was concluded.[7]

Settling In

Conditions on the plantations were less favorable than the immigrants anticipated. What they found was generally *trabajo y tristeza* — work and sorrow. They found variable living conditions, strange customs, a multiethnic population, and few who could speak Spanish. To make matters worse, the arrival of these willing workers from Puerto Rico also served to defuse the demands of the Japanese strikers.[8]

When the immigrants arrived in Hawaii, the HSPA clerks changed their Puerto Rican names to names with Portuguese spellings or to newly invented names. Because they were not really aliens — nor were they yet citizens — no lists of names of these immigrants were preserved. They were classified as Caucasians — unlike the Portuguese — although often they did not look Caucasian. They did not become American citizens until the passage of the Jones Act of 1917, after which they began to be recruited for military service.[9]

Because the Puerto Ricans were listed as Caucasians and were often experienced plantation workers, some became *lunas*. And because they were not bound by individual contracts, they could — and did — freely go from one plantation to the next in search of a small boost in pay or an extra ten minutes for breakfast. Their relative mobility, however, gained them a reputation for being unreliable. Some went to California in search of a better life. In 1902 only about 58 percent of the 1900–1901 male Puerto Rican immigrants were still on Hawaiian plantations.[10]

The Puerto Rican immigrants maintained their traditions and sense of identity and continuity through the food they prepared, music and dance, and their celebration of festivals. The Puerto Ricans were Catholic, a reflection of the years of Spanish rule. Moreover, the first-generation immigrants spoke Spanish though it was spoken to a lesser degree in the second generation. As Catholics, the most important celebration of the religious calendar was Navidad, Christmas Day. Serenading during the Holy Season, once widely practiced, has virtually disappeared since World War II.[11]

Music and dance were a central part of Puerto Rican culture, one of the brighter features in lives otherwise marked by hardship and struggle. After an arduous week of manual labor, the Puerto Rican immigrants looked forward to Saturday night dances. These dances were features of urban life in the 1930s and 1940s.

Immigrants brought with them three musical instruments: the *quatro*, which was developed from the Spanish guitar; the *quiro*, which was fashioned by carving one or two holes on one side of a gourd and shallow grooves on the other; and the *maracas*, round gourds hollowed out, dried, and filled with beans or seeds.[12] Parents and grandparents

Fig. 9.1. Five generations of women. *No. CP77304. Courtesy of the Bishop Museum, Honolulu, Hawaii.*

taught their children, most often boys but sometimes girls as well, to play the *quatro*.

Their song, dance, and folk poetry sustained and entertained the Puerto Ricans on the plantations. Many of the immigrants, even some who were illiterate, composed *decimas*, Spanish poems of ten lines that they sang to musical accompaniment. The poems were initially sung in Spanish, but English and Hawaiian words later crept in as workers labored beside Hawaiian- or English-speaking hands in the fields. Early *decimas* relate their feeling for the homeland they left behind, tell of the hazards of the journey, and describe the land in their new home. The singing of *decimas* and storytelling were major forms of amusement in the days before television and movies. Folk tales relayed in *decimas* about the deaths of young children and about witches who assumed human form also preserved tradition and enchanted children. The music that accompanies the Spanish lyrics of the *decima* is usually repetitious — to the point of monotony to the untrained ear.[13]

Women

Puerto Rican women worked in the fields initially, as did Japanese and Filipina women. Like those women, they also devised survival strategies as their families grew. The Puerto Rican women we met were imbued with a strong Catholic faith and a sense of service to others. The importance of religion to these women was reflected in the fact that many of them concluded statements they made with "Thanks to God." Whatever their financial status — and they were not well-to-do — they articulated a sense of responsibility for helping others. Their mothers had served in the camps as midwives, in the absence of trained nurses or doctors. Some of their mothers were Mothers of Mercy, who worked through the church to help others.

They also learned from their mothers numerous needlework skills: knitting, crocheting, embroidery, and sewing clothing for families and friends. Some of this handwork provided basic necessities or augmented family incomes and part of it embellished their clothing and homes.

When they were not caring for their own families, they cooked, sewed, laundered, and ironed for bachelors in the camps. Some of the first-generation women worked in the fields as well. The women worked for long hours, and the requirements of survival left them little time for refinements. Nevertheless, they retained some of the Spanish Catholic traditions they grew up with, such as the proscription that girls should be, if not cloistered, at least chaperoned when in mixed company.

Life was not all drudgery for these Puerto Rican women. They were self-sufficient in entertainment, as in the rest of their lives, and when they found spare moments, they enjoyed music, singing, and dancing. As one repondent who raised a large family put it, "We had no TV those days. We used to sing. We had our own choir."

MARIA

Maria was born on Maui. She had to leave school after less than six years so that she could help raise several siblings. She and her Filipino husband had two children, but she also raised the children of relatives. In addition, she worked at several jobs.

I was born April 19, 1903, on Maui. I lived on Maui all my life. I traveled, yes I did, but back to Maui again. I love Maui. My parents were born in Puerto Rico. They came here 1901, immigration. . . . I was born 1903. They brought my grandmother with them, on my father's side. Grandma passed away before my mommy came to Hawaii, but she left many sisters. You wanna know the reason my grandma came? They had a terrible typhoon in Puerto Rico before that, and people was having a hard time. They didn't have food or anything like that. It was the biggest and hardest typhoon they ever had. . . . [In] 1901 when my parents came, that's the first Puerto Ricans. The second was in the twenties. I cannot remember, '22 or '23. Nothing between that, that I know.

This is what my grandma told. That she knew that my father was going away. . . . She told me that she was living a poor life, like my mother was. This is exactly how my grandma told me. They had this flood, and there were hard times and all that. So she heard that my father was going away too, see. So when the immigration truck was coming down . . . I went to see the immigration office, and the truck, how they put them in, and the building was still there twelve years ago, but nobody goes in it now. [They just go] to look at it. And I could see the galvanized iron on top. That's where they put them — then they go in the boat. My parents were coming down, and my grandmother was walking toward them with her two sons, and they met on the way and stopped. My father said to the man in Spanish, "Stop the car," or wagon, whatever they were riding. They stopped. Then my father said, "Where are you going, Mommy?" And she told him, "I'm coming with you and Tina. Because you folks going to Hawaii, because I don't know where's that, and I'm not gonna leave you. I'm going with you folks." And then my mother said, "Why not?" And then they hugged each other and kissed. She got in the wagon and said, "I'm going where you go. And I'll take my two boys with me." Because my grandmother was young then. She had one bundle, whatever it was. She lived a poor life, a very poor life.

Grandma was a widow — she was a widow twice. A very young lady, I remember, she was white and blond hair. She never got married anymore because she told me she went to the house of God and said, "God help me. I don't want no more men in my life." Up to the day she died, she was away from men. Must be happy because she got married twice. Not only that, she said she didn't want more men, she was going to raise her two sons, last sons. . . .

My grandma was a first-class cook. Oh yes, I learned from her and from my mother. We still keep the tradition. The special one is *pasteles*, and then you make brown rice, *ganduri* rice. That's very special in Puerto Rico. And chicken, *con pollo*, and *sopas*, I ate in Puerto Rico . . . made out of chicken, not out of pork. Make thin noodles, spaghetti, and put oregano and put *comino* [cumin] and things like that in it. I learned all that from my mother. And I have one granddaughter, and she follows me in everything that I can cook. The one that takes the tradition, she cooks on holidays. . . .

My father was one of the ones that helped make the immigration come to Hawaii. When he landed, he became foreman right away on the plantation. *Luna*, they called it. HC&S [Hawaii Commercial & Sugar] . . . My mother was what they called Mother of Mercy among the Puerto Ricans. You like to help. . . . She used to be midwife in Puunene, you know. And a dressmaker. . . .

My mother was a great help to me. . . . My mother lived separate in a big house. You know, the plantation always gives big houses for the *luna*. That's why. But at first, when they came from Puerto Rico, it was sad. I remember that first house we were living. It was hard to get milk. Not like today. Very hard. You know, we used to eat in the morning — wake up and drink half a cup of coffee with one sweet potato. Because my father planted — he took time to grow. Flour, they wouldn't give you pure flour, just medley from the pigs, mixed up with flour. And brown bread. We used to eat brown bread. We called it *midlin*. I don't know what it was. Dinner we always had — poor food, whatever it was. I don't go boasting around like some people, saying, oh, we had this . . .

There was no mangoes, those days. I know in the haole clubhouse they had a mango tree and a pear tree, and you cannot pick them. In Puunene they had it. Only haoles could go. When they opened the second haole clubhouse. It's the only one I remember, because I was a small girl. And the teachers in school taught us how to make one ring like that and then put in paper flowers. And we went to Puunene: "Good morning, and how do you do? We came all the way from Puunene School to sing a song to you." And we bowed. I remember that song. "Oh, we are the sunbonnet babies. We came all the way from school."

I went to night school. I used to live by the Japanese school, so we went to night classes. I studied English. Not the writing, the writing I learned in public school. I studied nursing at home, correspondence. I kept on learning. No, I didn't go to high school. High school was in H'poko . . . transportation from Kahului. And how could I go when my mother had so many children? In summertime I worked in the cane field, when I was about thirteen, fourteen years old. To save. You know, that was wartime [and] schoolchildren would go and do the best they could. For $13 a month — how you like that?

I remember when I was going to school, every weekend I had to go clean my grandma's house. I used to go in the afternoon, help her wash dishes. They used to cook outside, you know, on the plantation. She cooked for about six men. She was smart lady. After school — not much homework those days — I would go help her wash the copper tins. And on Saturday, the water run by the ditch, I would go help her wash the *kaukau* [lunch] bags. . . .

I never was allowed to go swimming. None of us. No swimming. I don't know how to swim. None of our three sisters know. The boys could learn in the ditch if they wanted. How could my mother, with all this bunch of children, let us go down the road like crazy people? My mother was a very particular woman. The park's so near. We could never see baseball. This is not for girls, the way she was raised up. . . .

Oh dear, I had five brothers and three sisters, but one passed away. . . . Oh dear, only two sons, but I worked hard, raising other people's children. Oh, my brothers' children. I had two brothers divorced, so I helped them out with their children. I worked very hard. My brother had three. Wait, when I took his children in, there were three boys and one girl. Yes, I raised them until — the girl was three — she graduated high school. . . . My husband was sick already. . . . He told me to take in the children. . . . The son wanted them to live with him, but they were not fit to keep these children. I wouldn't let them go. But the boys, I had to let them go. But they came back to me after that. The stepmother wasn't good to them. . . . I lived in Honolulu a year and seven months because of these children. I raised two sons, three boys, and one girl of my brother, and not only those. I love children, see. I love children. . . . That's my grandson next door. He's German–Puerto Rican–Filipino, and I raised his sister too, for two years and a half. She was the most beautiful little thing. I don't know how that mother could part with her.

Oh my goodness, listen. If I'm gonna tell you from the beginning . . . and I can put my right hand to God and tell you. My mother was a type that loved children. Ah, dear me, she had five boys, eight girls, ya. Plus that she raised up two girls from somebody else. . . .

My first husband was Filipino. . . . Second, I didn't marry that man. I didn't marry in my life, never. I stayed almost ten years widow before I accepted this other man. Puerto Rican. But I didn't marry him. I didn't marry him because when I found out something wrong, I wouldn't marry him. Well, he was divorced about five years. But I wouldn't marry him for nothing. I'm a good Catholic, you see. He used to drink too much. . . . I didn't marry him, poor man. . . . But I still take care of him. A very sick man, very sick.

At first when I was widowed, I was gonna give them up [children]. And I wanted to go as a nun. I never expect to marry. I wanted to become a nun. But I didn't because Father D. told me that what is more worth is the work that I am doing, and stay home and take care of those three boys in my house, and the girl. So he advised me not to leave the Islands. Stay and raise up these children. . . .

I kept on helping the Red Cross — sewing you know we do. Sewing and knitting, you know, because I was in the sewing department. I was a dressmaker, not to brag about it. I was really a dressmaker before the Japanese began to make a business as dressmaker. Everyone would come to me. How cheap! Fifty cents I believe it was to make a dress for the children, and the highest price was a dollar. Stay home night and day. And then handwork, you can see that there. And not only that. I used to crochet and embroider in my spare time and all that. My mother taught me.

I used to help my mother out when I was married. Midwife. Many, many children were born under our care. Not one died, thank the Lord. Not one. There was one case was very hard, so they called for the doctor, and he came and helped. My mother said, "I'm not a licensed woman. . . . And then he said, "Lady, we don't need a license, but you have done wonderful work in the camp." We didn't have camp nurses then. No doctors. You gave birth at home. . . . One time my mother knew it was coming out wrong. It was the neck. It come sideways. . . . She knew about that. I didn't know anything about it. That interested me to take Chicago School of Nursing. I studied in the book. . . . I worked for the Red Cross three years before the war break out. . . .

I would interpret sometimes for the camp nurse when she would come to the camp, to my camp. She always stops in my house. . . . This is God's truth I'm telling you. I was the highest-paid widow in the plantation. I was getting pension — $65 a month from the plantation. Before he died, he made me promise not to keep up my dressmaking. But quietly I used to help people in sewing. And I couldn't collect Social Security when I was young. [There was none.] So then I took laundry . . . had a haole lady, she used to bring. Schoolteacher. Start with two [baskets] because she loved the way I iron clothes. So well ironed. She fooled me, the teacher. She bring me about two baskets of clothes and then she wants [to pay] only $10 a month. . . . I did laundry for nine people. And you know how much a month? For each people, $6 a month. That's how I could keep these kids, my brother's. I call them my kids because I raised them up, my brother's children. . . . My husband was sick, you know. For a while I had to do something to earn more money. Plus my sewing. . . .

Then I went work with the navy in the laundry. I took my examination — I passed. Floor lady. Being that I had a good reputation from the Red Cross and all the third day they called me for packages. Wrap packages. They taught me in the Navy. . . . They put me for inspector, because I could dispatch ladies. Being a Puerto Rican, you do good ironing. . . . Go over white uniforms, see the spots.

One of my brothers, the youngest one, was a priest. I didn't want him to be a priest. Being a great religious boy. I wrote him a letter, try to live a life for himself. But he was chosen by God . . . this I can say, he was chosen by God. . . . Because this boy of mine, he wanted to be a priest, and he seen something. One priest with one woman. All my kids that I raised up, I sent them to learn about the church, about the things of God. And this one didn't want, so I wouldn't tell him to go. You do what you think is right. I didn't force. . . . St. Joseph, but I cannot go to church now. The last thing I have in my heart is about the church. For two months now I wanted to go forward. I wanted to go out with the church. My church is in my heart, like my mother used to teach us. Your church is in your heart. If you cannot do right, don't go to church, because our church is in our heart.

My brother would go and kneel down by my mother's feet and ask for her blessing if he don't come back [from war]. And my mother said, "Go with God." The same thing she did to the priest. My mother was very strong. Half-Indian. . . .

That's the saddest day in my life when they bombed Pearl Harbor. And I had five brothers in there. . . . You know, America wasn't prepared for that war. So we had hard time. I was brave lady all my life. I met some sassy soldiers too. I said, "I have my son in the Pacific, and if he'd do what you're doing, I'd be ashamed of the American flag." Cool them down. I worked in the navy yard over here. . . .

Whatever I had, I spent with them [children]. Now, if somebody come to my door, if it's welfare or whatever, I would give a dollar. I would give a little. I keep some for me. But before, I would give all. My mother would give. And then I had a brother like that. She was Mother of Mercy. I did too. You see, in Puunene they had . . . You see, if these old ladies were dying in the camp, I would help. In the night. I took it more after my husband passed away.

Now I'm going to tell you a short story. Japanese used to call me gifted mother. Gifted Mother. Even now, Japanese come to me sometimes for prayers, or younger women have troubles. They ask me, broken homes, for advice like that. I enjoyed helping others. Oh, there's a little girl cripple, Kula Sanatorium. Go and ask her about me. From the day she was born, I went visit the mother. I know the whole history. Every time I cook brown rice, I would send her and mother a little bowl. She had father and brothers and sisters, and they don't hardly go to visit. I go to Kula San[atorium]. . . . Because always if people ask me for something, I like to help. It's funny, but I'm that way. I always think of others. . . . But if I had to live all over again, I wouldn't change my life, because I've been so good to my grandchildren. They are all so good in return to me, the nicest grandchildren. And, thank God, even if they have hard luck, they always come.

ROSA

Rosa was not able to attend school because her parents could not provide clothing or spare her from household chores. She raised eleven children and one grandchild in the plantation house where she still lived at the time I met her.

I was born in Puerto Rico, October 23, 1899. My husband arrived in Hawaii 1901. First in Kohala on the Big Island. I was twenty days old when I left Puerto Rico by ship. I don't know how many days the ship took to get here. I came with my mother. My father didn't come. He was supposed to come, but he didn't like to come. She never did tell me why.

You know, that time they no used to get married, just common law. So she [mother] find another husband and get together, and then she start to get the other children. She had from my father just one. Then from the other man she had three. Three boys. Then we came to Koloa. And then from there she caught another husband. She had three husbands. That one was the last one, and then she passed away. My mother passed away young. I don't remember how old she was. I was already married — I had my third child when she passed away. And she got this man, and this man used to be alcoholic too, you know. She used to work, and most of the time he used to take the money away from her, you know. He beat her up. Yeah, beat her up. My mother had a mean life before she died. . . . I used to be scared of him. After she passed away, he took another wife.

My mother used to go work to the other neighbors and make little money to support us. Housework, cook, wash. Just to support us. Some people, they don't give money — they give food. They could afford to help her 'cause she help.

She [mother] never send me to school. I didn't go to school. That's why I can't write. Well, I was home all the time. And that time, you know, we were short of clothes and she don't have the money to buy clothes. Plus, you know, I never admit was that poor way, you know. Not enough money. Sometimes we was short of food too, you know. We didn't use to wear shoes. I remember the day I wear shoes — only when I get married. They had a hard time to find shoes for me because, you know, my feet were so big. Even when I was raising my children, many things I couldn't give them because he [husband] was working on the plantation. His salary was very small. And at that time he was foreman, and then he was working so hard. Only $70, the whole month. . . . I have three children that went to college. And I have a son working as schoolteacher, and his wife is a schoolteacher there.

I stay with my husband. I live sixty-six years with him . . . before he passed away. He was ninety-two years when he passed away. So I gonna be eighty-five. I was young. He was a good man, and he wasn't alcoholic, and he was the kind of man to respect and to raise the children in a nice way. Not to talk about him, but he used to be spoiled. Even my daughter like to come and take care of him [but] he never like to. Have to be me, everything.

I had eleven children, and I raised one grandson. I figure twelve, you know what I mean? . . . When I go to Honolulu and my sons tell me this way, "Mama, I can't raise children like you folks used to raise" — 'cause you know the kids today, they tell their parents what to do — I'm ashamed to tell, but I have very nice children. . . . I count sixty-five grandchildren and great-grandchildren. And now I don't know how many great-grandchildren, because we can't keep track. Too many . . .

Sometimes my other daughters-in-law tell me . . . "Mama, I'm not gonna spoil you son just like you spoil the father." So I say, "Well, that is up to you. You folks can [be less spoiling] because my sons already, you know, more cooled down, but my daddy used to get, well, his temper." Bad temper. Everything was bothering him. But he was alright, you know. So we get along sixty-six years. I remember the last days, couple years, he was very nice to me. He let me go out, and he used to stay home. . . . I couldn't go out before that. He wouldn't let me go. And if I go even — I'm ashamed to tell — even my neighbor . . . I used to go to visit . . . oh, when I come home, oh, the big noise! So I just keep my mouth shut. 'Cause you know what happen to some women. Some women just start with the husband. The husband say one word, and they say two, and that's how they get tangled. . . . But I used to be that quiet. . . .

Sad time was, you know, plenty of my children was sick children. They was sick. Sometimes we thought they was gonna pass away, so sick that they was. I go to the hospital . . . Well, in my whole life I don't used to get too much happy because I used to have my children sick. And my! You know. So not used to be so happy for me.

Well, the first marriage, I married in Koloa. You know, they used the courthouse. They used to have Hawaiian priest over there. One used to give you license, and the other one used to marry you. So after a couple of years, I had my children, I came to Eleele. The priest said, "Why don't you get married by Catholic?" So I get married by Catholic. . . . So I had two marriage, just one husband.

My husband used to work in the plantation. I was home and I used to do laundry, when they had the soldiers over here from the Army. I used to make a little money. I used to iron those shirts, and they used to give only 75¢ for one. . . .

The plantation no put me out but right now I'm alright over here. They say I can stay as long as I want [in the plantation house]. . . . At Eleele plantation house I had four rooms over there. When I started the children, quick we tell the plantation, and they add another room. And there's a toilet, and, you know, people used to get toilet outside. There's a toilet inside the house for us. Everything. Oh, the plantation was very nice. But not anymore. . . . We used to have free life before — free water, free house, free wood for the fire, yeah, everything free. Kerosene. All those things we used to have here, thank God.

Every Sunday I go to church. I give my donation — and sometimes have special mass. First time I went to church was when I get married. I was sixteen already. . . . Six o'clock I have to get up because my neighbor pick me up. I put my alarm clock, I get my card, those cards where you put your donation.

My son comes every night and he stay couple hours, and he left, I lock all the doors. In the morning, first thing, he calls me up. "How you, Mama?"

My life is over, and I thank God. I'm happy. Not happy that he left [husband], but he live his life. He live ninety-two years. About ten years before he left, he join this other church. But he no used to force me to go to his church . . . Seventh-day Adventist. The pastors used to come here and tell him, why I don't this and why . . . but I never change. Thank God, I'm over there, I don't need . . . Still I keep up with my religion, to my Catholic church. . . . And I paid every year — I paid $12, so I gonna be buried over there by him, too.

ALMA

Alma was born in Puerto Rico and was brought to Maui with her family when she was an infant. She attended school through fifth grade. She married, raised nine children, and also worked for Dole Cannery for twenty years.

I was born in Puerto Rico on a plantation, 1898. I came here when I was two years old — to Maui — in 1901. They had a cyclone, and everybody was so poor. They had to walk about fifteen miles to get a few pennies for food, and they really had a hard life. My mother used pick up coffee whenever there was a job, you know. After the cyclone was very difficult, you know. As I say, they immigrated because they had to, for which we are thankful. They were wise enough to do that, for a better life. And they came to Maui. . . .

My grandma said they had the hard times. She used to cook for the rich people. She had apron, big pockets, and the food that they don't eat, used to put, poor thing, in her big pocket. Put 'em in paper and put 'em in her pocket and bring it for her children. For her two children, ya. They really had hard times. That's why we were so proud of my parents. They made the right decision to come. . . . My father used to say he was glad that he made that decision to come over, ya. 'Cause it was better for all, everyone.

My father was on his own — seven years old he was on his own. So this old man . . . he was an alcoholic, he was alone. But he had a place to stay, and my father used to work, and he gave my father a place to sleep. . . . Many years later he found my mother's house, and my father took him in because he took in my father.

My grandmother was a good cook. She used to take in boarders. She used to cook for about seven or eight persons. All men, single men. And every day, about four o'clock I used to walk over to my grandmother's house to help her with the dishes and things.

My mother could read, but that's funny because she couldn't write. I think she learned her own self. In those days, they couldn't go to school. My mother was a midwife, I remember. On the plantation. She helped a lot of women, ya. Must have learned from her mother.

I heard, sometimes, mother talk stories to us about her life, you know. And they had a sickness . . . what-you-call? And my mother used to help. She'd go out to the people's house, and when she went out she used to change clothes. And when she came back she used to change again. She used to help that way. That's the story I used to remember. . . .

I remember when the train used to carry all the cane, ya, and we used to run, hanging on to get pieces of cane to chew. It was delicious. But then it spoiled our teeth. In those days, we never used to brush so often, like now. Ya, we had a good time. Running barefoot all around. Oh ya, we had a plantation house, comfortable. Ya, it was very comfortable. Oh yes, there were Japanese. I remember when the Koreans came in. And if they didn't go to work, I remember the foreman used to come in the morning and give them marks, hit them. The head policeman used to come and beat them up. My father used to work out in the fields. And I remember seeing this Korean . . . My mother had ruffles around the beds. They used to be very careful about the beds — they used to make them up nice. In those days, you used to keep your doors wide open. And this Korean came running in and hid under the bed. My mother and I were frightened. What's the matter? And he couldn't talk in English, of course, and he said they were going to take him to jail or what. So my mother said, "Stay there, stay there." So after they came out, my mother said, "Everyone is gone, so you can come out." So he came out and ran. In those days, the head ones used to be mean to — some, not all — they used to treat the workers very bad, ya. . . .

I remember when I was old enough to know about something that he [father] was a foreman in a plantation. I used to keep his books because he didn't know how to read or anything. When I was a child she [mother] used to sew, do a lot of sewing. Even men's suits she used to sew. I guess she learned by herself.

Oh, I had to quit at sixth grade 'cause my father got sick. In those days you graduate at eighth, but I had to quit at sixth. Because my mother couldn't take care. I had to help feed him. Help my mother around the house and take care of my father. Because he wasn't able to walk for quite a while, but finally he got well. But it was already too late to go to school, because it was over two years. So then I just study, borrowed books and studied, and help myself as I could. I always like to read. I read a lot. . . . Those days I wanted, you know, do something more. Become something important, like go out to school, but I wasn't able to do that. Of course, after work if I had wanted, I could have [gone to school], but I got married and I started to raise children. . . .

We used to dance. We used to get a big hall. Two-step, any kind of dance. And we used to dance sometimes until three or four o'clock in the morning. We used to love that. They played all kinds of music. That's where I met my husband. I met him in a dance. I got married [when] I was eighteen, almost eighteen. And in those days, when a boy comes to the house, he asks permission to see the girl, and if the parents agree, which they didn't like very much — you know, my father didn't like very much . . . You know fathers, always protective of their children. And finally he had to give in. He didn't like him at first. I said, "But no, he seems to be a nice guy, and I like to talk to him." So finally they agreed, and he came to the house. But then he would sit there, and I would sit here, far, far apart, and that was for two years. No, we didn't go out. Oh no, they didn't allow you to go out to no place. . . . Then he found himself a job working in the electric company — that was better off. Then we decided to get married. And already about two years we knew one another.

I used to sew my own dresses, and my girlfriends'. For 25¢ I used to sew for them. The older ladies, for 50¢ I used to sew one dress. I used to help a lot with my sewing. And during the war, I worked in Pearl Harbor. I was an electrician in Pearl Harbor. We did very well, and so we was able to save some money. I stayed home two years after that. Then I went back to work at Pearl Harbor. Then I went back to the cannery and worked another year. I worked hard in the cannery, Dole Cannery. I worked to help educate my children. Oh, I worked for about, gee, I think twenty years. And then I had varicose veins from working, from standing up. And I had to quit because the doctor says for my own health. . . . Then I got operated from varicose veins, and I had to get a disability. . . . And as my husband was working at Pearl Harbor every week, I would put so much . . . he used to let me take care of the budget. . . . At the cannery, we used to work even Sundays, ya.

My husband was a very bright, smart man. He studied himself. He was always buying books and borrowing books. He educated himself way up, ya. . . . He was president of the Puerto Rican club. My oldest daughter, she went to the University of Hawaii. My husband and I worked very hard — you know, in those days you had to work hard to educate. She was a very smart girl. . . . My husband believed in education, and me too, but if the children don't want to educate themselves, you can't do no more. So they quit school at eighth grade after they graduated, and they found themselves a job . . . which today they say they sorry. Oldest, after college, she went to Queens' Hospital, nurse. . . .

Somebody told my husband to do the bootleg, so he did and tried to make some money to build up the house. Ya, he was making whiskey. From the hop. Ya, he had one underground tunnel. It was against the law. The other neighbor reported. I guess he thought my husband was making business, but he didn't get to sell once. So the policeman came to the house. . . . My husband told the policeman, I admit I'm making, but I done this for my family. I want to make one time and no more. I quit. So the policeman, they look at me and they felt sorry for me and the kids, I guess. They told me, "That's okay, lady. We have to take him down, but we'll bring him home." About two hours later they brought my husband home. . . . He was lucky. Had to face court the next day, and he got free. He told the judge . . . "I have seven children. Give me a chance." And the judge let him go. Lucky! He was just lucky.

I remember we had a stone wall, and we used to sit over there and we all sing, my husband and all, we all sing, just like crazy people, you know. We got no TV. All kinds of songs, English songs. We didn't know no Spanish. Yes, my children still sing. I got one son — he got a beautiful voice. We had our own choir, yes. . . .

I taught my children [that] while I was working, no one could leave the house, and everyone had their chores to do, and they would do it. And we had a big stone wall like that, and they were all sitting by the stone wall waiting for me to come home, when they used to run down the steps and meet me. . . . Then, of course, [when] it was payday I had to . . . get goodies for them. And I would tell, "Okay, let me go and inspect the house." I used to go, and they had everything done, do the wash, put away, the beds all fixed. . . .

I had nine children. The older ones spoke Spanish because my mother and father speak Spanish. So the older ones had to speak. Well, I have two granddaughters that learned how to sew. I taught them, yes, and crochet. . . .

Well, I guess everything has changed. Things have changed. Now everything's so easy. The washer . . . I think I was the first lady that had a washer in Palolo Valley. Ya, and we were the first ones to get electricity. Kerosene lamps before, ya. But I remember we had those ovens, ya, outdoor ovens. I used to bake my bread, which was delicious — those nice big loaves of bread. And the children used to enjoy. I used to make small, little bread out of that, and we'd butter. And my friends used to come around and enjoy that. . . .

I have two sisters and five brother. . . . I had nine children. They're all living. I have so many grandchildren, I can't even count. I got over fifty. And great-grandchildren, and great-great. I got one great-great! Whenever I used to give birth of my children, and I see they were so perfect, and that made me very happy. We worked very hard raising nine children, but we had a beautiful life together. Very happy.

CELESTA

Celesta was born on Kauai and attended school through fourth grade. However, she often missed school because of a hearing problem and because she was needed at home. She later entered a Salvation Army training program in San Francisco and then worked twenty-seven years as a hospital cook in addition to raising a family.

My parents came from Puerto Rico, 1901. They were the first immigration from Puerto Rico. They came as immigration, and they work in fields, contract for the fields. I was born in Kekaha, in 1906.

My mother and my father always used to tell us about Puerto Rico and things when she was a young girl. She had to go be a cook for the higher Puerto Rican, wealthy. So they were on the poor side. So they took her to be a cook. And then my father too, my father when he was in Puerto Rico . . . He said he never . . . my father, he never like to go back to see Puerto Rico. Never, he said, because he know what the suffering, what he did in Puerto Rico. Hawaii was better. He used to be a field worker — cane and coffee and bananas and all those products they make in Puerto Rico.

I remember my mother. I always picture when I was very young [she was] sitting down and mending clothes. That I remember very well. Sitting in a chair, mending some clothes. Yeah, plantation house. We had three bedrooms. That's what all the plantation homes had. It was a Puerto Rican group. We had the Puerto Rican camp and Filipino camp, a Japanese camp, and I remember we had two German families. Norwegians and all that.

My mother was a midwife. That's why when we were about ten, eleven, twelve years old, we never could see our mother at night. No, I never went to help her. She never want us to go out. None of my sisters went. I was the only one who learned how to midwife, from her. I midwifed a few women here after I was married. After I had my children. I had, I think, about four children that I brought into this world. I helped the mother. No, no hospital. The doctors wouldn't come to the house, so they had to choose a very busy woman. Every night. Most every night. And I remember they used to come in horse and buggy to come and get her. There she goes. That's what I remember from my mother. She was a very hardworking woman. Very hardworking woman. . . . She taught us. That's one thing I'm thankful. She taught us how to do our own cooking. When we were young, very young, all Puerto Rican dishes, she taught us. Crocheting, my mother taught that.

Yes, I wanted to be like my mother. I get along with everybody, you know. When there is a group and I get there and I don't know the people, I try to love them and to make friends with them. That's the way my mother was. My brothers and sisters all care for others.

Celebrate Christmas, yeah, we did. We used to put up a Christmas tree. We used to go cut any tree. They never taught us to have a nice Christmas tree in those days. So we go and cut a pine tree, and we put all kinds of things. We used to have a wonderful time, a beautiful time. We used to go to church, midnight mass. We come back, and I remember my mother used to have a lot of food cooked. Well, she used to get ham and turkey, chicken, all kinds of pastries. We used to sit and we pray, and I remember we prayed together, and then we eat. During the day we used to have a wonderful time. I remember [we] had an old Puerto Rican man who would come and serenade. Sing, sing Christmas songs, with guitar, sing Spanish songs. We spoke Spanish. We had to speak Spanish with the parents. My children understand a few words, but I couldn't make a long conversation to them. Always in English.

I quit school when I was fourteen years old. Because my parents, you know, couldn't meet the demands of the home and the cultivating of the fields. . . . So then, after that, we used to go to school one day a week, or two days a week, and then the rest had to be work, in the fields, because that time they didn't get no laws. . . . I know how to read — not so good — but at least I get along. I can go anyplace and read and write. My brothers couldn't finish school. My older brother, neither my second brother, neither my younger brother — couldn't finish school. They couldn't finish — only eighth grade, yeah. And then my sisters, my oldest sister finished eighth grade. She died. My second sister, she finished seventh grade. Then I finish only to fourth grade. You know why? I am hard of hearing. So I got very discouraged when I go to school. . . . That's why I quit school. You know, they couldn't do anything for my ears. All of my sisters didn't go to high school. Neither brothers. . . . My children all finish high school. My youngest boy went to college. . . . You know, at that time they no used to force the children to go to school. But I'm thankful that I went to those days, because I learn a lot. When I used to go to school, I really try to learn. The only thing is, I used to get discouraged when the teacher used to have some kind of subject she used to be teaching. I couldn't really hear it. . . .

When I was nineteen years, I left home and went to the Salvation Army training college, in San Francisco. So I spend two years in the college, learning. You know it was real hard, a battle for me, 'cause I didn't get education, but I graduated as a lieutenant. After that I was sent into New Mexico for preaching — to preach the gospel, the word of God. So then I didn't stay there too long. They send me back to Kohala, Hawaii. I stationed there for about a year, and then they transferred me to Maui. But when I left Kohala, I was sick. The Salvation Army wanted someone to go in the camps to show the mothers to feed the babies, what food to feed the babies. So then I stayed doing that with other nurses, other camp nurses. Then I got sick and stayed one year away from the Salvation Army. . . . Then they sent me back to work in Honolulu. Then Lihue called headquarters. So they send me here, and I started to work hard again. Then I lost weight again and the doctor said, "I think this job is not good for you." So they send me home, and after being home for two years, I got married.

I was twenty-three years old when I got married. So then I had two boys and one girl. . . . My husband died when he was fifty-eight years old and I was sixty-three. He was younger than me. . . . Then twenty-seven years hospital work, as cooking. When I had a chance, I go in the wards and help the nurses fixing beds. . . . I used to run to the nurses' cottage and I used to start cleaning the cottage. They used to tell me, "Celesta, don't do that."

My daughter loves to learn a lot of words. And then sometimes I speak the Puerto Rican language, Spanish language. But I don't know how to read it. But my daughter, she try to. She tried to spell, because she had a better education than I had, so she is able to. She went to college, and she teaching too.

I was Catholic. I was always a Catholic. I was guide in the Catholic church, but I lost the Salvation Army. So my mother accused me of being . . . "You change your religion and that's why you sick." I said, "No, Mom, not that, because I love my Catholic." So anyway, I started going to the Catholic church, and I'm still going to the Catholic church. I help the Salvation Army very much too, still. . . .

I give thanks to the Lord for the good times and the bad times, because with the bad times I learned a lot. Suffering. That's the only way we can learn. I didn't learn only the good times, you see.

I wanted to be a woman that could help everyone. And all those who in need, I wanted to be there and help them. But I wasn't so well off. I wanted go ahead. I wanted to be a nurse too, but I always was afraid of my hearing. But when we went two years in the Salvation Army, we learned how to make a first aid, 'cause I have a certificate. I always wanted to be one that could help. Help someone that really need. I still do that. I still want to help. Lots of people come to me. . . . I meet a lot of people with selfishness in them. No love. Doesn't want to share. They don't want charity, nothing. So I tell them, "You know, love, charity, is the most important thing in this world." . . . For us, love. We must love.

X   Filipinas

Immigration

Stories of immigration from the Philippines, in 80 percent of the cases, begin in the barrios of Ilocos, a comparatively poor agricultural region in the northwest corner of the main island of Luzon. There, high population density and scarcity of land and resources prompted a pioneering spirit that took Ilocanos to many parts of the globe. Because of the scarcity of land, the custom of equal inheritance, by which land was divided equally among all sons, was replaced in the mid-nineteenth century with the custom of inheritance of all land by one son.[1] Other sons were thereby encouraged to emigrate, either to other parts of the Philippines or to other countries.

The Ilocano dream was that by working on the Hawaiian plantations one could save enough money to buy land for a dowry, to marry, and to establish a family in Hawaii, on the mainland, or back in the Philippines. Many Filipino immigrants to Hawaii realized this dream or, at least, continued to think they might. By 1940 half of those who had emigrated to Hawaii had left, two-thirds to return to the Philippines, the other third to relocate on the mainland.[2]

The U.S. annexation of the Philippines coincided with its annexation of Hawaii, and these two events, coupled with the recruitment of laborers by Hawaiian sugar planters, caused an influx of contract laborers from the Philippines in the first three decades of the twentieth century. Soon after annexation, the HSPA began to turn from recruiting Japanese labor to recruiting Filipinos. In 1906 the Oahu strike by Japanese workers closed down most plantations there. Planters realized the danger inherent in depending on a single ethnic group for field labor, though in actuality they never discontinued this pattern. But they sought an alternative to Japanese and Okinawan labor.

For Filipinos, annexation made Hawaii an immediately attractive destination. The Philippine High Commission, which was the American governing body in the Philippines, in an attempt to protect Filipino recruits, required the HSPA to furnish a model individual labor contract. According the contracts, plantations were required to furnish Filipino laborers with housing, fuel, water, medical care, and $16 per month, and laborers were required to work ten hours a day, twenty-six days a month, for three years.[3] This rate of pay was far more than they could earn as dockworkers at home and thus provided added incentive to accept HSPA contracts. The contract did not specify schools, but there were not many children among the first Filipino arrivals.

During the decade following both annexations, 109,928 Filipino workers and families immigrated to Hawaii.[4] The exodus of labor from the Philippines was so great that in 1915 the Philippine government passed laws restricting and regulating labor recruitment. For example, the Philippine Assembly passed a bill in 1915 compelling the HSPA to guarantee free return passage after 720 days of work.[5] Yet despite these laws, the exodus continued, and in 1926 over half the sugar plantation labor in Hawaii was Filipino.[6]

It was also in 1915 that the HSPA stopped paying passage for plantation labor; the planters felt that incentive was no longer necessary. Moreover, despite the efforts of the Philippine High Commission to protect Filipino labor, the results of their efforts, once workers reached Hawaii, were minimal. The housing of Filipino workers was inferior, and there was almost no possibility for a Filipino worker to become a *luna*.

Another consequence of the U.S. annexation of the Philippines was the ambiguous legal status of Filipinos in America and in Hawaii. Attorney General Matthewman ruled that Filipinos were neither citizens nor aliens. They had no legal protection. Moreover, the Philippine Independence Act of 1934 proclaimed them aliens and placed a quota on immigration of fifty immigrants per year.[7]

As the most recently arrived ethnic group, the Filipinos were incorporated at the bottom of the socioeconomic plantation structure, the ethnic class hierarchy created by the plantation system. Even in the 1980s, Filipinos in Hawaii were lower on the socioeconomic scale than mainland Filipinos or non-Filipinos in Hawaii. Measured by education, only about half of the Hawaii Filipinos were high school graduates in the 1980s, in contrast with 79 percent of the mainland Filipinos and 77 percent of non-Filipinos in Hawaii.[8] The same order of difference was seen in the 1980s with regard to the proportion of employment in the service sector and as laborers. Despite these inequalities, over half the

Filipinos in Hawaii in the 1980s were born in the Philippines, which suggests that this ethnic immigration is continuing at a rapid rate.[9]

Labor Unrest

Among the growing Filipino community in the early twentieth century, living conditions were poor and the pay far below what was necessary to support a worker if he were married. It was not long before signs of discontent appeared.

Like immigrants from other ethnic communities, Filipinos, on arrival in their new home, organized societies for various purposes — social interaction, mutual aid, savings, and security. The most successful clubs were those based on hometown origin. Clan ties were also important in motivating Filipinos to join relatives in Hawaii. Of importance for the plantation laborers, these groupings served as a focus for the expression of grievances. By the end of the first decade of the twentieth century, Japanese workers had organized strikes on several islands. The advantages of organizing to express dissatisfaction were not lost on Filipino workers.

One individual who arrived in Hawaii from the Philippines in 1910 was to change the working situation of his compatriots. His name was Pablo Manlapit. He was born not in Ilocos but in Batangas and could not speak Tagalog or Ilocano. Like other Filipinos, he was recruited by the HSPA. He worked briefly on a plantation but was soon dismissed. He then began two newspapers, ran a pool hall — the focus of Filipino male sociability, especially for bachelors — and worked as a stevedore and salesperson. After that, he found a job as an interpreter and a janitor in a law office and began to study law.

In 1919 he inaugurated the Filipino Labor Union and began to organize sugar workers. In 1920, in cooperation with Japanese workers, he formed the Higher Wage Association and presented wage demands to the HSPA. When the HSPA rejected the demands, Manlapit and the Japanese labor organizers called a strike of sugar plantation workers. About eleven thousand workers were evicted from their plantation homes and became homeless and jobless, living in tent camps in Honolulu. The strike ended after several months, when the HSPA increased wages and improved conditions. In 1923 Manlapit asked for a forty-hour work week and pay of $2 a day; the HSPA again refused. The workers struck, and when the strike spread to other islands,

Fig. 10.1. Field workers, dressed today as seventy years ago. *Courtesy of Wayne M. Tanaka, photographer.*

Manlapit and sixty others were arrested and convicted of conspiracy. Sentenced to a two-year prison term, Manlapit chose exile instead. He returned to Hawaii in 1932 and reorganized the Filipino Labor Union. In 1935 he was banished to the Philippines permanently. Another union leader, Fagel, took the union underground.[10]

But Manlapit's example and leadership had caught on. The HSPA's dictates no longer went unchallenged. Filipinos participated in nine strikes between 1909 and 1925. Those who left the plantations, however, were blacklisted by Honolulu firms and were unable to find alternative jobs. Moreover, the Organic Act of 1900 had barred non-American citizens from public employment.[11] Some Filipinos managed to find jobs as gardeners in the employ of well-to-do haoles, but generally it was difficult for Filipinos to move up in the socioeconomic hierarchy.

Women

The gender ratio among Filipino workers was more asymmetrical than among most other ethnic groups, with the possible exception of the Chinese. The ratio was variously reported as being from four to seven males to every female. One result of the excess of men was what was known as *coboy-coboy*, the abduction of married women by bachelors, some of whom managed to keep their illegally acquired wives. At that time, the husbands had, in practical terms, no recourse. Another result of the imbalance was a lowering of the average age of marriage for girls; being in great demand as wives, most married in the early and mid-teenage years. This low marriage age correlated with a low educational level, as most girls quit school when they married.

One strategy to reduce the imbalance paralleled the picture-bride influx of Japanese and Korean women. Before 1930 women arrived posing as the wives of workers already in Hawaii — a strategy that enabled them to bypass the immigration quotas. There were also dockside marriages of women who wanted to enter Hawaii with recruits seeking wives.[12] Later immigrants tended to bring their families with them, which helped to alleviate the earlier gender imbalance. Yet the number of Filipino pool halls in parts of Honolulu today attests to the large number of bachelors. In some areas on Oahu, near the old sugar plantations, for example in Waipahu, the Filipino male population is still disproportionately high.

The Filipinas shared with the Portuguese and Puerto Ricans a strong religious faith, and the church was the focal point for many of their social and organizational activities. Unlike the Portuguese and Puerto Ricans, however, many Filipinos left the Catholic church for Protestant churches when they arrived in Hawaii. Some of the women whose interviews follow discussed their conversion. One respondent suggested that she converted because Protestant churches were more helpful to early immigrants than were Catholic churches, at least where she lived. As Protestants, nevertheless, they remained as close to their churches as they had as Catholics. Today, for these respondents, as for octogenarians of other ethnic groups, the senior centers often vie with churches as centers of social interaction and concern. The church was the focus of welfare work within the Filipino community, and the help many women gave to others was a result of their strong religious convictions.

These women arrived in the Islands without much education but with high hopes. That they were disproportionately few and in great demand as wives led them to marry early, which further reinforced their low educational level. Virtually no Filipinas remained unmarried. They married early whether or not they were born in Hawaii. Establishing family life in their new homes absorbed most of their time and energy, although on some plantations women worked in the fields with their husbands. As with first-generation women of other ethnic groups, work was more arduous and living conditions more primitive than they had been led to believe.

ANGELA

Angela was born in Ilocos Norte, married there, and bore four children. She immigrated to Hawaii with her husband and two of their children. She raised sixteen children in Hawaii — all her own — and, in addition, did cooking, laundry, and ironing for fifteen to twenty bachelors. She still lives in the house near a sugar mill where she and her family settled.

I was born 1901, Ilocos Norte, Philippines. My father's mother, I remember, take care us, because we have big family, as a good grandma. No more school our place. We did not go to school. . . . I went only first grade, second grade. After that, the typhoon take the school. After that no more. We live by the river, but the river come big, like the ocean. But plenty fish, beautiful, delicious. Grandma teach us cook, and I watch if she cook. That time we have plenty sister, ten of us. Back and forth go to my grandma, because close to my house. She teach us how to do this, do that, cook, wash the clothes. Everybody had to work.

My father is a carpenter. My father-in-law, he work for the government. My husband go to school all the time in Manila. But after the father pass away, he came home. He was elected lieutenant governor in Ilocos Norte.

We [had] beautiful place, our place, but the money not too good. Hard time. You got family, enough food, plenty. Vegetables growing, and fish in the river. Only meat was hard to get. You had to keep your own chickens, keep your own pig, cow. No more market like in Hawaii. Raise your own animals so you can have meat. . . . It was a good time, a nice life. It wasn't a hard time. The only problem was clothing. It was hard to get clothes. You had to plant the cotton, harvest it. Because we had to make our own cotton — we had to weave the cotton, all that. And plant the rice. We did all that, because there were no boys. So we all helped to plant the vegetables and rice, pound the rice. We washed clothes in the river. There was soap, but we couldn't buy it. We used rice husks to wash clothes. It was just like soap.

After he come back from Manila, we meet each other. We knew each other anyway. We lived in the same place. Second cousins. My mother and his mother, first cousins. Close relatives. There weren't many people in our place. Small town, and only family lived there. Nobody came there. I was seventeen when I married. If your parents wanted you to marry, you married — especially relatives, because they wanted children. Parents on the two sides talk, then you can marry. I had to follow my parents. Even if someone didn't want to marry, if the parents tell you to marry, you marry. That was the style then. But not now. It was okay because my mother and mother-in-law were first cousins — because there weren't enough people there, because we lived in the country. We married, 1917. Nineteen eighteen I had a baby boy already, in January. My husband died, 1971. Always I set a place for him and a cup of coffee and fruit in his memory.

I have one uncle, the first Filipino to come to Hawaii. Nineteen twenty-three was when I came to Hawaii. He came before. He came back to pick up his family. He said they need ladies because they don't have any ladies, plenty of men. He said, "Oh, if you wash clothes in Hawaii you'll make 25¢ for one pantaloon. I told him, "Uncle, oh I can wash plenty," I told him. "Well, that's why I came to get my family," he said. But people were making a dollar a day yet, then. I was going to leave my husband and come by myself with my two babies, because he was lieutenant governor. I didn't want him to quit his job. So I told him, I talked to my uncle. "Oh uncle, I want to go. Washing clothes is easy for me," I told him. "Well, I don't know, if your husband lets you come." "Oh, I'm going to tell him that I'm going to go to Hawaii, and if I can make money I'm going to send for you to come to Hawaii," I said. My uncle laughed. I told my husband too, "Oh, Daddy, I want to go to Hawaii because Uncle said it is easy to make money in Hawaii." "Okay," he told me, "Okay." Oh, I felt happy.

So I hurried to make preparations, because my uncle was about to leave. I had one day to pack, and the next morning we were supposed to leave. During the night my husband called his mother, his sister, his grandma, grandpa. But I didn't pay attention because I was making preparations and packing. But I listened to what he was saying to the parents. Then, after that, in the middle of the night, because we couldn't sleep, "What were you saying to your mother, your grandma, your sister, 'Take care of the land, the house'?" I asked him. "Why?" "I want to go to Hawaii too," he said, just like that. It was easy to come to Hawaii then. Not many questions asked. So he came with me. And he couldn't do the work, because when he was growing up he never worked — he was sent to school by his parents. Because his parents were rich. They had everything — land, not too much money, but they had servants to work on the land. So he did nothing, only go to school.

The trip was very hard. I cried many times, ask myself why I leave the Philippines. I was glad my husband was with me. My daughter was only three months old. I was so sick, could not get out of bed. My husband wash the diapers and other clothes. He never help me like that before in the Philippines. I was happy to come to Hawaii. But after we arrived I cried when I saw the house they gave us. Had only one small room, and the floor had wide cracks in it. We had to cover with mats. The kitchen was a separate shack and had a dirt floor. The stove was a box filled with dirt. We cooked our food in half of a five-gallon can over the wood fire. It was so different. In the Philippines we were poor only for clothes. We were happy to see money [in Hawaii].

We came to the Big Island. My husband had six poles to carry the cane, because there were no trucks or trains then. They had to carry the cane and throw it in running water. There was a raft there. The men cut the cane, carried it to the river and put it on the rafts. The men carried it there, someone threw it on the rafts for transportation to the mill. That was life in the beginning. He had donkeys to carry the cane to the field for planting. No trucks. Cuttings for planting were carried to the field. Then my husband worked in the mill. His wage rose to $1.50. Before, it was $1. After that he got a bonus, 25¢, worked twenty-five days. By payday [because of bills that had piled up] there was nothing left in the pay envelope. Because they put the check in the envelope. We had enough food because what I did. We had friends — some of the old people gave food, and they had free land to keep animals. My husband plant vegetables, cabbage. But the kids like canned goods. They don't want eat fresh vegetables — only cabbage, fried with corned beef or meat, and we ate it. The boys went to school, and they got part-time jobs. The teacher gave them jobs in the school.

We had only one faucet for one camp, to wash clothes. Only one faucet for the whole camp. Not such a big camp, all newcomers. All Filipinos in that camp. Some Japanese, but mostly Filipinos, especially from Ilocos Norte. Because they work harder than the Visayan. They are better because they work harder. I had to iron with charcoal. No electricity anyway.

I have ten sons, but the number one and number two passed away young. I have six daughter, five alive, thirty-nine grandchildren, fifteen great-grandchildren. Too much! I teach them how to wash clothes. They have to learn how to cook. I told them what you do in the Philippines — how you cook, how you do the clothes, everything. "Oh, too hard for me," they said. "Well, you're lucky you're in Hawaii," I said. You can buy your clothes, but in the Philippines you have to make them. You plan the cutting, then pin them up.

It was a hard life, though. No one help in housework. Only me. Day and night I worked, day and night. I got laundry work. I did all the laundry for all the children, and still I took laundry from outside, from working men for only $2 a month. Sometimes I had fifteen or twenty men to wash for. We had to boil the clothes. The plantation gave an allowance for wood for fire, for baths too. I boiled them [the clothes] in a big pan outside. We bought soap. I don't know how I managed that life. And I fixed the lunch for all the men. I made between ten and fourteen lunches for the men each day. I got up two A.M. day after day, year after year, but never got sick. God help me.

One week after giving birth, I took in the laundry of five or six men, plus all my children. One week, one time [a week]. Nobody to help, only me. But I didn't want to go back to the Philippines — only at first, when I had to wash clothes outside, no faucets. You know, in the Philippines we washed in the river. Beautiful fresh water. I cried for that. We didn't have washing machines — we had to scrub and keep the water in the bucket. Sometimes the women argued with each other over who got the faucet first. I think we had fifteen families in our camp, and everybody had laundry to do.

I worked in the night too. It was almost as if I didn't even have one hour of sleep. I worked at night ironing clothes. And especially [be-cause] all my children go to school. Before, [unlike today] have to iron the clothes. Not wash and use. You have to iron, and I did that in the night. I wash in the day. I don't know how I can do it. Sometimes I went to bed at one o'clock, because I was still ironing clothes. Then after that, sometimes a baby cried. Sometimes a baby got sick. All the girls, thanks to God, they helped me. I wash the clothes, and after they came home, they had to iron clothes, men's clothes. So it was nice. Nice, beautiful life. But I never got tired. I never got sick, thanks to God. I give birth, I'm lively already. Today I give birth and then tomorrow I can do something.

Gave birth at home, one baby every year. One lady came. She came seven days and bathed the baby. Portuguese, big lady. They had a hospital but not many doctors or nurses. So that lady took care of everybody. Plenty ladies gave birth — Portuguese, Japanese — but no go hospital. Only home.

We go shopping, ride the horse. Or we catch the plantation truck [that] carry all the working men. And over here too, the first time got a store [in] our place. We have one post office. Store got clothes, food. That time a little better. After the war, we have theater, got the church, got the school — in front my house, the high school. Wonderful place! We have the store, we have the church. Oh, so close, got the kindergarten there. The first grade there behind my house. . . . That's why I'm so happy, lucky, because all my children go to school. They don't need to pay a bus.

I cannot speak English right. Not much Tagalog, Visayan. I speak Ilocano with my husband. I speak Ilocano to children but they speak English. That's why I learned a little bit. They understand, but they no talk Ilocano.

Ten sons, six daughter, five [of the daughters] alive. They all went to high school except the first one. She passed away in the Philippines.

All eight boys [who lived] went to university. One daughter went into nursing after she graduated. I have a daughter — the oldest one in Honolulu — she went to study in the university. They all active — 4-H, Girl Scouts. All the boys [were] scouts. I have two Eagle Scouts. I helped the boys join clubs, scouts, Cub Scouts. "Mama, you can help us do this, do that," [they said]. Because some parents didn't pay attention to the children. I did. Because all my boys were scout captains. They knew all my boys worked. If they have some responsibility, they do it. I joined PTA for school. I joined the League of Mercy to visit people in the hospital. . . .

"Daddy, you wanta go visit your town [in the Philippines]? I can take you. You visit all your land." "No need to go look at the land because everyone will argue about it." "But you got land, Daddy. More better you go sell some." He said, "You folks let your relatives" — because I have plenty of sisters' children — "let the family, relatives take care of the land. In case you folks go, you have a house, somebody to pick you up." That's what my husband said. "You folks don't go and bother them." That's what my husband said. He did not go, only me. Well, I had a good time, because my son was in Clark Field [a major airfield and U.S. base]. I went to visit my place, but I only stayed half a day. Too hot! So hot! Too hard, a hard life, and my son was staying in Manila. So I stayed with them. So I stayed one day and visited around, but I don't appreciate going back. That's the best, stay in Hawaii. Well, the Philippines is nice. You can do what you like. You work, you no wanna work. But you no work, you no more food, you no more clothes. But over here, well, you wake up early to work. . . . No, I no tired.

ELNORA

Elnora was born in Ilocos Sur and was trained as a nurse in Manila. Her family was well-off and educated. She was brought to Hawaii by American missionaries to work in public health, and she helped to inaugurate the visiting nurse program. She married and raised five children.

I was born [in] Ilocos Sur. It means "the southern land." Luzon. I was lucky, because my mother was an educated lady. She was fortunate because she had the best education for ladies in those days. She played the piano well those days. They all had private tutor, instructors come in the house. My mother grew up in the convent, you know. In those days, you family are in the law school or in the priesthood. My mother spoke only Spanish. We were well-to-do. We were not considered poor. . . . You know, when he [grandfather] took the position — is Spanish governor of the city — when he was in office he was so honest that he didn't think that somebody going to be dishonest. Those Spanish days, your family either lawyers, then medicos, doctors, or priests. You know social classes, and they happen to be higher.

We were Catholic. My mother was. She grew up in the convent. Then the Americans came, the Protestant missionaries came. In our family, my mother was one of the early ones who joined the Methodist church. The reason why, she used to tell us . . . in the Spanish time, the eldest one is usually sent to become the priest. She said the Protestant and Methodist missionaries came to our town. "When the Americans came," she told us, "the missionaries said, 'We have the same Bible as the Catholics.' " She said, "Prove to me," because she spoke Spanish very well, and the priests were relatives. Up in the convent they had the copy of the Bible. The only difference is no graven image, not in the Protestant. When she was reading, she began to think about it. Of course, in the Roman Catholic, they did not. They took out where it says "Don't make any graven image," you know. When my mother compared, that was the one that was different. She joined the Methodists. My husband was a preacher in the Methodist church here. But in the Philippines in those days, the early time was the friars, they call friars, the ones who came from Spain. They said priests should not get married, but they have plenty of children outside of marriage. Oh yeah. And they could choose anyone they want. And they could choose upper class.

Well, I was the first graduate nurse from my town. Nobody could believe I would leave, because they said, "You're gonna be like that? You are too fussy." I was really a good nurse, and I made a point to work for the church for one year. "No," they said, "you cannot be a nurse — you are too lazy." Yes, I was, but I wanted to. When I was looking at this first nurse I saw, I was so attracted with what she was doing and her uniform. And I wanted to be like that, so nobody could believe it, but I said I want, so my mother said, "Let her go. She wants. I don't want any complaint." . . . So after I finish my training three years in a Methodist hospital, I went home. I spent a year.

I was the first in the Public Health Department, visiting nurse. One of the early ones when they open up. I gave one year to the Methodist mission in my hometown. I can go to work in the hospital, you see. It was only for women and children. I was the first one who went for nursing in my town. To Manila . . . it was the only place where they had nursing school and hospitals those days. You know, before, the ones who worked in hospitals were old persons, older women, doing Spanish-style. I was the first who understand medicine. I always say the Lord help me, because I never lost a patient and I was so thankful. After that, I stayed a year, and then there were many girls who take up medicine.

When I came here, the one in charge of the Filipinos was a missionary in the Philippines, of the Methodist church, and a good friend of ours. An American missionary, Methodist missionary. In fact, he was the one [who] came and said, "Come to Hawaii." So I said, "Sure, if you need me." I always work, trying to get advantage, trying to go anywhere overseas' places. So he said, "Yeah, we need you." So he made the arrangements to come. So I said, "I like to travel — I come." And my mother said okay.

I worked on Ewa Plantation, employed by the Hawaiian Board of Missions. I was one of those who started visiting nurse. No, I didn't stop when I had children because it was important to help. And, fortunately, the Lord has given me ability, too. Brothers, ya, they all came here. They went to the mainland.

We met here in Hawaii. I was working in Ewa Plantation. I got married here. The one that married me went over to my hometown, to my parents in the Philippines, you know. Before we got married, he went and ask. The nurses were his friends, and so we could trust him. I knew them because we were together in the Public Health Division. He must be alright if that is his friends. If they trust him, he must be alright. . . . We have to be really careful who we would like to get friends. I'm Ilocano but my husband was Visayan. So we use English at home. Because he could not speak my own. He can understand, speak little bit, but I couldn't speak his dialect. I was happy I had a good husband and good children. We were able to send them to school. My girls went to college. In fact, one was a nurse and one was a teacher.

. . . I'm a nurse and I learn to speak pure, pure languages. If you are a nurse, you have to speak Tagalog because we were in Manila. And I speak Spanish and my English. . . . I speak the three main Filipino dialects. I was really fortunate and happy that when the Puerto Ricans came, immigrated to Hawaii, the older ones no speak English, and I was glad that I could speak Spanish. And I practice my Spanish with them.

I was beginning to forget. Plus helping all the Spanish-speaking Puerto Ricans. It surprised me when they came. As a visiting nurse, you know, in the first place there are two words just the opposite in Filipino. "Medicine" in Tagalog is *gamut*. In Ilocano, *gamut* is "poison." I have to explain to the Ilocanos. You don't want to die yet, that's why you have to take. Good thing they believe me, what I tell them.

JULIA

Julia was born in Hawaii two years after her parents arrived from the Philippines. Despite having completed only six years of schooling, she has held several responsible positions. She raised two adopted children and enjoys helping others.

I was born here, Hawaii. My parents come from Philippines. My mother became converted soon after coming to Hawaii. She became Protestant, Congregational. She always help others. Go around and collect money for people who need help. My father died early, and my mother marry again, but he beat her and beat us too. My mother stay with him seven years because she took a vow, "in sickness and in health." But finally she separate to protect us, but she didn't divorce him. My older brother want to kill him and told him, after the last beating, that he better not show his face again. He always came back and apologized. He beat me when I got a letter from somebody want to marry me.

My mother kept a boarding house, did washing, cooking. And she help women when they have a baby. I had to wash out the bloody garments and cloths after the births.

The worst part [she did not use the word "rape"] . . . about twelve years old, by a relative. And I was put into the Salvation Army home because I was, you know, pregnant. I had a child, a boy. He was adopted by a family that lost a child. Today, yes, I meet him. Here, this is his family [she shows a photograph]. He has a wife, children. My husband wanted to marry me at age twelve, even after that. He said he still loves me. So I did not finish high school, even junior high school. We married early, probably I was about fifteen. He wait three years. When I married him I said, "Okay, but please don't beat me." He never did, and we don't argue much. Kind, gentle man. We discuss about everything. He was never jealous when we went to parties, not like other Filipino men.

In sixth grade, I worked for a lieutenant's family — housework. I worked at Dole seven years. In the war I worked for the navy in charge of linen locker. Then I worked in civil service, Fiscal Department, for the Navy Supply Center. People used to think I went to school more than six years.

Now my daughter lives with me with two children. Getting a divorce. I own three houses. I pray every day, and I get guidance from God.

I love God first, then my mother, then my husband, after that everyone else. Yes, I help in the church, like my mother. I handle several funerals — my mother, husband, and others. I help in the church and the senior center. I adopt many people. I invite black people and haoles in the church for lunch. I took care four retarded girls for three years, downstairs here. I did all their shopping and cooking.

ANNA

Anna was born on Luzon and came to Hawaii in 1923. She worked as a beautician both before and after her children were born. She enjoys showing photographs of her children and grandchildren, but she has lost count of their number.

I was born [in] Ilocos Norte. . . . I continued in school. Seventh grade, I was in Honolulu already. In Luzon we met a boy who was trying to come to Hawaii alone. And so he said, "If you go to Hawaii, I like to go as your son." And so my father said, "Okay, because I got only a daughter." . . . But when we really go, he never come with us.

My father, by the grace of God, went to work in the sugar fields. I think two years one time. Maybe about five, six years. I think when he was old already. Sugar. Was $1 a day, I think — their daily work.

I was a spoiled brat, you know, because I was the last one. My sister died when she was supposed to take the Veil of St. Mary on Easter Day. She was a good girl. My mother was so sad. She said, "Very obedient, not like you, lazy." She was strict, but she didn't want to be so strict, because I'm the only one left.

My mother was a hardworking lady. She took laundry and ironing, and she cook also. On the plantation. And not so many wives there. And that's when they kill because they want to take somebody else wife, like that. Suppose you say yes and then, after, you marry another one. That makes them angry. I was young, and they didn't bother me because I said, "Oh no." They know how to scare you. But as long as you believe in God, that's one thing. Because I teach Sunday school, my friend and I.

But I found out about religion. Because my mother told me to memorize all the prayers, Catholic prayers. Only the long one I could not. Then we came to Hawaii. Then, when I went Sunday school, the man preached that the God you are worshipping is made by hand. [I went] because I obeyed my parents. Then afterward . . . I realized that you cannot say a true God because it's made by hand, you see. They told them that this is Jesus, this is Jehovah, you have to kneel down. So I said, "No, that's not right." And so my mother said, "Well, it's up to you." I was about twelve, thirteen, fourteen. A Congregational church. Then they hired me and one girl, three girls to clean the church. We sing in the choir. My daughter directs it at the church.

I told, "Look, Mama, the statue that you are worshipping is idol. You see, that's clay. You like to worship that?" "Why you tell me those things?" She mad. Then afterward she realize it. Join Congregational church.

That's the way I notice my husband. He came to church, and he was dolled up, too. He was a mail carrier too — he come and give the letters. The way he courted me, he was smart too. You know we have a store, plantation store. There was one store, and there was a telephone, and you can yell we get the news. But then Mr. Chung, this Chinese man in the store, call me, "You get telephone." So I went, and it was him, calling for a date or something. Yes, can have a date, but you have to ask permission from your parents. They said okay, because they know his custom. They know him longer. According to his ways, they know he's a nice boy.

Boyfriends? Only by the eyes. Because I cannot promise or bambye [by and by] they kill you. They killed one girl, you know. I don' know how many she wen' promise, and they kill her. She live right above us. Even the police got no business. Because she make love with him and promise. And she accept, he say, like that. What they gonna do? The police, no more, no more. Even the parents. Even my brother tell them — he call them inside the house. "Don't meet in no corners." So I said, "How we gon' talk?" "Sit down, then we leave you," he said.

If I tell yes, quick, he say, "Get married," and I didn't want to get married. But then I think he see all the mail coming to me, love letters, and then he think he cannot go on unless he saw what it says. Ya, my husband was like that already, that time. "So if you really love me, you better make up your mind." So he came, and he talked it over with my mother and my father and my brother. Because my brother was here.

But I didn't obey the one thing that my mother asked. They liked a man, but I didn't like. He smoked a lot. I said I gotta marry the man I love. But they liked him, because his ways polite. Because when he came to propose, [they said], "Because you are the one wants it, we agree." . . .

I was supposed to go to school in town, but we got married. Then we moved to Waipahu, to a plantation. There my husband was the helper of the one that take care the post office. Then he went to work in the bank.

You know, I got married, and three years I got no baby, two years and half. And they said, "How come?" Well, cannot help. God never give us yet. Bambye. But I prayed. I said, "Oh Lord, give us a baby girl." There was a lady, she said, "How come?" I said, "Well, when the Lord give to me, I'll be happy." Then I had a baby. She said, "What kinda baby you got?" I said, "It's a girl." She said, "Tough luck." It was my first child, you know. Even the Filipinos think like that. I said, "You're not God. I hope and pray God will give her a good life." I always wanted a girl, you know, so I could make her play the piano. Boys are lazy, you know. I couldn't learn to play the piano. We had no money. Now my daughter, she's a teacher, and she teaches piano.

I wanted her to study music . . . and sure enough, I sit down on the bench with her, and she play quick, you know. "No, no, you wrong. I know the song." She said, "How do you know, Mama?" "I know the song." . . . My sister, she sing in choir, too. My mother has been a singer in her own way. In the old days, they had a big book for singing during Christmas and Easter. . . . Sometimes she sing alto and I sing soprano. She had a good voice. I like play piano, but I rather give to my daughter first. . . . Sometimes what you can tell to your daughter, you cannot tell to your son . . . the secret of us women.

I went to beauty school, and I work when my daughter was in college. In the beauty shop I stay ten, eleven, all the time. My boss too. My husband stayed downstairs waiting for me. We want our children to get ahead. Oh boy, we really worked!

JOSEFA

Josefa was born in Luzon and married a minister before coming to Hawaii in 1923. She attended high school in Hawaii and then taught. She raised five children. She now lives in a retirement home and organizes senior activities.

Grandmother was an active Catholic. Whenever someone died, she prayed nine days. Filipino custom, you know. So she led the prayer. She was a leader.

My first memory of my mother? Oh, she's very nice to us, you know. Teach us to go to church every Sunday. Ya, Catholic church those days, but [when] I married my husband I became Protestant, Congregational. But my mother say, "Never mind, that is Christian, because my father is independent, independent church." We call it *aglipayano* in the Philippines. It means we are not using Spanish, dakin' [that kind]. They use Filipino kind [chants from Tagalog mass].

We belong to Tagalog. My mother told me straight, "I cannot send you to school because we do not have enough money." I had to find a way so that I can earn it. So what I did . . . You know, over there, there is a lady who cooks some kind goodie goodie. And I used to bake and decorate, *lumpia*. It is rolled in a wrapper, and inside is chicken and pork. Until now I am doing it, because I know it helps me out. And whenever I have a party or birthday of my children, I make some. You can buy the wrapper — it's made of flour. It must be a frying pan that you cannot use for anything else. You can buy the wrapper in the market. Flour and little bit water, that's all. Inside is not the cow meat but pork, shrimp, and chicken, with water chestnut and sweet potato. I mean regular potato cut in pieces, little bit head cabbage, and garbanzos. Be sure that it will be uniform, the cutting, because you are going to wrap it in a wrapper, and it must be almost just like grinded. So garlic and a little bit oil in the pot and then put onion and all the meat, because boiled already. Yes, like national dish. Whenever we have party. And it is also good for when you have appetite, just like snack.

My uncle always give us fish. And my mother said, "You can cook *sarciado*." *Sarciado* is the one [where] you fry the fish and you must have scrambled egg and tomatoes and onion and you put on the top. You cover it and you call it *sarciado*. And I remember that now, I remember even now. And whenever I make that one for my children, "Grandma, teach me that one," and "Mama." I always tell my children, and especially my daughter. She tell, "Okay, I like eat *sarciado*." Like that, you know. My son, my oldest son, he is a major, retired already. Now he stay home. He do the cooking and he say, "Mom, you know what I cook today? I cook *sarciado*."

I tell them I like to finish high school, I like to buy books, I need money. [She tells them] "I no like stay like what you folks, in fact." "You high *paloko*, you high class, what you thinking?" "No, but I like to finish my schooling, and afterwards I like to do something different from you folks. I no like how you folks . . . I no like too much of all the work, go to the field, harvest, dakin'." [Harvest] corn and rice, *palay*, they call it *palay*. So they thought I was bragging because I tell them that I will not always pick up tamarind tree because get a stick to get the tamarind fruit and put it in a basket, and bring to the market and give to the one that they pay you, you know . . . I tell I am not going to do this one. Maybe I will do it now, two, three times, but I told them 'scuse me — I am not going to get mad in my own way of telling to them, you know. "I like to do something different than you folks, you know." "What are you going to do? This is our own way." "No, but in fact I like to go to the mainland — I like to go to America." That I said, you know. "I like to go New York," I tell to my sister. "I like to go New York." "Oh baloney," she said. She said I have too much wind in my head. Then I got married, and 1923 I come over here.

I went to high school, and after I finished I went to be a nurse. So I went to Manila General Hospital. Although I had a hard time to get the money, I tried my best to go and enroll to study that nursing. But I just could not take it because I was assigned in the ward [with] old men and old people . . . because they wet the bed and everything, so I thought maybe I cannot enjoy it. . . . The supervisor said alright, because it was only my fifth day. So I changed my mind.

So afterwards I went back to my town, and my two cousins are schoolteachers in the Malolos school, so I told my cousins that if there is any vacancy, I want to apply to be a schoolteacher. Then I was accepted. I was in Malolos Elementary School, teaching.

Then after about three years, this man who is from Hawaii . . . Neighbors, we were neighbors. The mother . . . When I was in school, we are using uniform, and his mother is the one washing my uniform, my clothes for me. Can you imagine? This is really the true story. And so the mother told me, "Gee, I want to write letter but I don't know how to write. I want to write to my son in Hawaiian Islands, so please write for me to my son." So I was the one doing. Because he already here that time. He came — I have the history over there — it seems to me second immigrants, when the Filipinos came, you know. He came himself, like he was twenty. He was young those days, finished high school. He was plantations man, you know. He worked on the plantation here in Hawaii. Then he cannot endure the hard work, so he changed his job. You know, he went to laundry. He studied here in Honolulu, and he is a minister. We were married in the Philippines. He is a missionary here already, and he went to the Philippines and married me. Because we contact each other with letters, because the mother always let me write. I happened to mention to him that please come home because your mother would like to see you. Because, really, count the years, and he was over here long time, you know. He was thirty years old when I married him. I was going to be twenty-two. He was a big *luna* man and a minister then.

When my daughter was born, I like her to be too educated. I like her to take a good job as possible so she no suffer like I suffered. Because she graduated from Mid-Pacific Institute. Because she has good mark, she continue in University of Hawaii. But then she wanted to have venture, to venture, to go somewhere. "Like me," that's what she said. She copy. So like unto the mother is the daughter. She like to follow me, she like to go another place. Not only Hawaiian Islands. Because like me, I like go far away. Not only Manila, because I had been in the city of Manila. I like see the United States. I like see New York. Can you imagine my mind is so high like that? Because I want to be a teacher. And it happened, you know. Until now I am teaching. Retired already, two years ago. Help, you know. I substitute, you know.

I told my daughter about cooking, but she's not very fond of cooking. But now she's married. She always call me long-distance telephone and ask me this and ask me that, like the *pansit*. *Pansit* is noodles, fried noodles, you know. And the *lumpia*, you know. Then she says, "Send me a cookbook, a Filipino cookbook," so I send her.

I depend all to my God, my Heavenly Father, you know. Every Sunday I go to church. I am a member of the Board of Deacon, Mrs. B. and I. She's a hustler to go all around and tell the people that "I miss you," or "How many Sunday I never see you." But me, I take my time, I no tell that one [those lines]. Sometime I say, "Did you tell that one? You got to make different conversation. You must say something, learn about her activity, and then afterward you tell the program of our church, what's coming up." And she said, "Ah, I just tell them." Sometime I go after her, you know, because, you know, I count her as my daughter.

We spoke Tagalog at home. No, not my children. My children doesn't know how to speak Tagalog, only dakin', joke. Oh, I get hard time to teach my children. We talk in Tagalog, but they say, "What are you talking, Mama? You better speak in English. You know how to speak English." So I all English — all English-speaking. Just look at the meeting we had last night!

[In] 1938 I went back to the Philippines, you know. No, my children we left to my brother. My husband has a brother over here and we left them. And my madre, well call it madre . . . She is not my mother but something like to me, and I treat her nicely, and so she keep my children. So I went to the Philippines, and not that I am bragging, but I had been in the mainland, you know. So I am telling that story to the Filipinos when I went home. Because three times already I went home. But my first time, [I had been] only around here in Hawaiian Islands. But they always ask me to speak in Tagalog. I went to the mainland and to see New York. I went! It happened! And I brought some cards and some pictures of mine, and then they believed me, because some of the old folks in the Philippines, they will not believe you. So I showed the pictures. I had plenty album that I could show the pictures to them. And they said, "Oh, you look rich!" And they gave me a reception. And they make this kind *lechon*, what do you call it here in Hawaiian Islands? Roast pig, but it's a small pig, you know. You can put on the table. My sister said, "Are you telling the truth? You had been in America?" They don't use "mainland" over there. "Had you been in America?" Sure, I have been in America.

XI   Conclusion

The history of the settlement of Hawaii by diverse Asian and European ethnic groups and the rich cultural heritage they have left with us have been chronicled elsewhere. What has been recorded here is half of that history, the half of the story created by women who pioneered new and unfamiliar surroundings with great courage, energy, and adaptability. Their voices reveal the harsh, unremitting circumstances of their lives, their sadness, and also their joys and satisfactions.

They came to Hawaii not always through personal choice. The decision to immigrate to the Islands was made more often by parents or husbands than by the women themselves. Some were Hawaiian by birth. The impetus for immigration was provided by policy decisions of planters to import labor serially by ethnic group.

Nor was marriage always a matter of personal choice. In East Asian ethnic groups, parents and families usually made the marriage arrangements, often without consulting the preferences of the daughters. In such marriages, girls had few expectations; disappointment, if it did occur, was endured and seldom led to divorce.

Families were large in all ethnic groups, including the haoles, particularly in the first generation of missionaries. There is little evidence among these respondents that Catholic families were significantly larger than non-Catholic, although the largest number of children born by any respondent here was born to a Catholic woman: eighteen children. Nor is there much to suggest that family size was determined by conscious planning.

The large size of their families and the fact that their husbands worked away from the home meant a heavy burden of domestic work for the women represented here. Only one of the respondents remained single, and she did so out of a decision first to help her younger brothers and then, after they married, to help raise their families. She did this of her own volition despite several marriage proposals and never regretted her choice. The women whose lives we examined worked long hours, not only caring for their own children but also doing laundry, ironing, cooking, and sewing for bachelors on the plantations. Labor-saving appliances were nonexistent.

Many also worked outside the home. Workdays were prodigiously long, and the economic roles played by women were multiple. The most extreme case was the Filipina who, besides raising her own sixteen children, took in laundry and ironing and prepared lunches for Filipino bachelors in her camp. She averaged, by her account, not more than two hours' sleep a night and did so without becoming ill, even without complaint. Although her case was extreme, many other respondents reported rising at 3:30 or 4:00 in the morning to start an arduous round of chores. It was not possible for husbands to help with these domestic tasks — even had it occurred to them to do so — since the men had their own heavy work loads in the fields.

In some ethnic groups, the definition of family was flexible. This was particularly true of the Hawaiian family, with its *hanai* custom that ensured that all children be cared for and that grandparents and childless aunts would have children to raise. A family with no child does not have much joy, by this Hawaiian sentiment. In a similar, though less institutionalized, custom, Puerto Ricans and others in this study also often raised the children of relatives.

Most of the respondents showed a strong sense of family obligation. Dutiful daughters who went to work as teenagers did so to help their families and generally gave part or all of their paychecks to their parents. When parents were no longer living, these women continued their support and concern for siblings, commonly sacrificing their own interests or education for younger brothers and sisters.

That the state of Hawaii has more highly developed and extensive services for the aging than do other states is no accident. It reflects the strong Asian sense of responsibility to family and to the elderly, as well as to community.

Surely these women displayed great endurance in their strenuous lives. In addition, they demonstrated ingenuity and adaptability in devising strategies that enabled them to survive and raise their children in unfamiliar surroundings. Survival was the overriding concern in situations in which bare subsistence called forth all the imagination and energy they could summon. Survival strategies did not depend on one's ethnic group. Taking in sewing, laundry, or ironing; operating a board-inghouse for bachelors; preparing meals for bachelors; opening a restaurant — women from all the ethnic groups took on these additional jobs to help support their large families. As they moved off the plantations, several of these respondents worked with their husbands in small retail stores.

Although it is true that many children of missionary fathers soon succeeded in business and were able to enjoy the help of domestic servants, in the first generation all women were faced with the common problems of survival in a strange land, initially without basic necessities, such as food, housing, and essential language skills. By the second generation and beyond, haole women had solved these critical problems in survival and enjoyed the economic and social advantages of their elite status, not the least of which were attending private schools and employing servants from more recently arrived ethnic groups.

If there is one thing the nonhaole women in this study most regretted, it was their lack of education. Gender asymmetry was the rule. Their brothers' education came first, particularly in Oriental families. The large family size typically meant that children, usually the older girls, had to stay home to help their overburdened mothers. There were many instances in which teachers or priests approached parents to urge that their able daughters be allowed to continue to higher grades in school only to be turned down regretfully by the parents. Although eight years of schooling was common at the time, many of these women had less education. There is no question that boys were given priority in education, even among haoles. In no ethnic group were there career expectations for girls. Thus, many respondents in this study had not been able to attend high school, and several remarked that they regret it to this day. But although they did not have as much education as they would have wished, they uniformly took pride in the education of their children, which in nearly all cases surpassed their own by several years.

By contrast, none of the haole respondents complained about not having had enough education or about a lack of opportunity for education, and their stories support their sense of economic freedom. Most respondents in the Scottish-English group in this study attended private schools, either in Hawaii or on the mainland. Most of the haole women did not aspire to a college degree. With the exception of a few who became teachers or nurses, the women in this study — both haole and nonhaole — did not go into professions, a generalization common to women of their generation.

A fundamental issue that should not be overlooked is the expendability of female children among certain ethnic groups. Two of the respondents in this study were raised in orphanages. In two cases, when one parent died and there were many children, it was suggested that the children be given away. This was particularly evident in families that had mostly girls. "Give them all away — they're only girls," said one father, in an attitude found in those Asian cultures that value male children more highly than female. In this case, the father totally rejected any responsibility for raising his family of girls.

Every group of settlers, regardless of origin, sought to sustain its identity and to provide for the welfare and well-being of its members through the organization of a variety of societies. These societies served to perpetuate the group's language and to preserve its customs in food, costume, religion, music, and dance. Many also performed specific economic functions by serving as savings and loan societies. In all cases, they offered a means of social interaction and support sorely needed by people separated from familiar surroundings.

When such support groups were lacking — when the ethnic group was yet too small, or for whatever reason — public-minded women took it upon themselves to see that those less fortunate than they were not without basic necessities. An apt example were the women who served as midwives; they performed this role in the absence of hospitals, doctors, and often even nurses. Typically, these midwives had been trained by their mothers, if they were trained at all, and acted in this capacity out of a sense of service and compassion rather than for pay, though they sometimes accepted food or assistance in return.

The churches, whether Buddhist, Catholic, or Protestant, became the focus for many of the social and support functions. All respondents in this study had been, and many still are, regular churchgoers. The churches played a vital role in the acculturation of these immigrants — not to mention the survival of individuals and their customs — and the churches in Hawaii generally still appear to be more vital than is the case in many other states. Certainly they are more numerous. The ethnic diversity of Hawaii is reflected in the number of languages in which church services are still held.

When male and female labor in turn-of-the-century Hawaii is examined, it can be seen that the household — and all the tasks performed therein — was female space. Yet the cane and pineapple fields were not exclusively male space. For first-generation later arrivals — Japanese, Okinawans, Filipinas, and Puerto Ricans — work in the fields was often added to the multiple domestic roles of women. Thus, the burden on women in the plantation economy was often heavier than the burden on men, who were themselves overburdened. Moreover, for those women working as field hands, all work was done by hand; as in other colonial and developing economies, if machinery was used, it was used by men.[1]

Ideological heritage also bore differentially on men and women. Confucian ideology, transmitted across the Pacific by East Asian immigrants, exempted male scholars — scholars by whatever definition — from the kinds of manual labor necessary to survive in the new Hawaiian environment, or at least made male scholars reluctant and at times unable to engage in such work. The burden of family support thus in some cases rested squarely on the shoulders of wives or even daughters. This Confucian dispensation, coupled with the Confucian preference for male rather than female offspring, had ramifications for women in access to schooling and in other areas of their lives. We can see this Confucian ideological diaspora operating in the lives of respondents from China, Korea, Japan, and Okinawa. The obvious social and economic value of women for communities with more men than women never outweighed the Confucian ideological heritage. Although the ideological strictures of Catholicism may not have been as onerous as those of Confucianism, women from Portugal, Puerto Rico, and the Philippines felt their ramifications in terms of access to schooling, as preference was similarly accorded to males.

For all these reasons, we see these women as doubly or triply colonized in Hawaii's plantation economy at the turn of the century. In this context, the words of these women attest to their extraordinary lives and contributions.

Notes

Chapter I

1. Andrew W. Lind, *Hawaii's People* (Honolulu: University of Hawaii Press, 1967), pp. 15–16.

2. John Charlot, *The Hawaiian Poetry of Religion and Politics: Some Religio-Political Concepts in Postcontact Literature*, Brigham Young University Monograph Series, no. 5 (Laie: Brigham Young University, Hawaii Campus, Institute for Polynesian Studies, 1985), p. 29.

3. Lind, *Hawaii's People*, p. 28.

4. *Haole* originally meant "stranger" in Hawaiian or, more literally, one without a voice, without knowledge of culture. At first it was used for all visitors, though today it is used only for Caucasians. Lind, *Hawaii's People*, p. 16.

5. Lind, *Hawaii's People*, p. 28.

6. Romanzo Adams, *Interracial Marriage in Hawaii: A Study of the Mutually Conditioned Processes of Acculturation and Amalgamation* (New York: Macmillan, 1937), pp. 145–146.

7. Ibid., p. 146.

8. Quoted from correspondence of the president of the Bureau of Immigration, June 6, 1887, in Lind, *Hawaii's People*, p. 28.

9. Lind, *Hawaii's People*, p. 30.

10. Ibid., pp. 30–35.

11. Adams, *Interracial Marriage in Hawaii*, 16–20 passim.

12. Lind, *Hawaii's People*, pp. 30–31.

13. Lawrence H. Fuchs, *Hawaii Pono: A Social History* (New York: Harcourt, Brace and World, 1961), p. 42.

14. Ibid., pp. 14–37.

15. Ibid., p. 30.

16. Gavan Daws, *Shoal of Time: A History of the Hawaiian Islands* (New York: Macmillan, 1968), pp. 269–282; Fuchs, *Hawaii Pono*, p. 39.

17. Ronald Takaki, *Pau Hana: Plantation Life and Labor in Hawaii, 1835–1920* (Honolulu: University of Hawaii Press, 1983), p. 3.

18. Ibid., p. 13.

19. Daws, *Shoal of Time*, p. 109.

20. Noel J. Kent, *Hawaii: Islands Under the Influence* (New York: Monthly Review Press, 1983), p. 59.

21. Takaki, *Pau Hana*, pp. 76–78.

22. Fuchs, *Hawaii Pono*, p. 56.

23. Takaki, *Pau Hana*, p. 78.

24. Daws, *Shoal of Time*, p. 314.

25. Fuchs, *Hawaii Pono*, pp. 252–253.

26. Takaki, *Pau Hana*, pp. 146–148.

27. Ibid., pp. 148–150.

Chapter II

1. Martha Warren Beckwith, *The Kumulipo: A Hawaiian Creation Chant* (Honolulu: University of Hawaii Press, 1972).

2. Martha Beckwith, *Hawaiian Mythology* (Honolulu: University of Hawaii Press, 1970), p. 168.

3. Ibid., p. 169.

4. Ibid., p. 154.

5. Ibid., pp. 403–404.

6. David Malo, *Hawaiian Antiquities* (Honolulu: Bishop Museum Press, 1971), p. 19.

7. Beckwith, *Hawaiian Mythology*, p. 325.

8. Ibid., pp. 321–326.

9. Antoinette Withington, *Hawaiian Tapestry* (New York: Harper, 1937), pp. 36–38.

10. Ibid., p. 40.

11. Ibid., pp. 59–61.

12. Malo, *Hawaiian Antiquities*, pp. 104–105.

13. Withington, *Hawaiian Tapestry*, pp. 267–271.

14. Katherine Luomala, "Phantom Night Marchers in the Hawaiian Islands," *Pacific Studies* 7, no. 1 (1983): 22.

15. Quotation from Lawrence H. Fuchs, *Hawaii Pono: A Social History* (New York: Harcourt, Brace and World, 1961), pp. 74–75. Further discussion in Noel J. Kent, *Hawaii: Islands Under the Influence* (New York: Monthly Review Press, 1983), pp. 32–33.

Chapter III

1. Clarence E. Glick, *Sojourners and Settlers: Chinese Migrants in Hawaii* (Honolulu: University of Hawaii Press, 1980), pp. 5–15.

2. S. W. Kung, *Chinese in American Life: Some Aspects of Their History, Status, Problems and Contributions* (Seattle: University of Washington Press, 1962), pp. 83–85.

3. Joyce Lebra and Joy Paulson, eds. *Chinese Women in Southeast Asia* (Singapore: Times Books International, 1980), pp. 177–178.

4. Kung, *Chinese in American Life*, pp. 30–41.

5. Tin-Yuke Char, *The Sandalwood Mountains: Readings and Stories of the Early Chinese in Hawaii* (Honolulu: University of Hawaii Press, 1975), p. 117.

6. Glick, *Sojourners and Settlers*, pp. 101–110.

7. Ibid., p. 256; Calvin Lee, *Chinatown USA* (New York: Doubleday, 1965), p. 135; Leo J. Moser, *The Chinese Mosaic: the People and Provinces of China* (Boulder: Westview Press, 1984), pp. 239–240, 247–248.

8. Glick, *Sojourners and Settlers*, pp. 187–189; Fei-Ling Davis, *Primitive Revolutionaries in China* (Honolulu: University Press of Hawaii, 1971), p. 12; Jean Chesneaux, *Secret Societies in China in the Nineteenth and Twentieth Centuries* (Ann Arbor: University of Michigan Press, 1971), pp. 16, 30.

9. Glick, *Sojourners and Settlers*, p. 274; Carl Glick and Hong Sheng-hwa, *Swords of Silence: Chinese Secret Societies — Past and Present* (New York: McGraw-Hill, 1947), pp. 172–173, 104; Chesneaux, *Secret Societies in China*, p. viii.

10. Glick, *Sojourners and Settlers*, pp. 228–229.

Chapter IV

1. Gavan Daws, *Shoal of Time: A History of the Hawaiian Islands* (New York: Macmillan, 1968), p. 169.

2. Caledonian Society of Hawaii, *Speaking of Scots in Hawaii* (Honolulu: The Scot in Hawaii Project Committee, 1986), p. 14.

3. Noel J. Kent, *Hawaii: Islands Under the Influence* (New York: Monthly Review Press, 1983), p. 23.

4. Caledonian Society, *Speaking of Scots*, p. 3.

5. These quotes are from notes made by my mother, Helen S. Chapman, a resident of Honolulu in the 1930s, from reports by early missionaries.

6. This information is also recorded in Helen S. Chapman's notes.

7. Ibid.

8. Lawrence H. Fuchs, *Hawaii Pono: A Social History* (New York: Harcourt, Brace and World, 1961), p. 253.

9. Andrew W. Lind, *Hawaii's People* (Honolulu: University of Hawaii Press, 1967), pp. 6, 30–31.

10. The Wilson-Gorman Tariff restored all sugar except Hawaiian to the schedule and had the added advantage of giving Americans ultimate control over the kingdom's foreign policy. William Adam Russ, *The Hawaiian Revolution, 1893–1894* (Selingrove, Pa.: Susquehanna University Press, 1959), p. 11; Kent, *Hawaii: Islands Under the Influence*, p. 59.

11. Lind, *Hawaii's People*, p. 9.

12. Daws, *Shoal of Time*, p. 181.

13. Merze Tate, *Hawaii: Reciprocity or Annexation* (East Lansing: Michigan State University Press, 1968), p. 262.

14. According to Eleanor C. Nordyke, the original, literal meaning of *haole* was "without breath," which, she said, meant "ignorant of Hawaiian language and culture." Nordyke, *The Peopling of Hawaii* (Honolulu: University Press of Hawaii for the East-West Center, 1977), p. 29.

15. Fuchs, *Hawaii Pono*, pp. 44–46.

16. Ibid., pp. 142–143.

17. Lind, *Hawaii's People*, p. 32.

18. Fuchs, *Hawaii Pono*, p. 152.

19. Ibid., p. 153.

20. Russ, *The Hawaiian Revolution*, p. 49.

21. Fuchs, *Hawaii Pono*, pp. 154–172; Kent, *Hawaii: Islands Under the Influence*, pp. 74–75.

22. In the Massie incident, a Navy wife was raped and beaten, and blame was put on a group of local boys. In the trial that followed, both the Attorney General's Office and the Navy raised questions about the administration of justice in Hawaii and about the territory's ability to govern itself. It was later learned that the crime was committed not by the group of local boys but by a Navy officer, a fact not admitted by the Navy. In the unraveling of the incident an innocent Hawaiian boy was murdered by Navy men and the mother of the raped Navy wife. See Dennis M. Ogawa, *Kodomo no Tame ni: The Japanese American Experience in Hawaii* (Honolulu: University of Hawaii Press, 1978), pp. 113–114; also see the account of the incident in Norman Katkov's novel, *Blood and Orchids* (New York: Signet, 1983).

23. Fuchs, *Hawaii Pono*, p. 188.

24. The quotations in this paragraph are from Fuchs, *Hawaii Pono*, pp. 263 and 269, respectively.

25. Fuchs, *Hawaii Pono*, p. 294.

26. Kent, *Hawaii: Islands Under the Influence*, p. 130. See also Fuchs, *Hawaii Pono*, pp. 263–264.

27. Kent, *Hawaii: Islands Under the Influence*, pp. 104–111.

Chapter V

1. Leo Pap, *The Portuguese-Americans* (Boston: Twayne, 1981), pp. 66–75.

2. Quotation from Ronald Takaki, *Pau Hana: Plantation Life and Labor in Hawaii, 1836–1920* (Honolulu: University of Hawaii Press, 1983), p. 35; also see Pap, *The Portuguese-Americans*, p. 74.

3. Pap, *The Portuguese-Americans*, p. 74.

4. John Henry Felix and Peter F. Senecal, *The Portuguese in Hawaii* (Honolulu: published by the authors, 1978), p. 35.

5. Ibid., pp. 27–31.

6. Pap, *The Portuguese-Americans*, p. 74.

7. Reported in Takaki, *Pau Hana*, pp. 35–36.

8. Quoted by Andrew W. Lind in *Hawaii's People* (Honolulu: University of Hawaii Press, 1967), p. 28, from the correspondence of the president of the Bureau of Immigration, June 6, 1887, Archives of Hawaii, Interior Dept. File 52.

9. Pap, *The Portuguese-Americans*, pp. 74–76.

10. Ibid., p. 78.

11. Ibid., p. 112.

12. Felix and Senecal, *The Portuguese in Hawaii*, pp. 56–57.

13. Pap, *The Portuguese-Americans*, p. 112.

14. The ukulele was not a native Hawaiian instrument but a Portuguese import.

15. Felix and Senecal, *The Portuguese in Hawaii*, pp. 73–74.

16. Hawaii Foundation for History and the Humanities, *Portuguese in Hawaii: A Resource Guide* (Honolulu: Honolulu Multi-Cultural Center, 1973), pp. 15–16.

17. Lind, *Hawaii's People*, p. 76.

18. Ibid., p. 75.

19. Ibid., pp. 27–28.

20. Felix and Senecal, *The Portuguese in Hawaii*, p. 117.

21. Romanzo Adams, *Interracial Marriage in Hawaii: A Study of the Mutually Conditioned Processes of Acculturation and Adaptation* (New York: Macmillan, 1937), pp. 137–138.

22. Ibid., p. 219.

Chapter VI

1. Dennis M. Ogawa, *Kodomo no Tame ni: The Japanese American Experience in Hawaii* (Honolulu: University of Hawaii Press, 1978), pp. 2–3.

2. Ibid., p. 5.

3. Quotation from Ernest K. Wakukawa, *A History of the Japanese People in Hawaii* (Honolulu: Toyo Shoin, 1938), pp. xiii, 55; also see Leonard Lueras, ed., *Kanyaku Imin: A Hundred Years of Japanese Life in Hawaii* (Honolulu: International Savings & Loan Assn., 1986), pp. 30–40.

4. Lueras, *Kanyaku Imin*, p. 30 passim.; Patsy Sumie Saiki, *Japanese Women in Hawaii: The First 100 Years* (Honolulu: Kisaku, 1985), ch. 3; Ogawa, *Kodomo no Tame ni*, p. 6.

5. Ronald Takaki, *Pau Hana: Plantation Life and Labor in Hawaii, 1835–1920* (Honolulu: University of Hawaii Press, 1983), p. 42.

6. Ogawa, *Kodomo no Tame ni*, p. 7.

7. Wakukawa, *A History of the Japanese People in Hawaii*, pp. 92, 217; Takaki, *Pau Hana*, p. 25; A. Grove Day, *Hawaii and Its People* (New York: Duell, Sloan and Pearce, 1960), p. 226.

8. Takaki, *Pau Hana*, pp. 34–43.

9. Ogawa, *Kodomo no Tame ni*, p. 9.

10. Ibid., p. 145.

11. Dorothy Ochiai Hazama and Jane Okamoto Komeiji, *Okage sama de: The Japanese in Hawaii, 1885–1985* (Honolulu: Bess Press, 1986), pp. 62–63; Romanzo Adams, *Interracial Marriage in Hawaii* (1937; reprint, Montclair, N.J.: Patterson Smith, 1969), p. 308.

12. Hazama and Komeiji, *Okage sama de*, p. 66.

13. Franklin Odo and Kazuko Sinoto, *A Pictorial History of the Japanese in Hawaii, 1885–1924* (Honolulu: Hawaii Immigrant Heritage Preservation Center, Department of Anthropology, Bernice Pauahi Bishop Museum, 1985), p. 41.

14. Hazama and Komeiji, *Okage sama de*, p. 66.

15. Lecture by Barbara Kawakami at seminar, entitled Plantation Days: Our Heritage, at Koloa, Kauai, July 20, 1986.

16. John F. Embree, "New Local and Kin Groups Among the Japanese Farmers of Kona, Hawaii," in Ogawa, *Kodomo no Tame ni*, pp. 117–124.

17. Andrew W. Lind, *Hawaii's People* (Honolulu: University of Hawaii Press, 1967), p. 110.

18. Joan Hori, "Japanese Prostitution in Hawaii During the Immigration Period," *Hawaiian Journal of History* 16 (1982).

19. Hazama and Komeiji, *Okage sama de*, p. 94.

20. Ibid., p. 42. In Takaki, *Pau Hana*, pp. 148–150, the worker is described as having been blinded, not killed.

21. Ogawa, *Kodomo no Tame ni*, pp. 150–153; Takaki, *Pau Hana*, pp. 150–155.

22. Hazama and Komeiji, *Okage sama de*, p. 43.

23. Take and Allan Beckman, "Hawaii's Great Japanese Strike," in Ogawa, *Kodomo no Tame ni*, pp. 150–175; Wakukawa, *A History of the Japanese People in Hawaii*, p. 236.

24. Hazama and Komeiji, *Okage sama de*, pp. 45–47.

25. Ibid., pp. 47–50.

26. Yoichi Hanaoka, "The Japanese Language School: Is It a Help or a Hindrance to the Americanization of Hawaii's Young People?" in Ogawa, *Kodomo no Tame ni*, pp. 180–182.

27. Hazama and Komeiji, *Okage sama de*, p. 84.

28. Ogawa, *Kodomo no Tame ni*, pp. 144–146.

29. Hazama and Komeiji, *Okage sama de*, pp. 30, 78–81.

30. Ogawa, *Kodomo no Tame ni*, pp. 192–193.

Chapter VII

1. See, for example, Andrew W. Lind, *Hawaii's People* (Honolulu: University of Hawaii Press, 1967), pp. 28, 75, 100, 106, 110.

2. Dennis M. Ogawa, *Kodomo no Tame ni: The Japanese American Experience in Hawaii* (Honolulu: University of Hawaii Press, 1978), p. 232.

3. Ethnic Studies Oral History Project, *Uchinanchu: A History of Okinawans in Hawaii* (Honolulu: Ethnic Studies Program, University of Hawaii at Manoa, 1981), pp. 76–82.

4. Ibid., p. 96.

5. Ibid., pp. 110–119, 140.

6. Dorothy Ochiai Hazama and Jane Okamoto Komeiji, *Okage sama de: The Japanese in Hawaii, 1885–1985* (Honolulu: Bess Press, 1986), p. 76.

7. Ethnic Studies Oral History Project, *Uchinanchu*, p. 84.

8. Ibid., p. 101.

Chapter VIII

1. Wayne Patterson, "The First Attempt to Obtain Korean Laborers for Hawaii, 1896–1897," in Hyung-chan Kim, ed., *The Korean Diaspora: Historical and Sociological Studies of Korean Immigration and Assimilation in North America* (Santa Barbara: ABC-Clio, 1977), pp. 3–4.

2. Ibid., pp. 5, 18.

3. Ibid., pp. 18–19.

4. Wayne Patterson, *The Korean Frontier in Hawaii: Immigration to Hawaii, 1896–1910*, Part 1 (Ann Arbor, Mich.: University Microfilms, 1980), p. 113.

5. Ibid.

6. Ibid., p. 252–254.

7. Yo-jun Yun, "Early History of Korean Immigration to America," in Kim, *The Korean Diaspora*, pp. 35–36.

8. Ibid., p. 37.

9. Patterson, *The Korean Frontier*, pp. 412, 682. Andrew Lind lists the total as 8,000 or never more than 2.4 percent of the total population. Lind, *Hawaii's People* (Honolulu: University of Hawaii Press, 1967), p. 8.

10. Patterson, *The Korean Frontier*, p. 253.

11. Ronald Takaki, *Pau Hana: Plantation Life and Labor in Hawaii, 1835–1920* (Honolulu: University of Hawaii Press, 1983), pp. 47–48.

12. Kim, *The Korean Diaspora*, p. 70.

13. Ibid., pp. 37–38.

14. Ibid., p. 61.

Chapter IX

1. Norma Carr, *Puerto Rican: One Identity from a Multi-Ethnic Heritage* (Honolulu: Department of Education, Office of Instructional Services, 1980), p. 8.

2. Ibid., p. 9.

3. Blase Camacho Souza, "Trabajo y Tristeza — Work and Sorrow: The Puerto Ricans of Hawaii, 1900–1902," *The Hawaiian Journal of History* 18 (1984): 158–159.

4. Ibid., p. 160.

5. Ibid., p. 162.

6. Ibid., pp. 162–163.

7. Ibid., p. 156; Carr, *Puerto Rican*, p. 9.

8. Souza, "Trabajo y Tristeza," p. 167.

9. Ibid., pp. 156, 165; Carr, *Puerto Rican*, p. 9.

10. Souza, "Trabajo y Tristeza," p. 168. Souza cites the Report of the Commissioner of Labor in Hawaii, pp. 102, 32, which lists eleven Puerto Rican *lunas* among a total of 1,700 men employed on the plantations.

11. Souza, "Trabajo y Tristeza," pp. 13–15.

12. Ibid., p. 18; interview with Blase Souza, Honolulu, July 22, 1986. Much of the information regarding Puerto Rican culture in Hawaii was kindly provided by Souza.

13. Interview with Blase Souza, July 22, 1986.

Chapter X

1. Reuben R. Alcantara, *Sakada: Filipino Adaptation in Hawaii* (Washington, D.C.: University Press of America, 1981), pp. 8–9.

2. Ibid., p. 8; Luis V. Teodoro, *Out of This Struggle: The Filipinos in Hawaii* (Honolulu: University Press of Hawaii, 1981), p. 21.

3. Alcantara, *Sakada*, p. 3.

4. Ibid., p. 2.

5. Teodoro, *Out of This Struggle*, p. 11; Alcantara, *Sakada*, p. 4.

6. Teodoro, *Out of This Struggle*, pp. 14–18.

7. Ibid., pp. 28–29.

8. East-West Center and Operation Manong, University of Hawaii at Manoa, *Filipino Immigrants in Hawaii: A Profile of Recent Arrivals* (Manoa: University of Hawaii, 1985), p. 4.

9. Ibid., p. 5.

10. Teodoro, *Out of This Struggle*, pp. 21–22.

11. Ibid., pp. 28–29.

12. Alcantara, *Sakada*, p. 26.

Chapter XI

1. See the literature on women and development, such as Ester Boserup, *Women's Role in Economic Development* (New York: St. Martin's Press, 1970), and Irene Tinker and Michele Bo Bramsen, *Women and World Development* (American Association for the Advancement of Science, Overseas Development Council, 1976).

Selected Readings

Adams, Romanzo. *Interracial Marriage in Hawaii: A Study of the Mutually Conditioned Processes of Acculturation and Adaptation.* New York: Macmillan, 1937; Montclair, N.J.: Patterson Smith, 1969.

Alcantara, Reuben R. *Sakada: Filipino Adaptation in Hawaii.* Washington, D.C.: University Press of America, 1981.

Ashdown, Inez MacPhee. *Ke Alaloa o Maui: Authentic History and Legends of the Valley Isle.* Wailuku: Kamaaina Historians, 1970.

Beckwith, Martha. *Hawaiian Mythology.* Honolulu: University of Hawaii Press, 1970.

Beckwith, Martha Warren. *The Kumulipo: A Hawaiian Creation Chant.* Honolulu: University of Hawaii Press, 1972.

Caledonian Society of Hawaii. *Speaking of Scots in Hawaii.* Honolulu: The Scot in Hawaii Project Committee, 1986.

Carr, Norma. *Puerto Rican: One Identity from a Multi-Ethnic Heritage.* Honolulu: Department of Education, Office of Instructional Services, 1980.

Char, Tin-Yuke, *The Sandalwood Mountains: Readings and Stories of the Early Chinese in Hawaii.* Honolulu: University of Hawaii Press, 1975.

Charlot, John. *The Hawaiian Poetry of Religion and Politics: Some Religio-Political Concepts in Postcontact Literature.* Laie: Brigham Young University, Hawaii Campus, Brigham Young University Monograph Series, no. 5, Institute for Polynesian Studies, 1985.

Chesneaux, Jean. *Secret Societies in China in the Nineteenth and Twentieth Centuries.* Ann Arbor: University of Michigan Press, 1971.

Davis, Fei-Ling. *Primitive Revolutionaries of China.* Honolulu: University Press of Hawaii, 1971.

Daws, Gavan. *Shoal of Time: A History of the Hawaiian Islands.* New York: Macmillan, 1968.

Day, A. Grove. *Hawaii and Its People.* New York: Duell, Sloan and Pearce, 1960.

Dorita, Sister Mary, B.V.M. "Filipino Immigration to Hawaii." Master's thesis, University of Hawaii, Honolulu, 1975.

East-West Center and Operation Manong, University of Hawaii at Manoa. *Filipino Immigrants in Hawaii: A Profile of Recent Arrivals.* Manoa: University of Hawaii, 1985.

Ethnic Studies Oral History Project, *Uchinanchu: A History of Okinawans in Hawaii.* Manoa: Ethnic Studies Program, University of Hawaii at Manoa, 1981.

Felix, John Henry, and Peter F. Senecal. *The Portuguese in Hawaii.* Honolulu: published by the authors, 1978.

Fuchs, Lawrence H. *Hawaii Pono: A Social History.* New York: Harcourt, Brace and World, 1961.

Glick, Carl, and Hong Sheng-hwa. *Swords of Silence: Chinese Secret Societies — Past and Present.* New York: McGraw-Hill, 1947.

Glick, Clarence E. *Sojourners and Settlers: Chinese Migrants in Hawaii.* Honolulu: University of Hawaii Press, 1980.

Handy, E.S.C., and Kenneth P. Emory. *Ancient Hawaiian Civilization.* Honolulu: Kamehameha Schools, 1933.

Handy, E.S.C., and Mary Kawena Pukui. *The Polynesian Family System in Ka'u, Hawaii.* Rutland, Vt.: Charles E. Tuttle, 1981.

Hawaii Foundation for History and the Humanities. *Portuguese in Hawaii: A Resource Guide.* Honolulu: Multi-Cultural Center, 1973.

Hazama, Dorothy Ochiai, and Jane Okamoto Komeiji. *Okage sama de: The Japanese in Hawaii, 1885–1985.* Honolulu: Bess Press, 1986.

Highland, Genevieve A., and Roland W. Force, et al. *Polynesian Culture History.* Honolulu: Bishop Museum Press, 1967.

Hormann, Bernhard. *Community Forces in Hawaii — Readings from Social Process in Hawaii.* Honolulu: University of Hawaii Press, 1956.

Hoverson, Martha, ed. *Historic Koloa: A Guide.* Koloa: Friends of the Koloa Library, 1985.

Kent, Noel J. *Hawaii: Islands Under the Influence.* New York: Monthly Review Press, 1983.

Kim, Hyung-chan, ed. *The Korean Diaspora: Historical and Sociological Studies of Korean Immigration and Assimilation in North America.* Santa Barbara: ABC-Clio, 1977.

Kimura, Yukiko. *Issei: Japanese Immigrants in Hawaii.* Honolulu: University of Hawaii Press, 1988.

Kodama-Nishimoto, Michi, Warren S. Nishimoto, and Cynthia A. Oshiro. *Hana Hana: An Oral History of Hawaii's Working People.* Honolulu: Ethnic Studies Oral History Project, University of Hawaii, 1984.

Kotani, Roland. *The Japanese in Hawaii: A Century of Struggle.* Official Program Booklet of the Oahu Kanyaku Imin Centennial Committee. Honolulu, Oahu Kanyaku Imin Centennial Committee, 1985.

Kung, S. W. *Chinese in American Life: Some Aspects of Their History, Status, Problems and Contributions.* Seattle: University of Washington Press, 1962.

Kuykendall, Ralph S., and A. Grove Day. *Hawaii: A History.* New York: Prentice-Hall, 1948.

Lebra, Joyce, and Joy Paulson, eds. *Chinese Women in Southeast Asia.* Singapore: Times Books International, 1980.

Lee, Calvin. *Chinatown USA.* New York: Doubleday, 1965.

Levison, Michael, R. Gerard Ward, and John B. Webb. *The Settlement of Polynesia: A Computer Simulation.* Minneapolis: The University of Minnesota Press, 1973.

Lind, Andrew W. *Hawaii's People.* Honolulu: University of Hawaii Press, 1967.

Lueras, Leonard, ed. *Kanyaku Imin: A Hundred Years of Japanese Life in Hawaii.* Honolulu: International Savings & Loan Assn., 1986.

Luomala, Katherine. "Phantom Night Marchers in the Hawaiian Islands." *Pacific Studies* 7, no. 1 (1983): 1–33.

Malo, David. *Hawaiian Antiquities.* Honolulu: Bishop Museum Press, 1971.

Morrison, Judith Krow. *Being Chinese in Honolulu.* Ann Arbor, Mich.: University Microfilms, 1981.

Moser, Leo J. *The Chinese Mosaic: The People and Provinces of China.* Boulder: Westview Press, 1984.

Nordyke, Eleanor C. *The Peopling of Hawaii.* Honolulu: University Press of Hawaii for the East-West Center, 1977.

Odo, Franklin, and Kazuko Sinoto. *A Pictorial History of the Japanese in Hawaii, 1885–1924.* Honolulu: Hawaii Immigrant Heritage Preservation Center, Department of Anthropology, Bernice Pauahi Bishop Museum, 1985.

Ogawa, Dennis M. *Jan Ken Po: The World of Hawaii's Japanese Americans.* Honolulu: Japanese American Research Center, 1973.

———. *Kodomo no Tame ni: The Japanese American Experience in Hawaii.* Honolulu: University of Hawaii Press, 1978.

Pap, Leo. *The Portuguese-Americans.* Boston: Twayne, 1981.

Patterson, Wayne. *The Korean Frontier in America: Immigration to Hawaii, 1896–1910.* Part 1. 2 vols. Ann Arbor, Mich.: University Microfilms, 1980.

Russ, William Adam. *The Hawaiian Revolution, 1893–1894.* Selingrove, Pa.: Susquehanna University Press, 1959.

Saiki, Patsy Sumie. *Japanese Women in Hawaii: The First 100 Years.* Honolulu: Kisaku, 1985.

Takaki, Ronald. *Pau Hana: Plantation Life and Labor in Hawaii, 1835–1920.* Honolulu: University of Hawaii Press, 1983.

———. *Strangers from a Different Shore: A History of Asian Americans.* Boston: Little, Brown, 1989; Penguin paper, 1990.

Tate, Merze. *Hawaii: Reciprocity or Annexation.* East Lansing: Michigan State University Press, 1968.

Taylor, Albert P. *Under Hawaiian Skies: A Narrative of the Romance, Adventure and History of the Hawaiian Islands, A Complete Historical Account.* Honolulu: Advertiser Publishing, 1926.

Teodoro, Luis V. *Out of This Struggle: The Filipinos in Hawaii.* Honolulu: University Press of Hawaii, 1981.

Wakukawa, Ernest K. *A History of the Japanese People in Hawaii.* Honolulu: Toyo Shoin, 1938.

Westerveldt, W. D. *Hawaiian Historical Legends.* New York: Fleming H. Revell, 1926.

Withington, Antoinette. *Hawaiian Tapestry.* New York: Harper, 1937.

Young, Nancy Foon, and Judy R. Parrish, eds. *Montage: An Ethnic History of Women in Hawaii.* Honolulu: College of Education, University of Hawaii, 1977.

———. *Searching for the Promised Land: Filipinos and Samoans in Hawaii.* Honolulu: College of Education, University of Hawaii, 1974.

Index